ENGAGING THE ANOMALOUS

ENGAGING THE ANOMALOUS

COLLECTED ESSAYS ON
ANTHROPOLOGY,
THE PARANORMAL, MEDIUMSHIP
AND EXTRAORDINARY EXPERIENCE

BY

JACK HUNTER

www.augustnightbooks.com

Engaging the Anomalous

Copyright © 2018 by Jack Hunter. All rights reserved.

Published and printed in the United States of America and the United Kingdom by August Night Books; an imprint of White Crow Productions Ltd.

The right of Jack Hunter to be identified as the author of this work has been asserted by him in accordance with the Copyright, Design and Patents act 1988.

No part of this book may be reproduced, copied or used in any form or manner whatsoever without written permission, except in the case of brief quotations in reviews and critical articles.

For information, contact White Crow Productions Ltd.
at 3 Hova Villas, Hove, BN3 3DH United Kingdom,
or e-mail info@whitecrowbooks.com.

Cover Design by Astrid@Astridpaints.com
Interior design by Velin@Perseus-Design.com

Paperback ISBN: 978-1-78677-055-4
eBook   ISBN: 978-1-78677-056-1

Non Fiction / Body, Mind & Spirit / Parapsychology

www.augustnightbooks.com

Disclaimer: White Crow Productions Ltd. and its directors, employees, distributors, retailers, wholesalers and assignees disclaim any liability or responsibility for the author's statements, words, ideas, criticisms or observations. White Crow Productions Ltd. assumes no responsibility for errors, inaccuracies, or omissions.

Most of the chapters in this book have previously appeared in various journals and websites, as well as talks and conferences. The versions included here have been modified and updated slightly from their original forms. Most of the chapters are stand-alone pieces, so this book is intended to be something that can be dipped into, rather than read from beginning to end. Owing to this, there is a little repetition in certain parts of the book. However you choose to read it (if at all), I hope you find something of interest.

PRAISE FOR *ENGAGING THE ANOMALOUS*

"As I have lectured on both sides of the pond, I have noticed a kind of quiet renaissance of interest in the paranormal among intellectuals, especially among younger scholars of religion, anthropology, and literary criticism. Jack Hunter is a shining light among these emerging voices. His search for a non-reductive anthropology, for a "paranthropology" as his journal has it, is among the most hopeful and creative signs in our shared fields. With his trademark refusal to simply "bracket" away every honest ontological question and his balanced insistence that there is a third path forward between and beyond naive belief and equally naive debunking, Jack has blazed a trail through any number of intellectual and spiritual jungles. Here is a welcome record of that trail-blazing and that intellectual courage."

—JEFFREY J. KRIPAL,
AUTHOR OF *SECRET BODY: EROTIC AND ESOTERIC CURRENTS IN THE HISTORY OF RELIGIONS*

"A must-read for anyone interested in the study of anomalous, extraordinary, and paranormal experiences. The brilliance of Hunter's analysis is not just that he identifies how contemporary methods fall short of weighing in on the ontological reality of the paranormal… but in the construction of a new method, a new strategy, that acknowledges the "agency" of spirits and paranormal experience. Yes, spirits are ontologically real, surprise!"

—DIANA WALSH PASULKA, PH.D.,
PROFESSOR AND CHAIR OF THE DEPARTMENT OF PHILOSOPHY AND RELIGION, UNIVERSITY OF NORTH CAROLINA, WILMINGTON. AUTHOR OF *AMERICAN COSMIC: UFOS, RELIGION, TECHNOLOGY*

PRAISE FOR *ENGAGING THE ANOMALOUS*

"Throughout history, across all cultures, and at all educational levels, people have reported experiences labeled strange, bizarre, paranormal, or supernatural. Anthropologist Jack Hunter inspects these weird but common experiences in a collected set of crisp essays and interviews. Are such experiences real, despite their challenges to today's scientific worldview? Or should we take human experiences more seriously and use them as clues to help expand our sense of reality? These are among the endlessly fascinating questions explored in an engaging way in 'Engaging the Anomalous.'"

—DEAN RADIN, PH.D.,
CHIEF SCIENTIST, INSTITUTE OF NOETIC SCIENCES.
AUTHOR OF *REAL MAGIC*

"This book demonstrates a highly original approach not just to the anthropology of the paranormal but arguably to the discipline itself, which often lacks the conceptual tools with which to place our interlocutors' ontologies on the same footing as ours. Questions of belief become superfluous in this work—indeed, there are more important queries and extraordinary experiences cannot and should not be reduced to states of mind or representations. Furthermore, Hunter has had the courage to argue systematically for a destabilisation of ontological certainty which I find fundamental for scholars working with religious and spiritual processes. This he does despite the risk of ostracisation from a community which generally maintains rigid boundaries of methodological atheism. This is a book ripe with historical and theoretical considerations which provides the reader with excellent material, while it is nevertheless ethnographic in that it is ultimately grounded in Hunter's dissertation work with a spiritual lodge in Bristol."

—DIANA ESPÍRITO SANTO, PH.D.,
DEPT. ANTHROPOLOGY, LA PONTIFICIA UNIVERSIDAD
CATÓLICA DE CHILE

ACKNOWLEDGEMENTS

Thank you to the estate of Eugene Burger (1939-2017) for giving permission to publish an interview I conducted with him back in 2012 – 'It's so Eugene!' they told me. Big thanks also go to George Hansen for his wonderful Foreword, and to Dr. Diana Espirito Santo, Dr. Dean Radin, Prof. Diana Pasulka and Prof. Jeffrey Kripal for their kind words of support for this collection of essays. A special thank-you to Dr. David Luke, Dr. Fiona Bowie and Dr. Hannah Gilbert for their constructive comments on early drafts of some of these articles. Thanks also to Dr. Mark Schroll for providing me with the opportunity to contribute to the *Rhine Online Magazine*. Thanks to Michael Tymm for inviting me to contribute to *The Searchlight*, to Dr. Nicola Holt for inviting a contribution to *Paranormal Review*, to David Taylor for inviting an article for *Psychical Studies*, and to Jeremy Johnson for inviting the *Metapsychosis* microdose. Thank you to David Metcalfe, Robert Dickins, Sharon Ann Rowland, Alex Tsakiris and Dr. Christopher Laursen for giving permission to republish their interviews with me. I am also greatly indebted to ASSAP, who provided me with several early opportunities to publish and present my research when I was first starting out. The Parapsychology Foundation, Parapsychological Association and Society for Psychical Research have all provided invaluable support for my work. Huge thanks to Robbie Graham and August Night Books for making it possible to bring this book into existence, and to my loving family for putting up with my weird interests.

Several chapters in this book have previously appeared in the following publications, presented in the order they appear in this book:

(2013). 'Taking Experience Seriously: What are the Consequences?' *Paranthropology: Journal of Anthropological Approaches to the Paranormal*, Vol. 4, No. 3, pp. 3-8.

(2010). 'Anthropology and the Ontological Status of the Paranormal.' *Rhine-Online: Psi News Magazine*, Vol. 2, No. 2. pp. 4-5.

(2010). 'The Persistence of Spirits.' *The Searchlight: Newsletter of the Academy of Spirituality and Paranormal Studies*, Vol. 19, No. 3, pp. 8-9.

(2012). 'Contemporary Physical Mediumship: Is It Part of a Continuous Tradition?' *Paranthropology: Journal of Anthropological Approaches to the Paranormal*, Vol. 3, No. 1, pp. 35-43.

(2010). 'Contemporary Mediumship and Séance Groups in the UK: Speculations on the Bristol Spirit Lodge.' *Psychical Studies: Journal of the Unitarian Society for Psychical Studies*, No. 76, pp. 7-13.

(2010). 'Talking With the Spirits: More Than a Social Reality?' *Paranormal Review: Magazine of the Society for Psychical Research*, Issue 54, pp. 9-13.

(2011). 'Mediumship, Animism and Altered States of Consciousness.' *Anomaly: Journal of Research Into the Paranormal*, No. 45, pp. 128-142.

(2011). 'Ethnographic and Psychical Approaches to Spirit Mediumship.' *Seriously Strange Magazine*, Issue 137, pp. 13-15.

(2009). 'The Issue of Fraud and Performance in Mediumship.' *PSI: Journal of Investigative Psychical Research*, Vol. 5, No. 2, pp. 17-25.

(2010). 'Talking With the Spirits: Anthropology and Interpreting Spirit Communications.' *Anomaly: Journal of Research Into the Paranormal*, Vol. 44, pp. 34-39.

(2014). 'Can Science See Spirits?: Neuroimaging Studies of Mediumship and Possession' Daily Grail, 27th May 2014. Available from: https://www.dailygrail.com/2014/05/can-science-see-spirits/

(2012). 'Expressions of Spirithood: Performance and the Manifestation of Spirits.' *Anomaly: Journal of Research into the Paranormal*, Vol. 46, pp. 144-156.

(2014). 'Ectoplasm, Somatization and Stigmata: Physical Mediumship as the Development of Extraordinary Mind-Body States.' Presentation at *6th Exploring the Extraordinary Conference*, Gettysburg College, PA, USA. 21st-23rd March 2014.

(2016). 'Engaging the Anomalous: Reflections from the Anthropology of the Paranormal.' *European Journal of Psychotherapy and Counselling*, Vol. 18, No. 2, pp. 170-178.

CONTENTS

PRAISE FOR *ENGAGING THE ANOMALOUS* VI
ACKNOWLEDGEMENTS VIII
FOREWORD XIII
INTRODUCTION XXI
THE PROBLEMATIC PARANORMAL:
SUPERNATURAL OR NATURAL? 1
ANTHROPOLOGY AND THE PARANORMAL:
TOWARD AN INTERMEDIATIST APPROACH 11
TAKING EXPERIENCE SERIOUSLY 23
ANTHROPOLOGY AND THE ONTOLOGICAL
STATUS OF THE PARANORMAL 31
THE PERSISTENCE OF SPIRITS 35
CONTEMPORARY PHYSICAL MEDIUMSHIP:
IS IT PART OF A CONTINUOUS PHENOMENON? 41
CONTEMPORARY MEDIUMSHIP AND
SÉANCE GROUPS IN THE UK:
SPECULATING ON THE BRISTOL SPIRIT LODGE 53
TALKING WITH THE SPIRITS:
MORE THAN A SOCIAL REALITY? 63
MEDIUMSHIP, ANIMISM AND ALTERED
STATES OF CONSCIOUSNESS 69
ETHNOGRAPHIC AND PSYCHICAL APPROACHES
TO SPIRIT MEDIUMSHIP 81
THE ISSUE OF FRAUD AND PERFORMANCE
IN MEDIUMSHIP 85
TALKING WITH THE SPIRITS:
ANTHROPOLOGY AND INTERPRETING SPIRIT
COMMUNICATIONS 99

CAN SCIENCE SEE SPIRITS?
    THE NEUROPHYSIOLOGY OF SPIRIT MEDIUMSHIP 115

EXPRESSIONS OF SPIRITHOOD:
    PERFORMANCE AND THE MANIFESTATION OF SPIRITS 123

ECTOPLASM, SOMATISATION AND STIGMATA:
    SPECULATIONS ON PHYSICAL MEDIUMSHIP, STIGMATA
    AND THE DEVELOPMENT OF EXTRAORDINARY
    MIND-BODY STATES 131

ENGAGING THE ANOMALOUS:
    REFLECTIONS FROM THE ANTHROPOLOGY
    OF THE PARANORMAL 141

REFLECTIONS ON A 'DAMNED' CHAPTER 149

RETHINKING THE SÉANCE:
    MEDIUMSHIP IN A CROSS-CULTURAL CONTEXT 153

MAGIC, SCIENCE AND RELIGION:
    A CONVERSATION WITH EUGENE BURGER 167

INTERVIEW WITH ROBERT DICKINS FOR
    PSYCHEDELIC PRESS UK 171

IN AN OPEN-MINDED WAY:
    AN INTERVIEW WITH DAVID METCALFE ON AN
    ETHNOGRAPHY OF ANOMALOUS PHENOMENA 175

INTERVIEW WITH SHARON ANN ROWLAND
    FOR ODDITIES NEWSLETTER 181

INTERVIEW WITH ALEX TSAKIRIS
    FOR SKEPTIKO 185

INTERVIEW WITH CHRISTOPHER LAURSEN
    FOR THE EXTRAORDINARIUM 199

MISCELLANEOUS 205

BIBLIOGRAPHY 213

ABOUT THE AUTHOR 235

FOREWORD

The first issue of the journal *Paranthropology* appeared in July of 2010. Founded and edited by Jack Hunter at the very beginning of his graduate study, it is now in its eighth year of publication. The appearance of the journal was, in retrospect, a remarkable event. The academic study of the paranormal was foundering. Access to the pertinent professional journals was becoming more restricted.

Anthropological ideas were not entirely absent in those periodicals, but they had little impact. For a newcomer, a beginning graduate student, to start a journal in his field of study, well, that was simply audacious. The odds for its success were not good. Why? Let me describe the intellectual climate in both parapsychology and anthropology; that should explain why, and why *Paranthropology* is important. In this foreword I will:

- Illustrate the state of paranormal research in academia via snapshot descriptions of a few illuminating episodes
- Address anthropology's relevance for understanding psychic phenomena and the academic taboo against testing their reality
- Explain the significance of *Paranthropology's* open access policy

Many readers of this book are likely to be anthropologists. I am not one, so I should introduce myself. During the 1980s I worked in parapsychology laboratories for eight years, and a number of observations led me to study the trickster figure. That, in turn, led to reading anthropology and finding structuralist and poststructuralist perspectives especially useful. Edmund Leach, Victor Turner, and Rodney Needham are the anthropologists who have most influenced my thinking. Others who significantly informed my perspective include Claude Lévi-Strauss, Laura Makarius, Mary Douglas, Marjorie Halpin, and E. E. Evans-Pritchard. These anthropologists had insights highly pertinent to the paranormal, but they are infrequently cited today.

The State of Academic Paranormal Research

To appreciate Jack Hunter's articles, books, and editorship of *Paranthropology*, readers should know something about the state of academic paranormal research. I cannot give an adequate historical overview here; instead I will report a few revealing incidents from the last 30 years. These may give an inkling of the challenges facing academic study of the paranormal as well as attempts to introduce anthropological ideas to parapsychologists.

The 1980s were the high point for parapsychology in the United States. Six laboratories employed full-time researchers for the entire decade, and a number of other labs were productive for shorter periods. By 1996 only two of the laboratories remained dedicated to parapsychology (for details, see Hansen, 2001: 203-208).

In year 2000, social anthropologist Marilyn Schlitz served as president of the Parapsychological Association, the professional organization of parapsychologists. By that time, Schlitz had devoted nearly two decades of her professional career to the field, was known as a psi-conducive experimenter, and had been employed by four centers doing psychic research. In her presidential address, she stated: "Today I direct the research program at the Institute of Noetic Sciences. We have about 40 projects... A number of them fall into the area of parapsychology, although *I almost never use that word*" (emphasis added, Schlitz, 2001: 342). This statement was made directly to the Parapsychological Association and published in the *Journal of Parapsychology*. It was an astounding declaration. The president openly admitted, in her presidential address, that she avoids being identified with the name – it was a striking display of the stigma of parapsychology (Hansen, 2007).

Today, now seventeen years later, how many persons in the United States are employed full-time in unclassified positions, who directly attempt to elicit paranormal phenomena and observe them under controlled conditions and then report findings in refereed, scientific journals? I don't know the exact number, but I guess it to be 5 or fewer.

Parapsychology in the United Kingdom appears to have fared better, but one may doubt its vitality. The premier UK center for psi research has been in the University of Edinburgh's Department of Psychology. Parapsychology has had a presence there since 1962. In 1985 Robert L. Morris was appointed to the Koestler Chair of Parapsychology, and the Koestler Parapsychology Unit (KPU) was established. In 2004 Morris died unexpectedly. In 2008 his former student Deborah Delanoy gave a concise summary of his achievements at a conference titled *Utrecht II: Charting the Future of Parapsychology*. She reported:

> Currently, there are 27 individuals who were supervised to completion by Morris of which 18 are currently working as full-time academics or associated with university-based research groups, 12 of these at UK universities... In short, in 1985, when the Koestler Chair was founded, parapsychological research was being conducted at only two or three UK universities; today full-time staff at 16 UK universities have parapsychological training at the doctoral level, with some of these universities building sizable research groups (Delanoy, 2009: 292).

This was an impressive accomplishment. There is nothing comparable in the history of the field; it has been called the *Morris miracle*. But was the program really a success? Misgivings are justified. With 27 persons earning doctorates, 18 of whom are fulltime academics, one would expect the professional journals to be filled with reports of innovative experiments, theoretical insights, and incisive commentary. This is not the case. In 1985 there were four professional-level, English-language journals devoted to parapsychology. Today only two remain; one of which appeared quarterly is now published semiannually.

At the *Utrecht II* conference on parapsychology's future, an inflammatory charge was hurled by Harald Walach, one of Delanoy's colleagues at the University of Northampton. He declared: "Classical parapsychology, it seems, is dead" (Walach, 2009: 380). Though Walach included a few caveats, and his remark overstated the case, he pointed to a very real crisis.

The final session of the conference included reflections by the moderator. In the discussion that followed, Giovanni Ianuzzo commented: "something is lacking... that you did not mention. We have heard about psychological aspects of psi and also physical aspects of psi, but we have not heard about anthropological aspects" (Ianuzzo, 2009: 556).

Four years after the *Utrecht II* conference, in 2012, the *Journal of Parapsychology* published a special issue titled: "Where Will Parapsychology Be in the Next 25 Years?: Predictions and Prescriptions by 32 Leading Parapsychologists." There was scant mention of anthropology; in fact the word was not found in the text of any essays, though it did appear in two authors' biographical profiles. One essay briefly addressed shamans' use of altered states of consciousness.

The future of parapsychology is not promising. So how have anthropologists fared in organizing groups to study the paranormal?

Starting in the 1970s, substantial efforts were made to foster collaboration between parapsychologists and anthropologists. The endeavors finally birthed the Society for the Anthropology of Consciousness (SAC) in 1990. Many of its founders had a very strong interest in psi. From its beginning, the SAC published a professional journal and was affiliated with the American Anthropological Association – thus achieving a certain respectability.

Stephan Schwartz (2000) provided an informative history of SAC's tumultuous gestation and birth. Its short-lived predecessors were marked by infighting, broken friendships, schisms, and realignments. The SAC, however, continues to this day.

Fifteen years after SAC's founding, Mark Schroll, with Schwartz's input, reflected on its development in its journal, *Anthropology of Consciousness*. The article was titled: "Whither *Psi* and Anthropology?" (Schroll, 2005). In the abstract, he explained: "This essay... seeks to explore... whatever became of the interest in psi and anthropology that led to the founding of the Society for the *Anthropology of Consciousness*?" On the next page he wrote that he found "only a few papers and book reviews tangentially related to *psi* and anthropology in the Anthropology of Consciousness journal from 1990 to 2000... I began asking why [the group]... would all but lose interest in the topic." I verified Schroll's observation with a quick search for the word *parapsychology* in the journal using the Wiley Online Library search function. A total of 39 items were returned; 28 were from 1990 through 2005 – an average of 1.6 articles per year. From 2011 through 2016 the average was 0.50.

The cases presented above hint at something fundamental about the paranormal. The academy discourages discussion of its potential reality. Reports of the phenomena are subtly but effectively marginalized; the phenomena are quietly cast out, even by the believers. We see a taboo enforced – and taboo is the province of anthropology.

Anthropological Insights Into Psi

Paranormal phenomena are not new. Their existence and implications have been debated for millennia. Divination, magic, myth, and ritual are human universals (Brown, 1991). For thousands of years, humans have used rituals to influence, channel, and hedge off paranormal/

supernatural forces; they have used myths to describe, explain, and understand those forces.

The anthropological literature on these matters is vast, confusing, and contradictory. Structuralist paradigms, developed half a century ago, bring some coherence. They address classification, magic, ritual, supernatural power, social marginality, taboo, and how these are all interrelated. Throughout history taboos have surrounded rituals, myths, magic, the sacred, and the supernatural.

The intentional use of psi is magic. By definition, parapsychologists study magic. Academics, including anthropologists, enforce taboos against studying magic's efficacy. Adapting comment by Claude Lévi-Strauss, one might say that taboos operate in anthropologists' minds without their being aware of the fact.[1]

Parapsychologists try to account for the antagonism they face by proposing the notion of "fear of psi" – which, generating no insights, is sterile. In contrast, anthropologists' concept of taboo is fertile.

It is widely understood that extrasensory perception (ESP) and psychokinesis (PK) violate limitations imposed by space and time. These properties are difficult to reconcile with usual science. Research in the 1970s and 1980s identified additional aspects that were even more problematic. Psi-mediated experimenter effects, task-complexity independence, retroactive PK, and the source problem present extreme challenges to usual scientific assumptions. These issues are not quickly grasped; hence they are rarely discussed outside of professional parapsychology. The concepts can be reformulated in structuralist terms and analyzed with those methods.

Open Access: The Policy of *Paranthropology*

From the beginning, Jack Hunter determined that Paranthropology would be an open access journal, freely available to anyone with an Internet connection. This policy is in striking contrast to the two major English-language parapsychology journals as well as *Anthropology of*

---

[1] Adapted from Claude Lévi-Strauss's statement: "I therefore claim to show, not how men think in myths, but how myths operate in men's minds without their being aware of the fact." See page 12 of his *The raw and the cooked: Introduction to a science of mythology*: I., transl. J. & D. Weightman, New York, NY: Harper & Row; 1975. (Originally published in French in 1964).

Consciousness. Those remain behind high pay walls, even the volumes that are decades old.

The importance of journals in science and scholarship is difficult to overemphasize. Journals present new data and theories; they promote the critique, discussion, and debate necessary for sharpening and clarifying ideas. They alert readers to important books and developments. In journals one finds the most advanced thinking in a field. They are loci of institutional memory, archives for ideas and data that may be recognized as crucial decades after their publication.

For marginal fields with limited resources, effective communication is essential. Educational opportunities are limited. It is all too easy for newcomers to repeat mistakes of the past. Methodological and statistical issues are complex. The best discussions of them appear only in journals.

The paranormal generates an extraordinary level of attention from students, independent scholars, and academics who may keep their interests hidden. These are the people who may have insights that can advance the field. But the professional literature is becoming more and more difficult to access. As parapsychology has declined, university libraries have dropped subscriptions to its journals. Back issues are moved off library shelves and into storage facilities, making it more difficult for newcomers to scan contents and discover articles of interest.

I've known many productive researchers in parapsychology who began as students reading the professional journals. Today journals have become less accessible. This can only harm the long-term prospects for the field. I fear for the future. Jack Hunter's research, writing, and editorship give me hope.

Concluding Remarks

Paranthropology arrived when the academic study of the paranormal was in period of stagnation and decline. The establishment evinced little interest in anthropological approaches. Because *Paranthropology* was begun by a student at the start of his graduate study, I didn't expect it to last. It is now in its eighth year. Jack Hunter has devoted an enormous amount of time in a sustained effort. His initial (now fully justified) audacity has been eclipsed by his tenacity.

Jack had the drive to change things, and I believe it fortunate that he worked somewhat apart from the established institutions of UK parapsychology and psychical research. Standing outside the establishment one encounters less pressure to conform and can more easily pioneer new directions. It was his good luck to find a supportive advisor in Fiona Bowie, who has had an interest in related topics.

Paranthropology allowed new voices to be heard, voices that likely would have been ignored. It also provides a publicly accessible archive that anyone can reproduce. It thus ensures the survival of the work of its contributors, which can be built upon to advance the field.

Jack Hunter's own work has substantially advanced. I have witnessed a growing intellectual sophistication, an increasing grasp of historical research, a talent to identify and articulate key issues, and a much-sharpened critical judgment. Recently I have had the opportunity to read a draft of his doctoral thesis. It is impressive. I learned much from it, and I am pleased to have had a small influence on it. I look forward to reading his future works.

– George P. Hansen
November 2017

INTRODUCTION

This collection started life as a private project to gather my essays from the past few years together in one place so that I wouldn't lose them. In a way, they encapsulate the development of my thinking about spirit mediumship and the paranormal over the course of the writing and research for my doctoral thesis (Hunter, 2017), which was written in parallel to – and incorporates parts of – the essays contained in this volume. This book also includes a selection of transcripts of interviews I did for various magazines, blogs and podcasts over the years, which I feel help to clarify and expand on some of the ideas presented in the essay chapters. This book is not, therefore, a definitive statement on the paranormal – it is not a closed system – but rather should be thought of as a spring-board for furthering alternative approaches to thinking about the paranormal. It is open-ended and is intended to be encouraging of further research and innovation in this field.

All research presented here has been compiled in an effort to develop what I call a *non-reductive anthropology of the paranormal*. By 'non-reductive' I mean an approach to investigating the paranormal that does not seek *easy explanations*, and that emphasises complexity over simplicity. For example, my analysis of spirit mediumship practices and experiences at the Bristol Spirit Lodge, combined with reviews of the theoretical literature on spirit possession and mediumship, made it clear that I was dealing with a particularly *complex phenomenon* that could not be reduced to a *single* causal explanation. To name just a few of the most popular explanations for spirit mediumship, we have: outright fraud, Dissociative Identity Disorder, hysteria, social protest, spirit communication, psi or super-psi, bereavement counselling, cognitive category error, epileptic seizure, psychological defence mechanism, cultural performance, oral history tradition and transmission, and so on. Perspectives from psychology, neuroscience, performance studies, social-functionalism, biology, and parapsychology amongst others all offer *pieces of the puzzle* – and, taken together, move us closer (if not all the way) to a more complete understanding – but none of these perspectives is completely satisfying taken alone, which is precisely what most theorists seem to want to do. I would suggest that it is more likely that the 'truth' (whatever that might be) lies somewhere *in between*, in what Charles Fort might call an 'intermediate' space (Fort, 2008), or what I have called an 'ontologically flooded' state – a position that is open to the possibility of multiple influencing factors, processes, worlds and phenomena.

From this perspective, questions of *belief*, which have been the dominant focus of the social sciences, become problematic. If we focus only on the issue of belief, then what about all the other possible factors involved, not least of which is *direct personal experience*? This approach is particularly challenging to the dominant academic (materialist) epistemology and ontology, which assume that we can only gain valid knowledge (i.e. empirically verifiable and falsifiable knowledge), about the world through objective, quantitative methods. Moreover, this view implies that any explanation must *ultimately* boil down to a purely physical process, as all experience is *produced* by the brain. This perspective results in mind/consciousness being reduced to a by-product of physiological functioning, in spite of apparent experiential evidence to the contrary, which is further explained away in terms of 'delusion' or 'hallucination.' If we truly want to understand spirit mediumship, alien abduction, astral projection, shamanism, witchcraft, magic and religion then we must escape from this mode of thinking and engage with experience on its own terms. Taking experience seriously on its own terms, however, also means we must take the implications of experience seriously. Treating subjective experience as valid data for social scientific research means that we must take seriously the possibility that the experiences reported by trance mediums in altered states of consciousness (or indeed any other kind of paranormal experience), might tell us something useful about the world, about the nature of consciousness, and about ourselves.

Through adopting the open-ended and open-minded perspective that *there may yet be phenomena in the natural world that exceed the limits of current scientific knowledge and understanding* (psi/spirits/the personhood of ecosystems/something else altogether), it is possible to avoid the hegemonic dismissal of alternative belief systems, world-views and ontologies as necessarily unfounded and irrational (an attitude that has unfortunately dominated mainstream scholarly discourse around the paranormal, non-ordinary realities, magic and anomalous experience), and move forward toward a richer engagement with them than has hitherto been achieved in the social sciences. This is precisely the kind of open-minded, ontological approach advocated in the following chapters, and it is my hope that this book might inspire others to take a similar critical but open-minded leap into the intermediate zone of the paranormal.

THE PROBLEMATIC PARANORMAL:
SUPERNATURAL OR NATURAL?

Spirit mediumship is just one of many human experiences that, particularly in the context of post-industrial Euro-American cultures, frequently falls under the controversial banner of the 'paranormal.' Because of this classification, mediumship is often viewed as an inherently 'suspicious,' usually 'fraudulent,' and occasionally even 'dangerous,' activity. The reasons for this are deeply rooted in Western academia's struggle to distance itself from supernaturalism, and to establish materialist naturalism as its dominant metaphysical paradigm. Equally, many religious traditions (especially the Judeo-Christian traditions), also condemn the practice of spirit mediumship, primarily on the grounds that it is 'demonic,'[1] though perhaps more likely as a means of asserting the primacy of a particular mode of spiritual communication, i.e. through divine revelation, scripture, and through the priesthood.

Before we proceed, it is important that we take a moment to unpack the polymorphous category of the paranormal in order to get to grips with anthropology's historical attitudes towards the anomalous. This is done primarily with the aim of developing a non-reductive approach to spirit mediumship (or any other paranormal or magico-religious phenomenon) that is capable of side-stepping prevailing academic attitudes to the paranormal without bracketing

---

[1] See, for example, Deuteronomy 18:10-12: "Let no-one be found among you [...] who practises divination or sorcery, interprets omens, engages in witchcraft, or casts spells, or who is a medium or spiritist or who consults the dead. Anyone who does these things is detestable to the Lord, and because of these detestable practices the Lord your God will drive out those nations before you."

it out (or presupposing it), thus allowing researchers to move forward into new arenas of inquiry and understanding.[2]

The Problem of the Paranormal

The paranormal is a collective term for a wide variety of experiences and phenomena (cf. Cardin, 2015 for an example of this diversity). This diversity of experiences, combined with their liminal nature, render the paranormal particularly difficult, though not impossible, for both the 'hard' (physical) and 'soft' (social) sciences to tackle.

The paranormal can also be said to possess archetypal 'trickster' like characteristics (Hansen, 2001). Paranormal experiences are often simultaneously absurd and deeply meaningful, both ridiculous and highly significant, and frequently transcend cultural and personal spheres (Kastrup, 2011; Kripal, 2011).[3] Indeed, the paranormal is, by

---

[2] I have chosen to continue to use the term 'paranormal' in my discussions of spirit mediumship for several reasons. Primarily, it is used in the spirit of its earliest form as denoting phenomena that are not yet understood by science. I argue that the dominant anthropological theories of spirit possession and mediumship have been unsuccessful in providing adequate accounts of the phenomenon. Through employing the term 'paranormal' in this context I hope to make it clear that the mainstream theories have not yet fully comprehended the phenomenon in its totality (we do not yet have a sufficient theory of it), and aim to emphasise the fact that there is still a lot more to learn about it, some of which may go beyond, or transcend, the limits of the standard models usually assumed in the social sciences. I feel that the term, to paraphrase Rupert Sheldrake, helps to 'free the spirit of scientific enquiry.' Admitting the possibility of the paranormal is also a necessary first step in developing a new approach to such subjects.

[3] Its ambiguity is, in part, due to its liminal nature. Jeffrey Kripal has commented on this feature of the paranormal as a category of experience in his suggestion that the psychical can best be understood as the 'sacred in transit from a traditional religious register into a modern scientific one' (Kripal, 2010: 9) The paranormal exists, therefore, somewhere in the interstices between religion and science. Kripal has further defined the 'sacred' as homologous with 'consciousness' (Kripal, 2015). According to Kripal's view, then, in dealing with the paranormal we are also dealing explicitly with questions concerning the very nature of human consciousness. I tend to agree with Kripal's suggestion that we stand to learn a lot about the nature of human consciousness from taking

its very nature, 'multi-dimensional.' It operates on numerous different levels, including, but not limited to, social, cultural, psychological and physiological levels, and includes spiritual, mythic, narrative, symbolic and experiential dimensions. The paranormal might also be understood as implying the existence of other worlds, planes of reality and realms of consciousness yet to be fully described, or even recognised, by science. As such, there are numerous problems that come with any attempt at making a serious scholarly study of subjects that are classed as paranormal or anomalous, not least of which is the academic taboo against taking it seriously at all (Cardeña, 2014).

Defining 'The Paranormal'

The term 'paranormal' was first introduced into our lexicon early in the twentieth century by psychical researchers as a replacement for the much more loaded term 'supernatural,'[4] which had been used by theologians since the Middle Ages to refer to the explicitly religious phenomena documented in the Bible, and other religious texts. Miracles, such as Moses' vision of the burning bush, Christ's resurrection from the dead, and the revelation of the Qur'an to the Prophet Muhammed (Pbuh), for example, were understood as manifestations of the power of an almighty God altering the course of everyday 'natural' law with the aim of producing faith in those who bore witness to them, or heard stories about them.

The association of the term 'supernatural' with the direct action of God (and all of the doctrinal baggage that comes with the category of religion), coupled with the idea that such miraculous phenomena were somehow causally separated from the rest of the laws governing the natural world, did not appeal to the early members of the Society for Psychical Research, who founded their society in 1882 specifically with the goal of investigating similar claims (such as ostensible visions, apparitions, survival after death, spirit communication, telepathy and psychokinesis), using rational scientific methods (Haynes, 1982; Broughton, 1991; Blum, 2007).

---

paranormal experiences seriously, and this work is, in part, a response to this observation.

[4] Originally used in its Latin form, *supernaturalis* is used by Christian theologians from the Thirteenth Century onwards to refer to the miraculous events documented in the Bible (Bartlett, 2008).

The term 'paranormal' was originally, therefore, a sceptical one. It represented a scholarly reaction against the 'supernatural' as an unscientific designation for unusual phenomena. By implementing the neologism 'supernormal' (later becoming 'para-normal'),[5] defined as referring to phenomena beyond the scope of *current* scientific understanding (Myers, 1992; Kripal, 2011: 66), as opposed to 'supernatural,' which implies phenomena firmly *beyond the ordinary laws of nature* (and hence beyond the scope of human reason), psychical researchers were attempting to demonstrate that paranormal occurrences, if real, were as much a part of the natural world as anything else and, as such, were equally as amenable to scientific investigation, experimentation and theorising (Hansen, 2001: 21). The psychical researcher Frederic Myers, who first coined the term 'supernormal,' writes in his *Human Personality and its Survival of Bodily Death* that:

> The word supernatural is open to grave objections; it assumes that there is something outside nature, and it has become associated with arbitrary inference with law. Now there is no reason to suppose that the psychical phenomena with which we deal are less a part of nature, or less subject to fixed and definite law, than any other phenomena (Myers, 1902, as cited by Kripal, 2010: 67)

The term 'paranormal,' then, although by now associated with a wide range of pop-culture notions (not all of which are positive), *is*, nevertheless, a scientific one, implemented in the first place to bring anomalous phenomena back into the wider scientific discourse without 'supernatural' or religious connotations.

Naturalising the Supernatural

Ethnographic fieldworkers, immersed in the life-ways of cultures that do not share Western academia's aversion to 'anomalous' events,

---

[5] The pre-fix 'para' suggests phenomena that currently stand outside the limits of scientific explanatory models. Para-psychology, for example, deals with psychological phenomena that are not adequately explained by dominant psychological theories. A Para-anthropology might, therefore, be concerned with human experiences/abilities/practices that are not adequately explained by the dominant anthropological theories.

have frequently highlighted the inadequacy of Western distinctions between the 'natural' and the 'supernatural' when addressing the beliefs of their informants, whose worldviews often do not adhere to such rigid dichotomies (Bowie, 2011). In many cultures there simply is no distinction between natural and supernatural orders of existence. In considering Sudanese Azande beliefs in witchcraft, for example, E.E. Evans-Pritchard (1902-1973) noted that:

> To us supernatural means very much the same as abnormal or extraordinary. Azande certainly have no such notions of reality. They have no conception of 'natural' as we understand it, and therefore neither of the 'supernatural' as we understand it. Witchcraft is to Azande an ordinary and not an extraordinary, even though it may in some circumstances be an infrequent, event. It is a normal, and not an abnormal happening (Evans-Pritchard, 1976: 30).

Evans-Pritchard is suggesting here that Western Rationalism's usually assumed binary distinction between 'natural' and 'supernatural' should not be taken as a universal feature of human thought – in actuality it appears to be a distinctly recent construct. Phenomena that would be classified as supernatural, or paranormal, in 'modern' Western societies are not necessarily conceived in the same way in other cultural systems, and may be understood as *natural* components of everyday life (as witchcraft is for the Azande).

Founding sociologist Émile Durkheim (1853-1917) made a similar point about the category of the supernatural when he noted that it emerged relatively recently in the history of the development of modern thought, coinciding with the rise of the European Enlightenment and the gradual proliferation of natural science and rationalist philosophy. He writes:

> In order to call certain phenomena supernatural, one must already have the sense that there is a natural order of things, in other words, that the phenomena of the universe are connected to one another according to certain necessary relationships called laws [...] But this notion of universal determinism is very recent [...] This idea is a triumph of empirical sciences; it is their basic postulate and has been demonstrated by their progress. Yet as long as this notion was absent or was not firmly established, the most marvelous events never seemed inconceivable (Durkheim, 2008: 28).

In an encyclopaedia entry on the concept of 'Miracle,' Fiona Bowie makes another similar point when she suggests that '[f]or the majority of non-Western people practising a so-called traditional or indigenous religion [...] the term 'miracle' has little meaning, as the boundaries between the natural and supernatural, material and immaterial worlds are drawn rather differently' (Bowie, 2015: 164).

To a large extent, then, what an individual deems to be possible (the full extent of their conception of reality) is simultaneously restricted and facilitated by cultural norms and expectations. For those whose worldview (which is not to necessarily imply a 'Non-Western' worldview), allows for the possibility of paranormal phenomena they pose no threat, while for those whose worldview rejects the possibility of such phenomena they are a very real threat to established models.

Alternative Terminologies

In recent decades even the term 'paranormal,' originally (as we have just seen) employed as a means to naturalise the supernatural, has itself been subjected to scholarly attempts to further bring it into the domain of the natural sciences. Biologist and parapsychologist Rupert Sheldrake, for example, has argued that the so-called 'paranormal' is, in actuality, perfectly normal, owing to the extremely widespread belief in, and experience of, phenomena such as telepathy and precognition among the general population.[6] Sheldrake has, therefore, expressed his

---

[6] According to a 2001 US Gallup poll 54% reported belief in 'Psychic or spiritual healing or the power of the human mind to heal the body,' 50% reported belief in 'ESP,' 38% believed that 'Ghosts or that spirits of dead people can come back in certain places and situations,' 36% believed in 'Telepathy, or communication between minds without using the traditional five senses,' 28% reported belief 'That people can hear from or communicate mentally with someone who has died,' and 15% believed in 'Channeling, or allowing a "spirit-being" to temporarily assume control of a human body. All of these had seen an increase since the 1990 poll (Newport & Strausberg, 2001). A more recent survey of 4096 adults conducted in the UK in 2009 by Ipsos Mori found 24% of respondents reporting having experienced precognition, 12.8% ESP, 12.4% Mystical Experiences, 11.5% Telepathy and 10.4% After Death Communication (Castro *et al.*, 2014). These represent surprisingly high percentages for experiencing phenomena that are supposedly anomalous or abnormal. Such findings support the findings

preference for what he considers to be the more neutral term 'psychic' (2005: 12),[7] which does not aim to distinguish such occurrences from other normal and natural phenomena. For Sheldrake, the term holds open the possibility that the paranormal might actually be an everyday occurrence. Other scholars prefer to use terms such as 'non-ordinary' (Harner, 1980; 2013), or 'extraordinary' (Young & Goulet, 1994; Straight, 2007), when discussing these kinds of experience in an attempt to distance their discussions from the negative connotations of the 'paranormal,' which is unfortunately often associated with notions of irrational thinking and charlatanism.[8] Arguing along similar lines, Robert Shanafelt has proposed the term 'marvel,' which he defines as 'an event of extraordinary wonder, thought to have physical consequences, claimed to be the result of ultra-natural forces.' He prefers this term because it 'encompasses divine interventions, supernatural wonders, and other paranormal phenomena without the implied hierarchy of monotheism or traditional anthropology' (2004: 322).

The term 'xenonormal' has also been suggested as an alternative label for anomalous occurrences, and refers to phenomena that appear to be paranormal at first glance but that, on further investigation, turn out to have much more prosaic explanations, for example mis-observation, pareidolia, cognitive illusions, and so on (Townsend, nd.). Others prefer the term 'anomalous,' or 'anomalistic,' which come with the implication that such phenomena will one day find a place within our scientific understanding of the universe, whether as genuine occurrences or simple misinterpretations of otherwise mundane events (Wescott, 1977: 345-346; Holt *et al.*, 2012).

Parapsychologists have labelled these types of experiences and occurrences 'psi' phenomena. Social psychologist and parapsychological researcher Daryl Bem, for example, provides a useful definition of 'psi' as denoting 'anomalous processes of information or energy transfer that are not currently explainable in terms of known physical or biological mechanisms' (2011: 407). *Psi* is an umbrella term used in reference to the supposed human faculties of psychokinesis (PK – the influence of

---

of earlier sociological research, which suggests that such experiences are far from uncommon (Greeley, 1975).

[7] Though this term also carries negative connotations in the mainstream media.

[8] A state of affairs that is perpetuated by the vocal activities of the skeptical and new-atheist movements.

mind upon matter), and extrasensory perception (ESP), which itself encompasses telepathy (mind-to-mind communication), clairvoyance (distant viewing) and precognition (knowing future events before they come to pass). These are the building blocks of the paranormal, the theoretical mechanisms by which paranormal events occur. Such phenomena, if real (as the parapsychological literature would appear to suggest), must be thought of not as somehow separate from the natural world, but rather as inherent and fundamental aspects of it – not supernatural, but natural.

There is, however, a significant difference between the kinds of ostensible phenomena designated by the term 'psi' and the supposed action of spirits during séances. Indeed, parapsychological investigators have historically struggled with the difficulty of distinguishing between spirit action and psi in the context of spirit mediumship demonstrations. The debate is ongoing, and is often referred to as the 'survival vs. psi' debate (Beischel & Rock, 2009; Sudduth, 2013). Given that, in essence, both the survival hypothesis and the psi hypothesis seem equally to fit the data of spirit mediumship, it is entirely possible that the mediums I encountered during my fieldwork might actually have been in contact with deceased spirits. Equally as possible is the idea that they *might* have been employing (or attempting to employ) some form of psi in their mediumistic demonstrations.[9]

Irrespective of the nomenclature we employ, it is clear that we are referring to essentially the same set of experiences and phenomena, regardless of whether we call them supernatural, paranormal, extraordinary, ultra-natural, xenonormal, anomalous or psi phenomena (Marton, 2010: 11-13). It is very easy for scholarly discussions to get too caught up in debates over nomenclature and terminology. For this reason, I will be seen to use many of these terms interchangeably throughout the course of this book, but I am confident that the reader will 'know what I am talking about,' and that it will not have a detrimental effect on the accuracy of the research presented here. Through adopting the perspective that there *may yet be phenomena in the natural world that*

---

[9] We currently do not know enough about what is going on in cases of spirit mediumship to state definitively whether mediums are communicating with spirits or employing innate psi capacities. Even if it is a matter of spirits communicating through mediums, we might still expect some form of psi as a mediator between the spirit and the medium. We are back to the old problem of how mind/consciousness and matter/the brain interact with one another.

escape the limits of current scientific understanding (psi/spirits/more), it is possible to avoid the hegemonic dismissal of alternative belief systems as necessarily unfounded and irrational, and move forward towards a richer engagement with them than has hitherto been achieved in the social sciences. This is precisely the kind of open-minded approach I would like to advocate.

ANTHROPOLOGY AND THE PARANORMAL:
TOWARD AN INTERMEDIATIST APPROACH

The development of a non-reductive anthropological approach to the paranormal is not necessarily a new idea, having precedents throughout the history of the discipline (see Schroll & Schwartz, 2005; Hunter, 2009; Luke, 2010; Laughlin, 2012), and beginning with the efforts of Andrew Lang (1844-1912) in the late nineteenth century to promote what he termed 'comparative psychical research.'[10] Lang saw striking similarities, across time, space and culture, in narrative accounts of paranormal experiences and phenomena, which led him to conclude that something more than mere 'hallucination,' 'delusion' and 'fraud' was going on. He wrote, for instance, of similarities in descriptions of apparent spirit manifestations cross-culturally, commenting on their core-features and pervasiveness:

> [...] from the Australians [...] in the bush, who hear raps when the spirits come, to ancient Egypt, and thence to Greece, and last, in our own time, in a London suburb, similar experiences, real or imaginary, are explained by the same hypothesis. No 'survival' can be more odd and striking, none more illustrative of the permanence, in human nature, of certain elements (Lang, 1894: 19).

Lang considered these cross-cultural correspondences to be particularly important observations because they seemed to provide objective cross-cultural evidence for the reality of certain core phenomena. Much as his contemporaries E.B. Tylor (1832-1917) and J.G. Frazer (1854-1941) had catalogued countless examples of rites,

---

[10] The comparative method was the dominant paradigm in anthropology at the time (Harris, 1969: 150-157), and so must have seemed like an obvious methodology to apply to the growing literature on psychical research.

rituals and myths to formulate their anthropological theories, so Lang catalogued accounts of ostensible paranormal experiences, appealing to the sheer number of accounts for the plausibility of his observations.

In light of these observations, Lang was deeply critical of both his contemporaries in anthropology and members of the Society for Psychical Research (of which he was also a member), for not sharing ideas and insights. The anthropologists were unwilling to take the literature of psychical research seriously, and the psychical researchers were unwilling to investigate accounts of ostensibly paranormal phenomena documented in the ethnographic literature. It would not be until much later in the twentieth century that a real interdisciplinary dialogue finally began to take shape (see Swanton, 1953; Weiant, 1960; Huxley, 1967).

In 1968 a posthumously published book by Italian philosopher and anthropologist Ernesto de Martino (1908–1965), entitled *Magic: Primitive and Modern*, presented a synthesis of the findings of anthropology and parapsychology. De Martino was an early advocate of interdisciplinary collaboration in anthropology, arguing for the need for anthropologists to collaborate with psychologists, and some of his research was funded by grants from the Parapsychology Foundation in New York (Ferrari, 2014: 21).[11] One of his most significant observations with regard to the paranormal, in my opinion, was that laboratory investigations of psi phenomena regularly ignore the emotional, social and environmental contexts within which ostensible psi experiences naturally occur. He wrote that 'in the laboratory, the drama of the dying man who appears [...] to a relative or friend, is reduced to an oft repeated experiment — one that tries to transmit to the mind of a subject the image of a playing card, chosen at random' (de Martino, 1968: 46). This, he suggests, represents 'an almost complete reduction of the historical stimulus that is at work in the purely spontaneous occurrence of such phenomena' (1968: 46). In other words: the drama of real life is ignored in the parapsychological laboratory experiment. It is precisely at this juncture, so de Martino suggests, that the ethnographic methodology of anthropology succeeds in illuminating the nature of the paranormal as embedded within social life. Specifically, ethnographic accounts can document the social dramas in which ostensible psi experiences and phenomena manifest in their most elaborate forms, i.e. the socio-cultural conditions within which such experiences most frequently occur (regardless of whether they are genuinely 'paranormal' or not).

---

[11] Who have also provided funding for my own research.

De Martino's contribution to the development of an anthropological approach to the paranormal was an important one, though it is very often overlooked by contemporary Anglo-American researchers, primarily because of the scarcity of English translations of his work. It paves the way for the emergence of a processual approach to understanding the paranormal.

Interestingly, as an aside note, in 1969 the famed anthropologist Margaret Mead (1901-1978) became the main driving force behind the incorporation of the *Parapsychological Association* into the American Academy of Sciences. Mead had taken part in parapsychological laboratory experiments using Zener cards with psychologist Gardner Murphy (1895-1979) in the 1950s, and was particularly interested in understanding the social and psychological dynamics of psychic sensitives, and so was keen to see parapsychology taken seriously as a valid area of scientific inquiry. Like de Martino, Mead saw the potential for research into the socio-cultural and psychological conditions that give rise to ostensible psi experiences, again emphasising the importance of process.

Other significant contributions to this developing trend in anthropology were later gathered together and published in the book *Extrasensory Ecology* (1974), edited by Joseph K. Long (1937-1999), which was inspired partly by his own unusual experiences while conducting fieldwork in Jamaica in the 1960s, and in another important edited volume published by the *Parapsychology Foundation* in the same year (Angoff & Barth, 1974). Both books brought together papers from leading theorists in anthropology and parapsychology and were groundbreaking in their presentation of a seriously reasoned anthropological evaluation of the evidence from parapsychology. Both books took seriously the implications of the parapsychological data for theory development in anthropology, with contributors from both sides of the paranormal debate, and were the seeds for what would eventually emerge as the anthropology of consciousness in the 1980s (Schroll & Schwartz, 2005). Indeed, Joseph K. Long served as the president of the *Association for Transpersonal Anthropology* (1980-81), and for the *Association for the Anthropological Study of Consciousness* (1984-86), which immediately preceded the emergence of the anthropology of consciousness as an anthropological sub-discipline.

In 1989 the *Society for the Anthropology of Consciousness* was finally accepted as a member of the American Anthropological Association, and has subsequently developed its focus and specialisation through its stated interest in altered states of consciousness and consciousness studies, shamanic, religious, and spiritual traditions, psychoactive substances, philosophical, symbolic, and linguistic studies, and anomalous experiences. It could be argued that the roots of the anthropology of consciousness go right back to the early pioneering work of scholars such as E.B. Tylor and Andrew Lang, whose interests in the experiential origins of supernatural beliefs set a clear precedent for the movement.

The anthropology of consciousness also has roots in slightly more recent trends in intellectual thought, including specifically transpersonal psychology (cf. Lajoie & Shapiro, 1992), and, slightly later, transpersonal anthropology (Schroll & Schwartz, 2005: 6-24), as well as in the humanistic anthropology of Edith Turner. Transpersonal anthropologist Charles Laughlin defines transpersonalism as 'a movement in science towards seeing experiences had in life, that somehow go beyond the boundaries of ordinary ego-consciousness, as data' (Laughlin, 2012: 70-74). Such experiences may include any number of ostensibly paranormal experiences and alterations of consciousness, as well as including more common (though not necessarily any less meaningful) experiences such as dreaming (Laughlin, 2011; Young, 2012), *déjà vu*, synchronistic coincidences and so on.

Typical methods in the anthropology of consciousness include active and immersive participation in rituals and other magico-religious performances, and a deliberate attempt to attain the states of consciousness that are most important to the particular society under investigation. This might include, for example, consuming culturally significant psychoactive substances (cf. Jokic, 2008), or participating in other forms of consciousness alteration and ritual in order to move towards a comprehension of the 'experiential' component of alternative worldviews. Indeed, Charles Laughlin has defined the transpersonal anthropologist as one who is 'capable of participating in transpersonal experience; that is, capable of both attaining whatever extraordinary experiences and phases of consciousness enrich the [socio-cultural] system, and relating these experiences to [...] patterns of symbolism, cognition and practice found in religions and cosmologies all over the planet' (Laughlin, 1997).

Laughlin's broader 'biogenetic structuralist' approach has also gone on to inspire other anthropologists, notably Michael Winkelman, who has applied similar methodologies to the study of shamanic practices and experiences (Winkelman, 2000). Winkelman also put forward the suggestion that the longstanding anthropological debate over magic might benefit from parapsychological insights—essentially suggesting the possibility that magical systems around the world might be tapping into (or at least attempting to tap into) psi for their efficacy (Winkelman, 1982).

Another particularly important book in bringing about a new anthropological approach to the paranormal, and specifically with regard to taking the extraordinary experiences of ethnographers engaged in fieldwork seriously,[12] was David E. Young and Jean-Guy Goulet's *Being Changed by Cross-Cultural Encounters* (1994). In their introduction Young and Goulet suggest that their book attempts to do three important things:

> (1) provide personal accounts by anthropologists who have taken their informants' extraordinary experiences seriously or who have had extraordinary experiences themselves, (2) develop the beginnings of a theoretical framework which will help facilitate an understanding of such experiences, and (3) explore the issue of how such experiences can be conveyed and explained to a 'scientifically-oriented' audience in such a way that they are not automatically dismissed without a fair hearing (Young & Goulet, 1994: 12).

Participation and Experience

Susan Greenwood (2013) has proposed another alternative means of overcoming the conceptual difficulties associated with the academic study of the paranormal, broadly in line with the approaches favoured by transpersonal anthropologists. Greenwood advocates an approach centred around the notion of what she calls 'magical consciousness,' which she explains is 'characterized by the notion of *participation*, an orientation to the world based on persons and things in contact with a non-ordinary spirit reality' (2013: 211). She explains, for example, how 'it is possible to overcome the anthropological dilemma of the reality of spirits by adopting an attitude of spiritual agnosticism by not believing or disbelieving in their reality' (2013: 218)—a third-way between belief and disbelief.

---

[12] Many ethnographers do indeed seem to experience ostensible paranormal phenomena while participating in the life-worlds of their informants (see Hunter, 2011 for an overview of some particularly noteworthy examples).

This is an essentially phenomenological approach employing a form of bracketing about ultimate ontological questions, but not of dismissing paranormal claims and experiences outright, and bears resemblances to David J. Hufford's experience-centered approach. Hufford's approach does not *a priori* deny the significance of experience, nor does it necessarily pass an ontological judgment on the nature of the experiences it investigates. Hufford writes:

> A major advantage of the experience-centered approach for carrying out this task is that it does not require presuppositions about the ultimate nature of the events investigated, although it can provide some information relevant to investigations of that nature (Hufford,1982: 256).

Learning to See What the Natives See

The ethnographic approach I have endeavoured to utilise in my own research has been greatly influenced by the work of Edith Turner (1921-2016), an ethnographer who highlights the importance in the study of religion, and religious/supernatural experience more specifically, for the ethnographer to 'learn to see what the Native sees' (1993:11). She argues that it is only through attaining the kinds of experience deemed important by the host culture that the anthropologist is able to move away from making excessively reductive assumptions about their beliefs and experiences. This approach might be referred to as a form of 'transpersonal anthropology,' that is an approach concerned with so-called 'transpersonal experiences.' Through participating fully in the host culture, to the extent of accessing culturally relevant experiences, the transpersonal anthropologist is able to gain a perspective on a particular culture that could not be attained through any normal means of objective observation. This is what anthropologist Zeljko Jokic refers to as 'a point of intersubjective entry' into another 'lifeworld' (Jokic, 2008b: 36). In order to 'see what the Natives see,' and to make use of transpersonal experiences as ethnographic data, it is necessary to immerse oneself fully in the culture under investigation, to essentially 'go native' for the duration of the research. Fiona Bowie proposes a methodology to achieve this kind of immersion, which she terms 'cognitive empathetic engagement.' Cognitive empathetic engagement is defined as a method by which:

[...] the observer [...] approaches the people or topic studied in an open-minded and curious manner, without presuppositions, prepared to entertain the world view and rationale presented and to experience, as far as possible and practical, a different way of thinking and interpreting events' (Bowie, 2010: 5).

The ultimate aim of this type of approach, then, is to interpret religious, spiritual and paranormal beliefs and experiences from a perspective that does not, from the very outset, reduce the complexity of the phenomenon or ignore the significance of personal, subjective experience. Indeed, Deirdre Meintel, in her investigations of contemporary Spiritualist groups in Canada, has specifically noted the usefulness of such approaches in interpreting and understanding Spiritualist belief and practice (2007: 125).

Paranthropology

All of this falls quite neatly under the label of *paranthropology*, a term first coined by the linguist Roger Wescott (1977) to refer to an anthropological approach to the paranormal, but which was eventually superseded by 'transpersonal anthropology,' and later by the 'anthropology of consciousness' (Luke, 2010). In recent years the term has been revived and the idea further refined (cf. Hunter, 2012b, 2012c; Caswell, 2014). Social anthropologist Fabian Graham, for instance, differentiates paranthropology from more traditional approaches to the anthropology of religion according to the way in which the two approaches interpret the *objects* of religious and paranormal beliefs specifically. The anthropology of religion, Graham argues, focuses primarily on systems of religious *belief*, bracketing out or negating the ontological status of the objects of the beliefs themselves (which are generally ignored), while paranthropology accepts the *possibility* that the objects of supernatural beliefs *may* have some form of independent ontological reality. He writes that 'paranthropology [defines] itself in relation to the phenomena themselves, and not to the belief systems, scientific or religious, that have evolved to support the phenomena' (Graham, 2011: 21).

Arguing along similar lines, anthropologist Patric Giesler has proposed a step away from the bracketing out of questions of ontology in phenomenological and social-scientific approaches to supernatural beliefs with his 'parapsychological anthropology,' which is geared directly towards attempting to experimentally verify or disprove the reality of paranormal phenomena in the field. Giesler has proposed a methodology for investigating the social and cultural factors involved in the manifestation of psi phenomena, as and when they occur in the field, which he terms 'psi-in-process.' Such an approach attempts to overcome the limitations of classical laboratory based parapsychological research by conducting experiments in the field, as de Martino had earlier suggested, with minimal reduction of the natural environmental setting. Giesler's own research has, for instance, investigated psi phenomena in the context of Afro-Brazilian spirit possession rituals using standard parapsychological tests.

For example, in an experiment with mediums from the religious groups Candomble, Caboclo and Umbanda, Giesler modified parapsychologist Helmut Schmidt's classic random number generator psychokinesis (PK) experiments by using culturally meaningful target symbols rather than standard Euro-American symbols (which had little relevance to Giesler's experimental participants). Giesler's results were significantly above chance and were suggestive of PK (mental influence on physical systems), albeit on a small scale (Giesler, 1985). Such an experimental approach takes a significant step away from anthropology's more traditional bracketing out of questions of ontology; indeed Giesler takes the opposite perspective and suggests that:

> [...] one of the purposes of anthropology is to explain the ontology, development, and function of the beliefs, practices, and claims of magico-religious experiencers [...] it should assume that psi *could* exist and then proceed etically on that assumption (Giesler 1984: 302-303).

Unlike Giesler's work, my own research as presented in this book does not attempt to scientifically verify the claims of mediums, but it does take up his call to 'assume that psi *could* exist,' because, in Zeljko Jokic's words, this opens a 'point of intersubjective entry' into the lifeworld of our research informants.

The approach employed in my own research, therefore, has been predominantly experiential, and does not make any *a priori* assumptions as to the ontology of the objects of the beliefs it explores, maintaining Greenwood's agnosticism towards the ontology of paranormal phenomena, while remaining open to the possibility that they might, in some way, actually be real. This is a delicate balance to maintain, between being open to the possibility of ontological realities, while also remaining ontologically neutral. Rather than beginning from the assumption that spirits either do exist or don't exist, I take the position that spirits *could* exist[13] and proceed from there, asking 'if spirits exist, *how* are they communicated with and experienced?' This might be termed an 'as if' approach. Writing about the Ojibwa belief in 'other-than-human-beings,' Irving Hallowell took a similar perspective and emphasised the ethnographic importance of understanding such beliefs from an insider perspective:

> [...] if, in the world view of a people, 'persons' as a class include entities other than human beings, then our objective approach is not adequate for presenting an accurate description of 'the way a man, in a particular society, sees himself in relation to all else.' A different perspective is required for this purpose (Hallowell, 2002: 21).

In a recent ethnographic account of spirit possession rituals in Indonesia, anthropologist Nils Bubandt has argued in favour of treating spirits as 'methodologically real' informants, as to do so allows the anthropologist to 'get on with the business of studying the social and political reality of spirits' (Bubandt, 2009: 298). To treat the spirits as methodologically real does not require the ethnographer to verify or falsify their existence as ontologically distinct entities, nor is it necessary to attempt to prove that the spirits are who they claim to be, although, as Hufford suggests, such an approach 'can provide some information relevant to investigations of that nature' (Hufford, 1982: 256). Therefore, rather than attempting to verify the existence of the spirits encountered during my fieldwork, this research will, instead, deal with the social, psychological, performative and physiological processes through which spirits are expressed and interacted with in the context of the séance, as if they are real ethnographic informants.

Ontological Flooding

The epistemological frameworks outlined in this section pave the way for a destabilisation of ontological certainty, which could help in the development of a more culturally sensitive and ontologically receptive

---

[13] This is essentially assuming what neuroscientist David Eagleman has playfully labelled a 'possibilian' perspective.

approach to non-ordinary reality, an approach that does not rely on bracketing as a means of engaging with the supernatural 'from a safe distance.' I have called this approach 'ontological flooding.'

Intermediatism

Charles Fort (1874-1932) was famous in the early decades of the twentieth century as a collector of accounts of strange occurrences, from apparent poltergeist activity through to mysterious flying objects and rains of frogs, which he found ample evidence for in newspapers and scientific journals, and which he compiled into four extraordinary books (Fort, 2008). In order to accommodate such unusual phenomena (which he called 'damned facts' because of their outright rejection by mainstream science), Fort developed the philosophy of 'intermediatism.' Fort defined intermediatism as a position in which 'nothing is real, but [...] nothing is unreal [...] all phenomena are approximations in one way between realness and unrealness' (Fort, 2008: 14; Steinmeyer, 2008: 170; Kripal, 2014: 259). In this characteristically playful way, Fort sought to deconstruct the rigid boundaries between the real and the unreal, and instead placed all phenomena, from the mundane to the extraordinary, on a sliding spectrum where all things fluctuate between the real and the unreal. From this perspective nothing can be said to be entirely 'real' or 'unreal,' everything is in flux. Fort's intermediatism can also be likened to Gregory Bateson's 'middle-way.'

E-Prime and The New Agnosticism

Drawing on Alfred Korzybski's (1879-1950) writings on general semantics, and taking inspiration from Benjamin Lee Whorf's (1897-1941) work on language and the construction of reality (Whorf, 1956), the novelist and philosopher Robert Anton Wilson (1932-2007) sought to implement and popularise the use of E-Prime, a mode of using the English language that rejects the use of the verb 'to be' in all of its forms. In this way, E-Prime avoids definitive statements of certainty in favour of uncertainty, and a capacity for change (Wilson, no date). For example, rather than saying 'The sky is blue,' E-Prime would say 'The sky appears blue to me.' Wilson also proposes what he calls a 'new agnosticism,' sometimes also called 'model agnosticism' or 'creative agnosticism,' he writes:

In this state we "are" model-relativists [...] and [are] actively creative; all perceptions (gambles) are actively known as gambles. We consciously seek to edit less and tune in more, and we look especially for events that do not neatly fit our model, since they will teach us to make a better one tomorrow, and an even better one the day after. We are not dominated by the "Real" Universe [...] (Wilson, 1987: 231).

Like Fort's sliding spectrum between the real and the unreal, Wilson suggests that all perceptions are gambles, and our models to explain them are ultimately gambles, too. Wilson's 'new agnosticism' is an epistemology of probabilities, uncertainty and indeterminism that takes its inspiration from the uncertainty of Quantum Mechanics.

Possibilianism

Possibilianism is a recent term coined and popularised by neuroscientist and author David Eagleman. According to Eagleman's possibilian philosophy, which seeks to inspire creativity and exploratory wonder in the scientific enterprise, scientific researchers are encouraged to enter into the 'possibility space,' a frame of mind in which the researcher celebrates 'the vastness of our ignorance [and is] unwilling to commit to any particular made-up story, and take[s] pleasure in entertaining multiple hypotheses' (Jansen, 2010). Again, this playfulness in considering multiple possibilities is perfectly suited to the study of the paranormal, and resonates well with Charles Fort's intermediatist philosophy and Robert Anton Wilson's implementation of E-Prime and the 'New Agnosticism.' According to this perspective, all models are understood as 'made up stories' (scientific or otherwise), and all are open to creative and critical exploration.

❋❋❋

Although only a very brief sketch of some quite complex ideas, some of these epistemological frameworks for the destabilisation of ontological certainty could be of practical use for the academic and ethnographic study of the paranormal, allowing us to engage with it on its own terms without the need to impose arbitrary brackets, or to distinguish between what is suitable and what is not suitable subject matter for social-scientific research.

An ethnographic approach that makes use of tools that destabilise ontological certainty, at least in the context of the ethnographic text, but also experientially in the field, might lead to a more honest appreciation of the 'non-ordinary.' In a sense, then, what I am suggesting is an approach that is, in many ways, the opposite of the traditional bracketing approaches. Rather than bracketing out questions of ontology for fear that they might lead to truths ('damned facts' in Fort's terminology) that cannot, by their very nature, fit into the established order of Western academia's dominant ontology, I suggest that we essentially open the flood gates of ontological possibilities. This places all ontologies on an equal footing, so that while ontological bracketing protects and reinforces the mainstream 'consensus reality,' what we might call ontological flooding destabilises it, and opens it up to questioning, exploration and expansion— in essence such an approach places different ontological systems on an equally questionable footing.

Ontological flooding does not at all mean that we have to be any less critical in our approach. Many, if not all, of the same critical themes can continue to be examined and explored from the ontologically flooded perspective. The main difference is that we do not begin our investigation from the position of certainty that 'our ontology' is the only one that can really be taken seriously. Everything is equally possible, everything is equally questionable, and nothing is certain.

TAKING EXPERIENCE SERIOUSLY

Consciousness is one of the great mysteries of contemporary science and philosophy (Nagel, 2012: 35), and is currently undergoing something of a resurgence of interest as a field of investigation (Zahavi, 2005: 3). Many commentators have noted, however, that the bulk of research into the nature of consciousness proceeds according to a fairly restricted idea of the types of approach that can be fruitfully be applied to it (Jahn & Dunne, 1997: 204). Recently emerging as chief amongst the dominant approaches is the neurophysiological approach, which attempts to understand consciousness as either identical with, or as an epiphenomenon of, physical brain function (Churchland, 1982). This kind of reductionism, often referred to as 'mind/brain identity theory,' that is the idea that consciousness and brain-function are synonymous, is becoming increasingly popular in both the professional academic literature and the popular science literature (Searle, 1998: xii-xiii). Such reductionist accounts of consciousness have proliferated to the extent that philosopher and neurologist Raymond Tallis felt drawn to coin the term 'neuromania' to refer to the belief that contemporary neuroscience *proves* that consciousness is identical with brain function, and that free will is an illusion (Tallis, 2012). The current debate over consciousness, and in particular the relation of consciousness to the brain (the mind/body problem), is therefore torn over the question of whether consciousness can be reduced solely to the functioning of the brain or whether it might be something more than this.

Whether consciousness can be reduced to brain function or not, however, the popular emphasis on quantitative, experimental, and neurophysiological approaches to the study of consciousness is not representative of the full spectrum of possible approaches. There *are* other means of investigation. Indeed, writing as long ago as the early twentieth century, psychologist William James (1842-1910) stressed the fact that any model of the universe that fails to take into account the complexities of subjective experience will ultimately be doomed to incompleteness (James, 2004: 335). Echoing this sentiment more recently, Thomas Nagel has written that '[t]he existence of consciousness seems to imply that the physical description of the universe, in spite of its richness and explanatory power, is only part of the truth' (Nagel, 2012: 35), the very existence of subjective experience implies that a purely physical explanation of consciousness is not possible, and that our current materialistic models are lacking. Consciousness is, after all, fundamentally entwined with experience (Blackmore, 2005: 5), and it would seem counterintuitively detrimental to attempt to divorce experience from the study of consciousness. Indeed, the *Oxford Dictionary of Psychology* characterizes consciousness specifically as 'the experience of perceptions, thoughts, feelings, awareness of the external world, and [...] self-awareness' (Colman, 2009: 164). In the words of philosopher David Chalmers (1995) experience itself is the 'hard problem of consciousness.' It would seem reasonable, therefore, to take subjective experience seriously, and to explore what experience itself might tell us about the nature of consciousness.

Quantitative and Qualitative Approaches

Qualitative methodologies, defined as 'forms of data collection and analysis which rely on understanding, with an emphasis on meaning' (Scott & Marshall, 2009: 618), can provide a route towards investigating consciousness *as experienced*, and can reveal many aspects unobtainable through neurophysiological investigation. For example, an fMRI scan could not express the redness of a red apple, or the blueness of a blue sky, let alone what it is like to experience pleasure, pain, love or hate. This is not to deny the relevance and importance of quantitative, experimental or neurophysiological research; rather it is a reminder that there is more in the way of richness and meaning to the experience of consciousness than is often presented in neurophysiological accounts. Again, echoing William James, the richness and significance of experience are just as much a part of consciousness and the universe as any physical object, and, as such, demand to be taken seriously. In order to examine subjective experience, it is necessary to take a qualitative, phenomenological approach.

The phenomenological method was first developed in a systematic way by the German philosopher Edmund Husserl (1859-1938) as a means to investigate the 'structures of consciousness as experienced from the first-person point of view.' In order to investigate first-person experience in a meaningful way, Husserl developed the notion of *epoché*, a process of observation whereby all assumptions about a phenomenon are 'bracketed out' in order to understand it *as it is experienced* (Ashworth, 1996: 2), as 'pure consciousness,' without *a priori* conclusions about the ultimate nature of the experience, or biased interpretations of it (Heath, 2000: 56). Robert Sharf, for instance, writes of the aim of phenomenological bracketing in the study of religion:

> If we can bracket out our own presuppositions, temper our ingrained sense of cultural superiority, and resist the temptation to evaluate the truth claims of foreign traditions, we find that their experience of the world possesses its own rationality, its own coherence, its own truth (Sharf, 2000: 268).

The phenomenological approach, therefore, aims to understand experience (or religion, culture, love, the paranormal, and so on) as experienced and understood by the experiencer, in its own terms. This is the qualitative nature of consciousness: what it *feels* like to experience consciousness.

Anthropologist Hillary S. Webb has used the analogy of 'clock systems' and 'cloud systems,' first employed by the philosopher of science Karl Popper, to illustrate the different aspects of consciousness illuminated by quantitative and qualitative approaches respectively. Quantitative approaches focus on the 'clock systems' of consciousness, which provide 'insight into, and information about, the physiological and behavioral implications of consciousness'– factors that can be recorded and analysed using the standard methods of experimental science. Such research is useful in demonstrating the physiological correlates of consciousness, but ultimately cannot provide insight into the *lived experience* of consciousness. Research on 'cloud systems,' referring to those 'aspects of consciousness that are unpredictable and free flowing,' however, can begin to fill in the gaps left in our understanding by the quantitative methods (Velmans, 2007a: 724; Webb, 2012: 7). Qualitative data begin to fill the gaps left in the neurophysiological account. Without qualitative descriptions of conscious experiences, the physiological description of brain states will forever remain incomplete.

The Explanatory Gap

The neurophysiological (quantitative) and phenomenological (qualitative) accounts of consciousness are two sides of the same phenomenon. Firsthand, subjective conscious experiences are undoubtedly correlated to neurophysiological brain activity (Rees *et al.*, 2002), and yet a so-called 'explanatory gap' persists because it is not yet clear *how* physical brain activity can be associated with subjective experience. In his famous article 'What is it like to be a Bat?' (1974), Thomas Nagel argues that:

> [...] the subjective character of experience [...] is not captured by any of the familiar, recently devised reductive analyses of the mental, for all of them are logically compatible with its absence (1974: 436).

According to the dominant materialist view, physical matter is essentially inert, possessing no form of consciousness, which, naturally, is incompatible with the phenomenon of conscious experience. This problem is, therefore, a deep one, and runs at the core of the debate over consciousness: how can physical matter (such as the stuff from which we are made) have subjective experience?

Philosopher Max Velmans (2007b) recognises two distinct approaches to the issue of the relationship between matter and subjective consciousness, which he labels *discontinuity* and *continuity* theories. Discontinuity theories essentially take the physical materialist approach and suggest that consciousness emerged through the evolution of sufficiently complex biological systems (nervous systems and brains), and consequently is something that is only found in sufficiently complex organisms, hence it is *discontinuous in the universe* – occurring only where complex organisms are found. Of course, this still leaves open the question of how and why matter, once it reaches a sufficiently complex state of organisation, becomes conscious. The alternative view, which Velmans feels to be the most parsimonious, is the continuity model, according to which consciousness is a fundamental property of matter itself. This is a perspective that might be termed *panpsychism*. Velmans writes that according to this view:

> [...] all forms of matter have an associated form of consciousness, although in complex life forms such as ourselves, much of this consciousness is inhibited. In the cosmic explosion that gave birth to the universe, consciousness co-emerged with matter and co-evolves

with it. As matter became more differentiated and developed in complexity, consciousness became correspondingly differentiated and complex [...] Its emergence, with the birth of the universe, is neither more nor less mysterious than the emergence of matter, energy, space and time (Velmans, 2007b: 279).

Currently the explanatory gap that exists between the physical structure and functioning of our brains and the subjective nature of our conscious experiences remains open, though there are models that attempt to close it. Only time will tell which model will prove to be correct (if indeed any current model is correct, or ever can be). For the time being, however, research *must* continue, not just into the physiological structure of the brain, but also into the nature of subjective experience in all of its varied forms, in the hope that such research might contribute to the solution of these long-standing problems.

Taking Experience Seriously: What Are the Consequences?

Taking experience seriously, and using it as a means to approach the nature of consciousness, may present the researcher with novel aspects of consciousness that would otherwise go unnoticed. Indeed, there are many peculiar quirks of subjective experience that might point us towards unexpected facets of the nature of consciousness. For example, what might near-death and out-of-body experiences tell us about the nature of consciousness? What might the trance experiences of shamans and mediums, the visionary experiences of mystics, or paranormal experiences tell us about the nature of consciousness? What does the psychedelic experience tell us about consciousness? There are countless such questions, and we will briefly explore a few of them over the next couple of pages.

Near-Death Experiences

Near-death experience (NDE) researchers Sam Parnia and Peter Fenwick have argued that the NDE poses a significant challenge to the notion that consciousness and thought are 'produced by the interaction of large groups of neurones or neural networks' (2002: 9). They write:

[...] the fact that [experiences recalled during periods of severely compromised cerebral functioning and no electrical activity in the cerebral cortex and deeper brain structures] raises some questions regarding our current views on the nature of human consciousness (Parnia & Fenwick, 2002: 9).

Parnia and Fenwick suggest that the NDE experience opens up the debate over the nature of consciousness to alternative theories of the relationship between consciousness and the brain. As examples of alternative scientific models, they list Roger Penrose and Stuart Hameroff's theory of consciousness as a quantum process within neuronal microtubules (Hameroff & Penrose, 1996), Rupert Sheldrake's notion of consciousness as a 'morphic field' (Sheldrake, 1987), and the dualist idea that 'mind or consciousness may actually be a fundamental scientific entity in its own right irreducible to anything more basic' (Parnia & Fenwick, 2002: 9). Whether consciousness is any of these things or something else entirely, however, the important thing to note in the context of the theme of this anthology is that taking the phenomenology of the near-death experience seriously demands a reconsideration of the dominant mind/brain identity theory of consciousness, rekindles debate, and opens up new avenues for scientific inquiry.

Trance Experiences

As an illustration of the kind of insights that can come from taking the experiences of trance mediums seriously we now turn to recent fascinating neuroimaging research conducted by Julio Fernando Peres and colleagues (Peres *et al.*, 2012). During the practice of automatic writing (psychography), mediums claim to enter into a trance state during which their physical body comes under the influence of a discarnate entity, which then uses the medium's body to write out messages using a pen and paper. During the trance the medium experiences a state of dissociation whereby the physical movements of their body are no longer felt to be under their conscious control. The standard materialist scientific approach to such claims is dismissal, because, according to the dominant materialist paradigm, mediumistic phenomena are impossible, therefore automatic writing must be fraudulent. Nevertheless, Peres' research team did take the experiences of mediums seriously and used single photon emission computed tomography to scan the brain activity of ten automatic writers (five experienced, five less experienced), while in trance. The research findings have been summarised as follows:

> The researchers found that the experienced psychographers showed lower levels of activity in the left hippocampus (limbic system), right superior temporal gyrus, and the frontal lobe regions of the left anterior cingulate and right precentral gyrus during psychography compared to – normal writing. The difference was significant compared to the experienced mediums (Thomas Jefferson University, 2012).

The implication here is that during the trance state of the experienced automatic writers, activity is reduced in the areas of the brain usually associated with reasoning, planning, language, movement and problem solving, suggesting that the medium's dissociative experience during trance is far from delusional or fraudulent. Furthermore, the researchers conducted an analysis of the complexity of the writing and found that, contrary to what would normally be expected, the complexity increased as the activity in the areas of the brain usually associated with such complex behaviours was reduced. This raises the question of how, if the brain's functioning was reduced, such complex writing was possible. The spiritist interpretation suggests that it was spirits doing to the writing while the medium's consciousness was absent, and the data could indeed be read in this way. More cautiously, however, Andrew Newberg has suggested that this research 'reveals some exciting data to improve our understanding of the mind and its relationship with the brain' and calls for further research in this area (Thomas Jefferson University, 2012). Again, we see that taking experience seriously –, in this case the trance experiences of mediums –, instead of dismissing them as delusional or fraudulent, opens up new avenues for inquiry and provides tantalising insights into the relationship, between consciousness and the body, that might otherwise have gone unnoticed.

Psychedelic Experiences

Interestingly, a recent functional magnetic resonance imaging (fMRI) study of the effects of psilocybin (the active compound found in magic mushrooms), has revealed similar patterns of deactivation of certain brain regions while under the influence of the psychedelic compound. The study, conducted by Robin Carhart-Harris and colleagues (2011), found decreases of cerebral blood flow in the thalamus and anterior and postulate cingulate cortex after the administration of psilocybin to research participants. The researchers also found that the magnitude of the decrease in blood flow was correlated with the intensity of the subjective psychedelic experience, leading to the conclusion that the results 'strongly imply that the subjective effects of psychedelic drugs are caused by decreased activity and connectivity in the brain's key connector hubs, enabling a state of unconstrained cognition' (Carhart-Harris *et al.*, 2011: 2138). The association of heightened subjective experience with decreased neurological activity certainly poses interesting questions about the link between consciousness and the brain. Indeed, these findings, amongst others, have led some researchers to suggest a 'filter theory' of consciousness, as originally suggested by Henri Bergson (1859-1941), and borrowing from Aldous Huxley's (1894-1963) conception of the brain as a 'reducing valve' for consciousness (Luke & Friedman, 2010; Luke, 2012: 99; Kastrup, 2012; see also Carter, 2012 for an overview of the filter/transmission model). This position suggests that rather than producing conscious experience the brain acts as a receiver of consciousness, so that when, under certain circumstances (such as mediumistic trance states, or while under the influence of psychedelics), brain activity is decreased so conscious experience is increased, or expanded (Kripal, 2011). Once again, taking the psychedelic experience seriously has provided surprising insights into potential models of mind/brain interaction.

ANTHROPOLOGY AND THE ONTOLOGICAL STATUS OF THE PARANORMAL

At a talk about anthropological approaches to the study of the paranormal at the Society for Psychical Research, I was asked whether I thought that anthropology was in a position to comment on the ontology of the paranormal. This essay is an attempt to expand a little on the answer that I gave.

Anthropological approaches to the study of the paranormal have generally tended to focus on supernatural *beliefs* without any attempt at addressing the ontological status of the *objects* of these beliefs, that is what the beliefs are actually about (Giesler, 1984: 302). This trend began with Sir E.B. Tylor's nineteenth century claim that establishing the reality, or otherwise, of supernatural beliefs was beyond the scope of the anthropological endeavour. Consequently, any notion of the reality behind supernatural and religious beliefs has traditionally been 'bracketed out' in favour of studying the beliefs themselves.

As the discipline developed, however, the role of the anthropologist changed significantly. With the advent of the methodology of participant observation, as advocated by Bronislaw Malinowski in the early twentieth century, anthropologists became more than mere cut-and-paste academics. They started living amongst those that they studied, and, as they did so, found that the theories devised by armchair anthropologists in the previous century were thoroughly at odds with the facts of real "native" life. This was especially true for the idea that so-called "savages" were of a "primitive mentality," utterly devoid of reason and rationality. Fieldwork deconstructed the idea that the western world-view was somehow superior to other perspectives, and, in so doing, brought a number of fundamental assumptions into question.

A prerequisite assumption of dominant western scientific thought is that there is no supernatural order of reality. Positivism, an epistemological position that inherently denies metaphysical speculation of any sort (Comte, 1853), has been the point of departure for the vast majority of scientific thought since the middle of the nineteenth century. It has been a significant player in the secularisation and de-supernaturalisation of western culture. Anthropology, as an outgrowth of Nineteenth century European culture (like all of the social and natural sciences), has always worked from this perspective. It is understandable, therefore, that early anthropologists, although concerned specifically with notions of the supernatural, entirely ignored the possibility that the beliefs and practices they studied could have any basis in reality, or any efficacy that was not the product of delusion and faulty logic.

But what happens when anthropologists themselves are exposed to experiences that apparently exceed the explanations allowed for by dominant western rationalism, experiences that in themselves appear to support the idea that there is something more to reality than the physical, or that the dominant frameworks of Western positivism are missing something significant? How are such experiences to be interpreted and understood?

The anthropologist has several options when faced with such a situation. (1) The experience may be bracketed out in line with the position of theorists writing over a century ago. (2) It can be explained away in terms that accord nicely with positivist ideals, i.e. it was a hallucination with no ontological value. Or, (3) it can be confronted head-on and treated as a valid experience of an actual event, whether paranormal or not.

If this last route is chosen it must be admitted that there is a gap in the way that western science has looked at the world. In other words: that an aspect of reality has simply been ignored, even if this aspect turns out not to have an objective reality in a physical sense.

Now, all of this might be considered as hypothetical speculation were it not for the fact that anthropologists have indeed been privy to anomalous experiences while working in the field (McClenon & Nooney, 2002), and, to my mind, this is a fairly profound issue. It has significant implications for the way in which anthropologists interpret systems of belief and practices dealing with supernatural notions, and more broadly with the way in which science in general deals with the so-called paranormal.

The anthropological approach *is* a scientific one. In a sense, therefore, anthropologists are scientists. Their methodologies have been developed as a means to understand human beings empirically.

Participant observation, then, is a scientific technique. If paranormal experiences are achieved through participant observation then we must say that a fact of experience has been arrived at through the scientific method. If we can accept the conclusions of anthropologists concerning kinship systems, economic and social organisation structures and so on, why should we ignore their claims to ostensibly paranormal experience, which have been arrived at in the same way?

It becomes clear from all of this that participation is a fundamental and necessary requirement if paranormal facts are to be replicated. Rituals, for example, can only be fully understood only when they are engaged with on a participatory level: simple observation will not suffice. If we were to send an anthropologist into the field and they came back saying: *"If you properly participate in this ritual you will see a spirit form,"* we should send another anthropologist to do the same. In this way replication (or not) of results can be achieved and a hypothesis as to the ontological status of the phenomenon in question can be devised.

All of this, however, proceeds from the assumption that western science has discovered something *new* about the world. The truth is, however, that the rituals we see in existence around the globe today were not spontaneously created only very recently. In actuality, rituals as they exist today are the direct product of centuries, if not millennia, of constant practice and refinement geared, especially, towards attaining specific goals: the object of the ritual. An exceedingly long time has already been spent in ensuring the repeatability of ritual outcomes over the course of human development. Ritual practices would not have survived if they constantly failed to achieve their intended goals. Anthropologists have tended to ignore this fact, and this has led to a naive naïve innocence whereby we think that we have only just discovered that rituals *can* be effective. We have attempted, historically, to blank out what our informants have been telling us and only now are we beginning to realise how foolishly we have behaved.

In the same way that if one follows the recipe for a chocolate cake in detail, a chocolate cake will result from the procedure. If one follows a ritual properly the ritual outcome will be achieved. This is precisely what Edith Turner found when she participated in the *Ihamba* ceremony of the Ndembu in Zambia (the climax of which resulted in the apparent extraction of a spirit-form from the back of the suffering patient). Her experience led her to declare that in order to "reach a peak experience in ritual it really is necessary to sink oneself fully in it" (Turner, 1993: 9), and in doing so she presents a methodology by which anthropologists can approach the issue of establishing the ontological status of paranormal phenomena: engage with it, an experience it for yourself, and thus overcome what she refers to as "positivists denial."

What makes the issue even more interesting is the fact that Edith Turner is not the only anthropologist to have participated in "native" rituals, or to have had experiences that have gone beyond the boundaries of traditional positivist science. McClenon & Nooney (2002) describe several such instances. Replication of results is already, therefore, at least to a certain extent, being gained by experiential anthropological methods to a degree that laboratory parapsychological approaches have struggled to achieve.

The question as to whether anthropologists are in a position to comment on the ontology of paranormal phenomena is, in my opinion, to be answered in the affirmative. I believe that there is good reason to suggest that anthropological methodologies could be employed alongside those of parapsychology and psychical research as a means to approach the most important question related to the issue of the paranormal: does it have any form of reality?

THE PERSISTENCE OF SPIRITS

Belief in the existence of spiritual entities is arguably one of the earliest manifestations of modern human thought. In seeking the origins of religious ideas, anthropologists in the nineteenth century looked to indigenous peoples around the world for examples of bygone primitive beliefs. What they found were multitudes of cosmological systems that differed drastically to from the accepted mechanistic world-view of Victorian physics – worlds inhabited by spirits and other supernatural entities, where magic was both widespread and efficacious. Sir E.B. Tylor dubbed this near-universal acknowledgment of invisible agencies "animism," a term derived from the Latin word *anima*, meaning soul. Tylor became convinced, from his reading of the ethnographic data, that animism represented the foundation of modern religious concepts. Indeed, he defined religion *itself* as the "belief in spiritual beings."

Any examination of our modern popular culture will demonstrate that the supernatural still permeates our thoughts and ideas about the world. Flicking through television channels today we find countless programmes devoted to ghost hunting, as well as platform mediumship demonstrations. As often as we are told that we are living in a "modern," "secular" society, animism, in one form or another, is still very much an aspect of our cultural lives. The very idea of spirits appears to be a surprisingly resilient one. Why do we keep coming back to animism?

Anthropology: Spirits as Agents

Anthropology, in dealing specifically with the magico-religious practices of the world's cultures, has often come into contact with spirits. As such, there is a vast and fascinating anthropological literature pertaining to spirits and how best to understand and interpret them. Like any other scientific discipline, anthropology has been through many theoretical paradigms, in the Kuhnian sense, and will continue to do so. Each paradigmatic perspective offers a different way of understanding what spirits are. Some of the earliest anthropological theorisers, for example E.B. Tylor and J.G. Frazer, were of the opinion that spirits were nothing more than superstitious nonsense – outmoded conceptions long since "evolved out," giving way to more "advanced" ways of looking at the world. To the late Victorian mindset, European culture (British in particular), was of the highest order in terms of intellectual development, consequently the beliefs and practices of so-called "primitives" could be nothing more than illusory, based on false perceptions and self-delusion, and irrational. Tylor, for instance, hypothesised that belief in spirits arises from *incorrectly* assuming that the figures we encounter in our dreams are the disembodied spirits of the dead.

It would be an oversight, however, to suggest that all Victorian anthropologists were so embedded in their own culture that they could not, or would not, bring themselves to wonder whether there was any rational basis to the belief in spirits. Andrew Lang, a Scottish academic, saw parallels between the ethnographic reports of distant lands, and the development of the Spiritualist movement in the second half of the nineteenth century. Lang considered anthropology to be a unique tool in assessing the ontological status of the increasing number of paranormal claims, specifically through making use of the discipline's comparative approach.

Later anthropological paradigms continued to carry the torch of their nineteenth century predecessors. Functionalism, a position that understands social and cultural phenomena as mechanisms for maintaining social cohesion (e.g. shared rituals and beliefs bring group members together), looked upon supernatural beliefs from a perspective that *a priori* denied them any form of ontological reality. In this view, spirits are seen as nothing but social facts performing a specific function within a given society. Questions of reality are replaced by questions of function. Such perspectives have been dominant in anthropology for many years, and have led to social-protest interpretations of mediumship and spirit possession, providing a means for women in traditionally repressive societies to vent their frustrations in a socially acceptable manner.

During the twentieth century, anthropologists underwent a distinct shift in focus away from grand theories (such as "functionalism"), towards a much more experiential understanding of culture. Cultures are, after all, lived-in constructs, and human beings are by no means uni-dimensional entities: we experience life and culture in different ways, and our understanding is built on our experiences of the world (empiricism in its simplest form). Grand theories like functionalism are now often thought to be overly reductive, incapable of encompassing such complexity. In order to fit ethnographic facts comfortably into the functional framework, key aspects must be either omitted or explained away in terms that do not contradict or transcend the limits of functional theory. Anthropologists have realised that through participating fully in a culture, and immersing ourselves in other life-ways, we can come closer to *understanding* it the way a native of that culture does. This realisation was a significant step in anthropological method, which for a long time has tried desperately to maintain a sense of distanced objectivity: an assumption that somehow there was a distinct cognitive difference between the anthropologist and his/her subjects.

Edith Turner is, perhaps, the most vocal advocate of this new approach in anthropology. While participating, physically and emotionally, in a healing ceremony amongst the Ndembu in Zambia, Turner caught sight of an ostensible spirit form: the *Ihamba*. The experience came as such a surprise to Turner in that it pointed her to the realisation that anthropologists had long made the fundamental mistake of refusing to listen to their informants, particularly with regard to the supernatural. Since discovering for herself the efficacy of spirit rituals through deep participation, Turner has advocated an abandoning of "positivists denial" in favour of actually listening to what our informants have to say. To this effect anthropologists have begun to, at the very least, treat these issues with seriousness, some even to the extent of utilising spirits as informants for their research. In certain situations, therefore, anthropology has begun to treat spirits as vital sources of information about the societies through which they make themselves known. Spirits, like human beings, are now seen as active agents in their own right, and it has been realised that they cannot comfortably be reduced to fit within academic culture's preferred ontological viewpoint. Such an ethnocentric perspective simply doesn't stand up to scrutiny when applied to the world of lived experience.

Parapsychology: Survival vs. Super-Psi

Next to anthropology, parapsychology is a discipline that has long been concerned with trying to understand the nature of spirits. The initial founding of the Society for Psychical Research (SPR) in London in 1882, being essentially the birth of modern parapsychology, was inspired by the need to seriously study the claims of spiritualists and the increasing number of individuals claiming mediumistic abilities in the late nineteenth century. Nevertheless, despite nearly 130 years of strict objective investigation, psychical research is still tackling the issue of whether or not some sort of spirit survives physical death.

Parapsychology has not given the notion of spirits an easy ride, and especially not the idea that spirits of the deceased communicate through the bodies and minds of entranced mediums. A rival hypothesis has been suggested to account for the apparent successes of certain mediums in retrieving information that they could not possibly have known: the *super-psi* hypothesis. Put simply the super-psi hypothesis argues that, contrary to the belief of the medium, the information retrieved during mediumship sessions is not achieved through the agency of spiritual beings, but rather is affected effected by the medium's own psi abilities (clairvoyance, clairaudience, etc. See Stephen Braude's 1992 article "Survival or Super-Psi?" for a more detailed exposition). Information, therefore, is not dictated by discarnate spirits, but, is rather, is telepathically retrieved from the minds of living human beings. This hypothesis has sparked a great deal of debate within the parapsychological community, with some arguing that mediumship provides evidence in support of the "survival hypothesis," and others seeing these phenomena as evidence for the existence of super-psi abilities.

Despite the criticisms laid on the survival hypothesis (and there have been many), certain researchers have continued to support it. Advocates of survivalism have argued that the super-psi hypothesis provides an explanation that is far too convoluted, while the notion of distinct discarnates answers some of the most challenging issues associated with mediumship and other forms of spirit incorporation parsimoniously, with ease. Researchers such as Gary Schwartz, and Julie Beischel of the Windbridge Institute, for example, have been working towards the development of triple and quadruple blinded research procedures as a means to assess the validity of mediumship readings, with exciting results.

Conclusions

Whatever the case with regard to the definitive ontological status of spirits, their persistence in our thoughts is strikingly evident. Thus far they have succeeded in surviving not only the transition from the world of the living to that of the dead, but also the intense scepticism and rational inquiry of over a century's worth of psychical research and secular scholarship. Given the uncertain status of the ongoing debate, the spirits look set to puzzle and persist for a while longer yet.

CONTEMPORARY PHYSICAL MEDIUMSHIP:
IS IT PART OF A CONTINUOUS PHENOMENON?

"It is prodigiously strange, prodigiously unusual, and it would seem so unlikely as to be incredible; but we must give in to the facts [...] Yes, it is absurd; but no matter – it is true."

— Prof. Charles Richet on Ectoplasm

For many people, physical mediumship séances are a social phenomenon relegated to the history books: rising to prominence in the mid-nineteenth century and eventually petering out amidst high profile exposures of fraud in the first decades of the twentieth century. In recent years, however, physical mediumship has made something of a comeback with new circles working towards the manifestation of physical phenomena being established in private homes across the UK, Europe and the United States. This resurgence has been facilitated by the development of Internet forums promoting the subject, enabling private circles to disseminate their experiences and to exchange tips and procedures for the production of physical phenomena. This chapter will explore the issue of whether the forms of physical mediumship popular today are part of a continuous tradition beginning in the nineteenth century, or essentially modern phenomena with roots in the 1990s. The main point of the discussion will be to ascertain the extent to which the phenomena of contemporary physical mediumship resemble those documented in the early literature of psychical research.

Jon Klimo provides a fairly standard definition of physical mediumship as the purported ability of certain mediums to "channel unknown energies that affect the physical environment in ways that can be directly experienced by persons other than the channel" (Klimo, 1987: 200). Manifestations of these "unknown energies" can take a variety of different forms, including: the levitation and manipulation of physical objects (such as knocks and raps, table levitations, etc.); the production of anomalous environmental changes (such as breezes and unusual drops in room temperature); the generation of so-called "spirit-lights"; the "apportation" of physical objects into and out of the séance room, and the materialization of ectoplasmic forms (manifestations of limbs, heads or, occasionally, whole bodies), amongst others (Braude, 1997). Such phenomena are, by their very physical nature, particularly controversial, even within the parapsychological community. Nevertheless, there is an extremely large body of literature composed by highly credible observers that seems to support the idea that certain mediums have, even under strictly controlled conditions, been able to produce these strange phenomena (Braude, 1997: 23-48; Tymn n.d: 1; McLuhan, 2010; Haule, 2011: 122-125). Although the main focus of this chapter does not necessarily require these phenomena to be *real*, as it will be primarily concerned primarily with the "culture of physical mediumship" (which undoubtedly exists regardless of whether or not its phenomena are ontologically real), it is both interesting and important to note that apparently good evidence *does* exist to suggest that such phenomena *may* be possible in the presence of particularly gifted mediums.

The Spiritualist movement itself was founded upon physical phenomena. In the small town of Hydesville, New York State, in 1848 the Fox family was plagued by anomalous raps and knocks that seemed, once a practical code for communication had been devised, to demonstrate the continued spiritual existence of a deceased pedlar by the name of Charles B. Rosma, who had allegedly been murdered in the house some years previously (Doyle, 2006; Moreman, 2010: 161). This example of what would later be termed physical mediumship was found to be focussed around the three Fox children, and spawned a movement which spread rapidly across the United States and Europe, and which still persists today. The Fox sisters, Leah (1814-1890) Kate (1837-1892) and Margaret (1833-1893), became the first physical mediums and toured all over the United States giving demonstrations of their ability to produce anomalous knocks through which ostensible spirits were able to communicate. As the Fox sisters toured, new mediums began to appear in their wake, and with them came an increasingly varied array of different spiritual manifestations: from mental mediumship and deep-trance communication to the materialization of spirit forms (Moreman, 2010: 161).

Perhaps the most influential innovator in early physical mediumship was the Scottish-born Daniel Dunglas Home (1833-1886). After an early life allegedly filled with visions and premonitions, and coming from a long line of Scottish seers, Home conducted his first séance at the age of eighteen and swiftly gained a reputation as a powerful medium. By 1856 Home was conducting séances in Britain. In 1868 he performed his most famous paranormal feat - the levitation of his body horizontally out through a third-story window at Ashley House in London. This event was apparently witnessed by Lord Lindsay, Lord Adare and Captain Charles Wynne, all men of high repute and considered at the time to be honest in what they described (Doyle, 2006: 99; Lamont, 2006: 185-187).

In 1874 Home's mediumship received further support with the publication of Sir William Crookes' report, which seemed to confirm, after laboratory experimentation, that Home did indeed possess the ability to manipulate physical objects by paranormal means. Using specially designed laboratory equipment, Crookes tested Home's ability to change the weight of physical objects and to play tunes on an accordion suspended out of reach in a cage (Lamont, 2005: 204-207; Alvarado, 2006: 142; Melechi, 2008: 198-200). Home's séances also often featured the alleged materialization of glowing hands that would mischievously touch the sitters, though he never produced full-body materializations (Doyle, 2006: 106).

Arthur Conan Doyle considered Home to be something of a virtuoso medium in that he was proficient in four different forms of mediumship: the direct voice (whereby spirits communicate verbally, independent of the medium), trance mediumship (whereby spirits communicate verbally through the body of the medium), clairvoyance (the ability to see visions of the spirit world, the future and distant locations) and physical mediumship (the ability to psychically manipulate physical objects) (Doyle, 2006: 106). Although accusations of fraud were made, Home was never actually caught in the act of cheating (Moreman, 2010: 164-165).

Ectoplasm

The substance known as "ectoplasm" is, by now, practically synonymous with physical mediumship and is well documented in the early literature of psychical research. The term itself was first coined in 1894 by the Nobel-prize-winning physiologist Prof. Charles Richet (1850-1935) in reference to observations of anomalous limbs during experiments with the medium Eusapia Paladino (1854-1918). Writing a little later, in his book *Clairvoyance and Materialization: A Record of Experiments* (2006), the psychical researcher Dr. Gustav Geley (1868-1924) provides a good description of this mysterious substance:

> During trance a portion of [the medium's] organism is externalised. This portion is sometimes very small, sometimes very considerable [...] Observation shows this ectoplasm as an amorphous substance which may be either solid or vaporous. Then, usually very soon, the formless substance becomes organic, it condenses, and forms appear, which, when the process is complete, have all the anatomical and physiological characters of biologic life. The ectoplasm has become a living being or a fractional part of a living being, but is always closely connected to the body of the medium, of which it is a kind of prolongation, and into which it is absorbed at the end of the experiment (Geley, 2006: 176).

Ectoplasm quickly became an essential component of any good Spiritualist séance. Some of the most intensive studies of ectoplasmic phenomena were conducted with the medium Eva C. (1886-1922) under the supervision of Baron Albert von Schrenck-Notzing (1862-1929), and were published in the book *Materialisation Phenomena* in 1914, complete with numerous photographic plates. During séances with Eva C. the ectoplasmic substance, which Schrenck-Notzing termed "teleplasm" (Brower, 2010: 117), would be exuded from the medium's mouth, breasts, navel, fingertips, vagina and scalp. This substance was described as coalescing into crude limbs, referred to as "pseudo-pods," and human-like heads, which would move independently and were particularly sensitive to light and touch. These materialisations would later dissolve or be absorbed back into the medium's body (Sommer, 2009: 304). Eva C's ectoplasmic manifestations are graphically described by Mme. Bisson:

> On 2nd December 1910 a particularly interesting phenomenon occurred. As the by now exhausted medium asked me to give her more strength; she moved towards me, her hands outstretched, and I made a movement to take her hands. At that moment, and in full view of all the sitters, a fully modeled arm and hand seized the medium's

left arm around the elbow and thrust her roughly backwards. Eva, frightened, cried out and started to tremble; she had an attack of nerves that I had to calm. Some minutes later the arm and hand reappeared on the medium's knees; this time they were flat and motionless. This phenomenon is all the more remarkable in that it suggests a will operating independently of the medium, myself and others (as cited in Barrington, 2011: 5).

The Decline of Physical Mediumship

The so-called 'Margery' mediumship was arguably the real cut-off point for serious psychical research into physical mediumship. Margery was alleged, by a certain Dr. Crandon, to have produced a variety of impressive physical phenomena. Dr. Walter Franklin Prince, one of the chief investigators of Margery's (Mina Crandon's) mediumship, provides a survey of some of her feats:

> At hundreds of sittings, it is claimed 'ectoplasmic' limbs – extruded from her body and afterwards reabsorbed – have performed various acts, such as touching persons seated nearby in the darkness, shoving, lifting and throwing objects, overturning a small table, ringing the bell in a box activated by contact cover, producing phosphorescent lights, etc. (Prince, 1926: 431).

Mina Crandon's mediumship, however, was very publicly declared fraudulent by the escape artists artist Harry Houdini in a pamphlet entitled "Houdini Exposes the Tricks Used by the Boston Medium 'Margery'" published in 1924 (Polidoro, 2001). Over the course of his public debunking Houdini employed increasingly tight controls on the medium including, at one point, completely sealing the medium within a specially constructed wooden box, with only her head and hands visible (Polidoro, 2001: 143-145). Her ectoplasmic protrusions were called into question when, in 1925, the Society for Psychical Research sent Eric Dingwall to investigate Mina Crandon's claimed abilities and discovered that her ectoplasm was apparently composed of "animal lung material" (Polidoro, 2001: 155).

This form of public debunking likely contributed to the demise of physical mediumship. Nevertheless, ectoplasmic materialisations of varying quality were present, though becoming increasingly rare, in physical mediumship demonstrations right into the 1930s and 1940s. This later physical mediumship is, perhaps, best exemplified by the mediumship of Jack Webber (1907-1940) (see Edwards, 1978) and Helen Duncan (1897-1956) (see Gaskill, 2001; Hartley, 2007). The following is a description of the process of materialization and dematerialization during Jack Webber's séances:

> [...] at first a vague, shadowy form is seen, darker than the prevailing light. This form then becomes denser, and the hands and head are held to the red light for closer examination. The red light is about nine feet from the floor, yet the materialized people are able to rise to it from the floor and expose their heads in close proximity to the bulb [...] When a form has built up in the red light, its disappearance is of interest. Standing full length in the centre of the circle, it is seen to diminish downwards as if passing through the floor. The period of time necessary for the disappearance is about two seconds. After the disappearance of a form, throat action is heard from the medium – gulp like sounds, rather similar to those made when ectoplasm is returning to the medium's body (Edwards, 1978: 96-97).

Again, accounts from the séances of Helen Duncan – arguably the last of the "great" physical mediums/smediums – feature many of the same characteristic descriptions of ectoplasmic materialisations and dematerialisations as earlier accounts of other mediums:

> Witnesses used terms such as disappeared, vanished, melted, sinking towards the floor [...] Mrs. Lock stated her mother disappeared down to the floor when seeing her on the 17th and 18th of January and her friend Pinkie who did so displaying a clear face with a red complexion with hair. He drifted down to the ground. Mrs. Jennings was so struck by the way the figures disappeared she explained in her testimony that she took a special interest and stood to observe the method. She explained at the trial that the head portion went first, then the shoulders down. The last thing she could see was a lot of white on the floor. She explained they all disappeared in the same way. Mr. Lock also described this same method for a figure purporting to be his sister Sally [...] He described how the white form disappeared towards the ground (Hartley, 2007: 205).

The phenomena described so far (raps, levitations, the movement of objects and ectoplasmic materialisations), form the basic itinerary of what I will term "classical physical mediumship," which flourished roughly from 1848 onwards with a gradual decline in activity after around about 1945. Although Spiritualism by no means disappeared after this period, physical mediumship certainly suffered a lull in interest. Numerous explanations for this have been offered, including: the idea that, in our busy modern world, people no longer have the time or energy to devote themselves to the development of physical mediumship; the idea that the harsh ways in which physical mediums had been tested in the lab put people off developing mediumship, and the idea that the numerous exposures of fraudulent mediums had given the profession a bad reputation which put people off entering into it (Foy, 2007).

Physical Mediumship Returns

Whatever the reasons, it wasn't until the late 1990s that interest in physical mediumship returned to the popular consciousness. A reinvigorated interest in physical mediumship developed after the publication of Montague Keen and David Fontana's *The Scole Report* by the Society for Psychical Research in 1999 (Moreman, 2010: 164), and the popularised version *The Scole Experiment: Scientific Evidence for Life After Death* by Grant and Jane Solomon, also published in the same year. Montague Keen (2001) describes the basic claims made about the Scole experiments:

> Based on two years of regular séances, the Group's chief claims were that they had established contact with a "team" of spirit communicators comprising, or in contact with, a number of former scientists. These had been accessed through [...] a husband and wife team, both of whom entered swiftly into deep trance, remaining thus throughout the proceedings, of which they retained no conscious recollection. The purported discarnate contacts had facilitated the manifestation of spirit lights, moved furniture, created apports (objects appearing from no known source and by no known means), displayed shadowy figures described as angelic forms, and produced films, allegedly employing a novel form of energy not involving the traditional ectoplasmic extrusions with their enervating and sometimes physically hazardous, and invariably contentious, associations" (Keen, 2001:167-168).

One of the chief developments of the Scole group, in terms of the history of physical mediumship, was their claim that a new "form of energy," significantly different to/from the ectoplasm of classical physical mediumship, was the basis of the physical phenomena being produced. Ectoplasm, it would seem, was considered dangerous by the Scole group's guiding spirit team and so was necessarily replaced. Indeed, numerous mediums and psychical researchers have commented on the potential dangers involved in the production of ectoplasm. This shift towards the use of a "new energy" has been quite influential in the development of subsequent physical mediumship circles who have been inspired to conduct their own experiments after reading descriptions of those carried out at Scole. The Bristol Spirit Lodge, the group with whom I conduct my own fieldwork (Hunter, 2009; 2011), often utilises a glass bell-jar for the containment of "energies" directly inspired by the recommendations of the Scole group, for example. Nevertheless, while modern physical mediumship circles do claim to employ this "new energy," the use of ectoplasm continues to be a particularly common feature of physical séances along with other of the traditional physical phenomena, such as "spirit lights" and raps. Indeed, the founder of the Bristol Spirit Lodge was inspired by the experience of "traditional" physical mediumship on 24th May 2006 in Banbury, Oxfordshire:

> My personal evidence was followed by the display of a misty formation that was barely visible within the set red-light conditions. In these conditions I could see the shapes of sitters all seated in their chairs around the room. They were all there. There were no empty chairs. So, I could see a haze, of perhaps 'something else,' some partial materialized 'something' near the cabinet (Di Nucci, 2009: 23-24).

More elaborate descriptions of classical ectoplasmic materialisations produced in private home-circles are now emerging on the Internet. For example, the following is extracted from a report by Dr. Nahm of a séance conducted with the Felix Experimental Group in Germany (see Braude, 2010), in April 2011. The description focusses primarily on the process by which ectoplasm was seen to be produced by the medium. Many of the characteristics of the ectoplasmic productions in this account do seem to match descriptions from the earlier literature of psychical research:

When the red light was turned on for the first time, all sitters could plainly see a whitish cloth-like mass protruding from the medium's mouth. He bent to the front and seemed to facilitate the ectoplasm's outflow [...] by accompanying movements of both hands. During the first display, the ectoplasm was comparably short, perhaps, 30-40 cm; during the second display shortly after it had already reached the floor [...] The next two displays in red light simply showed the ectoplasmatic veil lying curled on the floor between and in front of the medium's feet. There was no connection to the medium's body [...] The next two displays showed the supposed hand of HB, who announced that he would sort of dip his own hand into the mass and aggregate the ectoplasmic hand accordingly, then waving to the sitters with it. The purpose of this was to show the autonomous quality of the mass, and its ability to move. Indeed, a hand-like shape had risen about 30 cm upward, continued to rise some other 10 cm, and performed jerky waving movements [...] This ectoplasm was of condensed matter, not the veil-like stuff from before. It looked more like solid cloth [...] The next two displays showed how a different column of ectoplasm moved upward on the mediums medium's body, from the belly region towards the right chest. It was again of the veil-like quality [...] It seemed to grow and move on its own behalf [...] the medium's body was perfectly still, his arms hanging straight down at the sides [...] HB announced that the medium would wrap the ectoplasmatic veil around his entire body (with his hands) to supply the body with energy. Indeed, when the lamp was switched on again, the medium was covered all over by an extremely fine and very thin white veil (the "cocoon" condition) (Nahm, 2011).

The following account is taken from a report of a séance held in England in October 2011 with the medium Stewart Alexander. It describes the apparent transformation of an amorphous "blob" of ectoplasm into a well-formed human hand:

Walter returned and asked that everyone return to their seats and away from the table. The table had a translucent top with a red light underneath it, so that we could see what was happening on its surface without harm to Stewart. Walter then invited Brian K. to sit at the table across from him. Soon a blob of ectoplasm could be seen on the illuminated table top. It slowly formed into a large hand which Walter said was his. It knocked on the table and Brian said that it was a big hand. Next, Walter asked Brian to place his right hand on the table with his palm downwards. We could see that the hand moved toward Brian's hand and he announced that it was holding his hand and that it felt like a human hand. (Butler & Butler, 2011).

My own encounters with visible ectoplasm at the Bristol Spirit Lodge, although not quite as dramatic as that produced by the Felix Circle, also appears continuous with the general tradition of physical mediumship. The following extract is taken from my field-notes dated 05/02/2011:

> The first time [ectoplasm] was produced on a glowing board and appeared like a sausage in silhouette. It moved as though pulled [...] The second example of ectoplasm production was a thin strip of the substance apparently protruding from the cabinet - – somehow attached to the top of the spirit trumpet (a cone of sheet aluminium). This took a while to develop in darkness, and when it was fully present the spirit voice told Christine to turn the red light up slowly. The ectoplasm looked remarkably like a thin strip of silk (on talking to Sandy in the car on the way home she too thought it looked like a piece of silk). The spirit voice asked if we would like to see it move, we of course replied with a resounding "Yes!" The light was asked to be switched off and when it was turned on again the strip of ectoplasm wagged about a little, quite unimpressively. The sitters were apparently impressed by this demonstration.

Degraded Phenomena?

Again, it must be stressed that regardless of whether or not the phenomenon observed in this instance was real ectoplasm, produced by paranormal means, is irrelevant to an examination of the culture of physical mediumship. This event, as well as the other descriptions of contemporary ectoplasm presented here, was clearly within the same tradition as the ectoplasmic manifestations of mediums at the turn of the nineteenth century, though they would appear to be of a much-diminished quality. In comparison with the dramatic and extravagant, and often full-body, materialisations described in the earlier literature of psychical research, the ectoplasmic manifestations of the modern world are distinctly lacking. Why could this be? Writing on the history of ectoplasm in volume two of his *The History of Spiritualism* (Doyle, 2006) Arthur Conan Doyle noted precisely the same thing:

> When we examine the descriptions of the appearance of ectoplasm in Spiritualistic circles forty and fifty years ago, and compare them with those in our own day, we see how much richer were the earlier results (Doyle, 2006, Vol. II: 47).

The explanation he offers for this apparent degradation in the phenomenon was that attitudes towards mediums had changed. He writes: "At least [...] the early researchers observed one golden rule. They surrounded the medium with an atmosphere of love and sympathy" (ibid.). By the time Doyle was writing his history of the Spiritualist movement, physical mediums were subject to increasingly severe forms of testing, perhaps best exemplified by the methods employed by the psychical researcher Harry Price (cf. Tabori, 1968: 90 for a description of Harry Price's electrically controlled séances). In addition to this testing, the popular image of the physical medium was becoming increasingly associated with the notion of fraud and dishonesty, which naturally did not bode well for the way in which mediums were perceived and treated by those who attended their demonstrations. A further reason might also be found in the shift in the perspective of psychical researchers towards a laboratory-based approach, inspired by the establishment of Dr. J.B. Rhine's parapsychological laboratory at Duke University in 1930, with its focus directed firmly on the much subtler mental phenomena of ESP and clairvoyance. Physical mediumship was, by the 1930s, simply out of fashion and has never really regained its status as a respectable practice for either mediums or researchers. Perhaps the renewed interest in the practice of physical mediumship that has developed over the last decade, coupled with the interests of serious psychical researchers to investigate such groups (for example Prof. Stephen Braude's investigations with the Felix Experimental Group), will lead to the reinstatement of some of the more elaborate physical phenomena described in the early literature of psychical research.

To conclude, then, I feel it is fair to say that contemporary physical mediumship is, in essence, a continuation of the late nineteenth and early twentieth century tradition, though it has degraded quite considerably due to a variety of factors, some of which have just been discussed. The situation is reminiscent of a similar scenario described by the anthropologist Zeljko Jokic (2008b) with regard to the practice of contemporary Buriat shamanism. Traditional Buriat Shamanism was banned in Buriatiia, Siberia, by the Soviet Russian authorities. Jokic writes of the practices of contemporary neo-shamans in Buriatiia, who are striving to reinvigorate the traditional forms of shamanism practiced before the Soviet period, and describes how the inability of the modern neo-shamans to recall their trance journeys is indicative of lost knowledge about the techniques of the traditional shamans who were able to remember and describe their trance experiences. Jokic writes:

> The apparently unconscious trance of modern shamans from the Tengeri association is the direct result of the stress and discontinuity that come from the inhibition of the system during the Soviet times, which has left a deep impact on Buriat culture. Fortunately, it appears that the shamans are well on their way to reclaiming the "eternal blue sky" over modern-day Buriatiia (Jokic, 2008b: 45).

Perhaps contemporary physical mediumship could be viewed in a similar way. The culture and practice has degraded under a bad reputation, and only with the dedicated work of those who are striving to reinvigorate, promote and develop it will physical mediumship become as dramatic as it was when the pioneers of psychical research described it in the nineteenth century. As anthropologists with an interest in the culture of physical mediumship, therefore, we are uniquely placed to witness, record and document the re-emergence of this unusual social phenomenon.

CONTEMPORARY MEDIUMSHIP AND SÉANCE GROUPS IN THE UK:
SPECULATING ON THE BRISTOL SPIRIT LODGE

There seems to be a void in the anthropological literature. While it is easy to find ethnographic accounts of witchcraft, divination, spirit possession and trance mediumship practices in "far off exotic lands," it is much more difficult to find ethnographies of such practices in the post-industrial West, bar of course a few illuminating sociological explorations (Nelson, 1969a; 1969b; 1972; Skultans, 1974), and some interesting examples from the US (Emmons, 2000; Wallis, 2001). This is particularly true with regard to the *private* practice of Spiritualism, especially in the form of independent home-circles, distinct from any organized body.

In an attempt to fill this void in the literature I decided to gain an insight into the hidden world of contemporary trance and physical mediumship, a form of mediumship quite different to from the platform mediumship associated with the religious Spiritualism of the Spiritualist National Union (SNU). Moreover, I intended to approach this subject matter through the lens of immersive participant observation, as advocated by anthropologist of consciousness Edith Turner (1993). I did this with the goal of understanding the root cause for belief in a supernatural reality: the anomalous experience itself. My investigations would focus on the Bristol Spirit Lodge: a private home-circle established in 2005 with the sole purpose of supporting those with an interest in, and facilitating the development of, trance and physical mediumship.

Perhaps now would be a good time to define what is meant by the term "mediumship." In the context of Spiritualism a medium is understood to be someone who provides a direct link between the world of the living and the world of the dead, often referred to as the spirit world, or just 'Spirit.' Charles F. Emmons defines mediumship as a process whereby information is purportedly transferred "from discarnate beings or souls to the living through another human who is sensitive to such information" (Emmons, 2000: 72). Trance and physical mediumship are distinguished from the more common form of mental mediumship, or platform mediumship, popularly practiced at SNU affiliated Spiritualist churches and centres. The messages received through mental mediumship usually take the form of clairvoyant (mental visualisations), or clairaudient (mental auditory) messages, and are often of a highly symbolic nature, hence requiring interpretation. By contrast, when practicing trance mediumship, the medium enters into an altered state of consciousness, usually referred to simply as 'trance,' during which the medium is seemingly unconscious of their surroundings. While in this state, apparently distinct spirit personalities communicate through the medium's physical body, a process sometimes also referred to as channelling (Klimo, 1987). While the medium is entranced, sitters are able to speak directly to the communicating entity, so the messages do not require interpretation.

Physical mediumship, in addition to incorporating trance communication (the physical medium usually performs while in an altered state of consciousness, and may also present as a variety of different entities), is believed to be associated with a range of extraordinary physical phenomena including, but not limited to: the materialisation of spirit forms through the manipulation of a semi-physical substance known as ectoplasm (Pilkington, 2004), dematerialisation of objects, apports (physical objects brought into the séance room apparently by spirit intervention), levitation of the medium and physical objects, transfiguration (whereby the facial features of the medium are apparently distorted by some form of energy manipulation), direct voice phenomena (when voices are heard to emanate from beyond the medium's body), and so on. Klimo (1987) defines physical mediumship as "the human ability to channel unknown energies that affect the physical environment in ways that can be directly experienced by persons other than the channel" (200).

Physical mediumship was the dominant form of mediumship in the nineteenth to early twentieth century, but the practice has seemingly been in decline since the end of the Second World War. Robin Foy, a leading name in the promotion of modern physical mediumship since the 1990s, has suggested a number of possible factors contributing to this decline, including scarcity of individuals with sufficient ability, the necessity for a prolonged length of time in order for abilities to develop, scarcity of circles willing to devote time to the development of physical mediumship, the danger of injury associated with such practices, and the mistreatment and abuse which historical physical mediums have been subjected to when under investigation (Foy, 2007: 226).

The Bristol Spirit Lodge itself was founded by Christine Di Nucci who, after a number of extraordinary séance experiences, made it her duty firstly to investigate the subject further and then to preserve and promote the practice of physical mediumship. To this end, séances with developing mediums are held twice weekly (often more frequently) in a specially constructed 12'x10' shed at the bottom of her garden. At present, there are three mediums in development at the Lodge (Jon, Sandy and Jerry) each working towards the manifestation of physical séance phenomena and trance communication. Occasionally, a more developed medium will perform a guest séance, which is generally thought to be of a much higher calibre, both in terms of strength of physical phenomena and consistency of trance mediated personalities.

The group as a whole is constantly changing, but maintains a core of regular sitters and mediums. At present the group is fourteen members strong (including both sitters and developing mediums), consisting of an even number of seven males and seven females from a wide range of socio-economic and religious backgrounds. It is interesting to note that, at the time of my initial fieldwork in 2009, the size of the group totalled nine individuals – evidence of the Lodge's fluctuating attendance. The transitory nature of groups engaged with the paranormal has been noted by Hansen (2001).

Belief systems within the Lodge are varied; not everyone adheres to the same interpretation of the phenomena they seek to develop. Indeed, Di Nucci states explicitly in her short autobiographical book *Spirits in a Teacup* (2009), that the group is a "non-denominational home-circle." Such a stance is in line with the anti-dogmatism of the Spiritualist movement in general, although Christine would not consider herself a Spiritualist "with a capital S." Members come from a wide variety of religious backgrounds, ranging from atheist through Church of England, Methodist, Quaker and Spiritualist perspectives. At the time of my research none of the attendant sitters or mediums considered the séances conducted at the Lodge to be specifically religious events. Spirit communications are understood to be a natural fact, spiritual but not supernatural.

Nevertheless, there remains a sense of differentiation between the sacred space of the Lodge and the profane world outside. The Lodge space is treated with great respect; the practices that take place within it imbue the building with a residual energy. It has even been noted that a distinct sense of presence is occasionally felt when one is alone inside. While the Lodge's practices are not considered religious, they do appear to partake of at least a semi-religious character.

As I was particularly interested in the role of experience in the formation of group practice and belief, I endeavoured to question members about their own paranormal/ supernatural/ anomalous experiences before they started attending the Lodge. Five of the nine questionnaire respondents reported that they had previously had experiences, which they interpreted as paranormal in nature: that is experiences they were unable to account for in rational terms. Out of nine individuals, six reported that they considered themselves to have some form of psychic (intuitive), or mediumistic (conveying messages from the deceased/discarnate) ability. Christine, does not consider herself to have either psychic or mediumistic abilities, but does have a spirit guide whose special sensitivity assists her, particularly in relation to the running of the séances. This would appear to suggest, at least to some degree, that prior anomalous experiences are conducive to attendance of a physical séance group; after all, it was Christine's initial encounter with physical mediumship that led her to establish the Lodge in the first place.

Perhaps most important in understanding the Lodge is the experience of the developing mediums themselves. Without mediums there could be no séances, and, without séances, no group. Mediums, therefore, represent a cohesive factor: they are the charismatic core. Mediums participate in a symbiotic relationship with their "guides" and associated "spirit teams," for, when in trance, it is not the medium at the heart of proceedings but the "entities" that communicate through them. A medium's success, therefore, depends to a certain extent upon the strength of his/her spirit entourage. High status mediums, like the special guest who occasionally demonstrates at the Lodge, will mediate strong and distinctive personalities (occasionally celebrities), as well as more highly developed physical phenomena (e.g. transfiguration, levitation, spirit lights, materialization and so forth). The most exceptional mediums historically, Daniel D. Home for example, were seemingly able to perform a variety of physical feats and paranormal effects, as well as channeling spirits. Generally, however, mediums tend to specialise in one or two forms of spirit presentation (e.g. materialization, transfiguration, healing, trance or direct voice for instance). Circles, then, form around individual mediums, the personalities they channel and the type of phenomena they manifest.

The mediums developing at the Lodge are working towards different forms of spirit manifestation. Unlike at the SNU Spiritualist Churches, mediums at the Lodge tend not to provide communications from deceased loved ones. The spirit communicators, often working as part of "spirit teams," are believed to come through of their own desire to learn, and are generally personalities unknown to the sitters. In addition to refining his trance communication, Jon's séances are focussed on the presentation of transfiguration phenomena, while Sandy's efforts are usually directed toward levitation, transfiguration and healing. Jerry's physical mediumship is much less developed than Jon and Sandy's, despite having many years of experience as a platform medium in Spiritualist churches, and, as such, his sittings are centred on stabilising communications from spirit personalities and the development of transfiguration.

Generally, the mediums report that they have little or no recollection of the events of séances when in trance; often they are surprised that sitters have witnessed anything unusual at all. In describing his experience of trance, Jon reported:

> For the first half of the evening I have absolutely no awareness of what's going on externally [...] I can't feel anything at all whatsoever. Occasionally, I go off into a 'day dream?' mode and visit places and people [...] but not every time. Recently I've started to feel strong energies around me (hot and cold breezes particularly on my legs), usually just before Charlie (or whoever) comes in to talk first [...] Often now, when they are talking I'll go back into myself and I get a strange sensation of vertigo & being detached from the conversation, not just intellectually but physically as well. As if I'm on the edge of a precipice or inside a vast canyon. It's a sense of scale I think., I feel very small in comparison to something very large? (Extract from interview in Hunter, 2009a: 75)

For those who do not go into trance themselves, the reports of mediums returning from their brief excursions to the spirit world represent tantalising proofs, not only of the validity of their experience, but of the existence of another more subtle world beyond our own. Such experiential proofs provide the bedrock for metaphysical speculation: the foundation for the Spiritualist cosmology.

The séances themselves follow a regular pattern. Christine begins the proceedings with an opening prayer that sets the intent and purpose for the séance. This point marks entry into a liminal zone (Turner, 1969), protected by a "circular canopy." Once the prayer has been performed the séance room becomes an ambiguous space, suspended between the world of the living and the world of the dead. Several writers have suggested that it is precisely in these times of liminality, when the normal order breaks down, that ostensibly paranormal phenomena occur (Taylor, 1998; Hansen, 2001). Following the setting of intent for the proceedings (i.e. for transfiguration, materialization, healing, etc.), music is played for a set amount of time during which the medium remains motionless, seated in the cabinet as his/her trance state sets in. It is usually in the time between the onset of trance and the surfacing of communicative personalities that sitters observe transfiguration and other visual phenomena taking place. Once stable communicators have made themselves known, a question and answer session takes place with sitters quizzing the visiting speakers on a wide range of subjects – spiritual, philosophical, scientific and everyday issues. The entranced medium becomes a vessel for knowledge and the séance a means to acquire this knowledge; an alternative way of learning, recalling the role of the "shaman" in certain traditional societies – retrieving wisdom from the spirit world for the good of the social-group (Eliade, 1989).

When it becomes evident that the medium's energy levels are being depleted, the incorporating entity usually announces the end of the séance. The "closing music" is played in order to lull the entranced medium back into "normal consciousness." When the medium has returned to drowsy wakefulness, a closing prayer is read which asks for any residual energies leftover left over from the séance to be used for the purpose of healing. This procedure effectively ensures that no entities become trapped in the Lodge, signals the end of the temporary liminal space, and indicates that sitters are free to leave the Lodge without inadvertently letting something out, or harming the medium.

It was important to my phenomenological approach that I actively engaged with the practices of the Lodge in order to expose myself to elements of experience that might otherwise have gone unnoticed. I participated in numerous séances as a sitter and in this capacity experienced some very interesting visual phenomena: apparent transfiguration of the face and torso, small shining lights, hazes, mists and so on. In addition to sitting as a witness I also engaged in mediumship development, and, to my surprise, underwent a couple of peculiar experiences. This is not, perhaps, the place to discuss them at length, but during one particular meditation session I experienced both a sense of presence approaching me and a dissociation of control in my left hand. These experiences demonstrated to me that notions of spirit incorporation are directly derived directly from physiological experiences that appear to indicate an external control of one's physical body. While the sensation that I experienced only took hold of my left hand, I can now imagine, having undergone the experience, an extension of this sensation affecting my entire body. When the experience took place, I was in a heightened state of physiological arousal – my heart rate increased, and I was breathing deeply – and yet, in myself, I was relatively relaxed and was still able to observe the sensations associated with my physical body, albeit from a detached perspective. It was as though I had relinquished control of my hand to an invisible other. This perspective offered significant insight into the processes and sensations associated with the development of mediumistic abilities.

In exploring this experiential aspect of the Lodge's practices I came to the conclusion that traditional sociological approaches to the study of mediumship and spirit incorporation have neglected to address the anomalous experiences associated with them. Emphasis has been placed on reductionist social-functional approaches, for example I.M. Lewis' (1971) conception of spirit possession as a form of social protest, and Vieda Skultans' (1974) interpretation of spiritualist circles as a means of escape for women trapped in their traditional roles as mothers, wives and sexual partners. While it is inevitable that such practices perform social functions (in that human beings are communing with one another), it is also true that there is an experiential basis for belief in their practices that cannot be reduced to the purely sociological. If Lodge attendees wanted to escape from the repetition of daily life they could just as easily go dancing, meet up for tea or go for a walk than go through the rigmarole of sitting in a garden shed to hold a séance every week. The purpose for gathering is to encounter the paranormal – it is inquisitiveness.

In the darkness (or red-light) of the Spirit Lodge, sitters engage with what Rudolf Otto (1958) termed the *numinous* – a sense of uncanny awe at a much wider, and hitherto hidden, perspective on a vastly mysterious reality. This, in the case of the Bristol Spirit Lodge, seems to be facilitated through a combination of stimuli – environmental and symbolic – aimed at the induction of altered states of consciousness in which a glimpse of that wider world may be caught. Symbolic and environmental cues would include:

Symbolic signifiers:

- Entering the Lodge and leaving the "everyday" behind
- Prayers clearly denoting entrance into a liminal zone in which spirit interaction may occur
- Setting the intent and desire for something to occur
- The medium as a symbolic half-way point between the realm of human life and spirit, effectively blurring the distinction between the living and the dead.

Environmental stimuli to assist in the induction of ASCs:

- Darkness (or partial darkness in red light) and its effect on perception; Noll (1985), for example, has suggested that many shamanic practices are concerned with cultivating the vividness and improving the control of mental visual imagery.
- The use of music within this context, also traditionally employed for both the induction and modulation of altered states of consciousness.

The combination of these factors, in addition to the generally relaxed and meditative atmosphere amongst the sitters, likely assist in the induction of altered thinking, what some might term "magical thinking," resulting in an increase in sensitivity, which may facilitate the manifestation of séance phenomena, as well as assisting the medium in the development of his/her trance state. This perspective, therefore, suggests that mediumship and its associated phenomena are collectively manifested – a fact attested to by spirits communicating at the Lodge; when asked about the nature of transfiguration phenomena, for example, Charlie, Jon's main control, stated that what we observe is the product of multiple causal factors:

> The energy around the [medium's] body is changing and being manipulated. This causes your perception to not see what it is used to seeing. At the same time you are within the same building in close proximity to this energy, and as that's such your perception is also being changed... It is a combination which results in what you perceive, but it is not reliant totally upon you (Transcribed from a séance recorded 18/2/09).

In depth participatory fieldwork can provide insights into the way in which séance phenomena manifest, and, as such, moves beyond the realms of sociological/anthropological inquiry, through phenomenology and psychology to a form of participatory psychical research. Indeed, a cross-disciplinary approach is essential if any head-way is to be made in furthering our understanding of this intriguing aspect of human life. We need to learn more than simply the mechanisms for the production of paranormal experiences, whether that mechanism be purely psychological or parapsychological; we need to understand how these experiences are lived with: the role and function they play in the everyday lives of those who engage with them. In addition, this endeavour needs to be undertaken in terms that are not alien to the understanding of the groups we investigate.

My experience at the Bristol Spirit Lodge has been fascinating and revealing on many different levels. The centre provides an interesting focus for sociological and phenomenological inquiry – an endeavour that has so far resulted in both my dissertation (Hunter, 2009) and a short book documenting communications with an apparent spirit entity called Charlie (Di Nucci & Hunter, 2009).

TALKING WITH THE SPIRITS:
MORE THAN A SOCIAL REALITY?

When I started my dissertation fieldwork at the Bristol Spirit Lodge, in January 2009, I was working from a sociological perspective: I was there to study the social reality of the *belief* in spirits, and not the spirits themselves (Hunter, 2009).

The social reality perspective has been a useful tool in the social sciences, particularly when researchers are investigating the so-called paranormal; it allows for examination of the way in which beliefs influence modes of living in (and understanding) the world, without necessarily approaching the issue of the validity of these beliefs. To a sociologist, then, it does not matter whether or not spirits actually exist, what is important is that people believe that they exist (Gilbert, 2010: 10; Klass, 2003: 54).

This is a fair position, up to a point. It provides a comfortable approach; one that will not be too controversial in the highly rational world of Western academia. However, a time arrives when it becomes clear that this perspective is limiting to the scope of an ethnographic inquiry, and hence causing detriment to the overall conclusions made about the beliefs and practices of a group of people.

While this approach appears to present a means to address the issue of supernatural belief in an objective and un-biased fashion, it continues to miss the point. To those who believe, the objects of their belief are not conceived of as "social facts," but as "facts of nature." Consequently, any conclusions that are drawn from the social reality perspective are immediately distanced from the actual understanding of the group under study. This must surely be a problem: if the conclusions drawn about a group fail to match up with the ethnographic evidence, then what has actually been achieved?

I feel that I reached this point with my research at the Bristol Spirit Lodge. The difficulties lay in the fact that the beliefs of those I was studying were not simply isolated ideas without any connection to the objective world; rather, their beliefs were grounded in everyday experience. Sitters at the Lodge were able to talk directly, via trance mediumship, with the objects of their beliefs, and so was I. As a consequence, the spirits became a component of my everyday life, in an objective sense. I, like those I was studying, was talking with the spirits on a regular basis.

Was I participating merely in a social reality, or something more?

The Reality of Spirits

The issue, therefore, was that the objects of the beliefs of Lodge members (spirits) were not insubstantial abstract notions, but were, in fact, fully communicable aspects of this reality: as real as any other conscious mind incorporated in a physical body. In other words, the spirits were as real as you or I and certainly not invisible (at least not while communicating through the entranced medium).

Trance and physical mediumship can be seen as techniques by which spirits, which are otherwise abstract suppositions, become objectified, or embodied. The medium's body serves as a vessel in three-dimensional space which may be temporarily occupied by discarnate entities (Crabtree, 1988: 105; Klimo, 1987: 2).

Traditions in which some form of mediumship, channelling or spirit possession takes centre stage have the concomitant effect of providing individuals with first-hand contact with what Rudolph Otto termed "the numinous" (1958: 5-7). Consequently, belief in a supernatural order is reinforced by direct contact with it for followers of that tradition.

Within such traditions it is understood that spirits exist because personal experiential evidence of their existence is provided during the performances of spirit mediums. James McClenon, in a discussion of shamanic healing, writes:

> Because practitioners perform wondrous events, observers subconsciously accept (or increase their faith in) a particular ideology (1993: 117).

I would suggest that a similar process is in action during trance and physical mediumship demonstrations like those conducted at the Bristol Spirit Lodge. Mediumship itself, as well as the variety of ostensibly paranormal phenomena associated with the practice, serves as an experiential proof to the sitters of the existence of spirits.

What are Spirits?

The issue now arises, therefore, of trying to come to some idea of what spirits actually are, and this is not an easy task. Over the years, countless explanations have been offered from a variety of different theoretical perspectives: from the esoteric to the psychological and anthropological; from perspectives that accept the reality of spirits to those that negate their existence entirely.

One of the most common explanatory frameworks of recent years, at least for the type of spirit that communicates via trance mediumship, is multiple personality disorder (MPD), now often referred to as dissociative identity disorder (DID). Crabtree describes this psychological disorder as:

> ...a condition in which two or more personalities manifest themselves in one human being (1988: 60).

These personalities, referred to as alters, are understood to be the product of psychological mechanisms protecting the individual from traumatic life experiences. These alters can eventually assume control over the life of the individual, thereby engendering a serious pathological condition.

Ethnographic data, however, do not support the idea that mediumship and spirit possession trance states are pathological in nature. Morton Klass (2001) has noted that in societies where such practices are commonplace they are seen as quite the opposite of pathological: they are seen as "normal" or even desirable attributes (2001: 110).

Another possibility is offered by the psychoanalyst Carl Jung. In a 1948 article entitled *Psychology and Spiritualism,* Jung wrote that spirits:

> ...are shadowy personifications of unconscious contents, conforming to the rule that activated portions of the unconscious assume the character of personalities when they are perceived by the conscious mind (2008: 165).

To Jung, therefore, spirits were aspects of the unconscious mind, brought forward and personified. In Jung's view, however, this did not detract from the independent existence of the spirits as autonomous beings, nor did it dismiss the apparently paranormal abilities of these spirits to communicate accurate information. Jung's view of the unconscious mind was far more expansive than we might expect; he claimed, for instance, that "a psychological truth is... just as good and respectable a thing as a physical truth, which limits itself to matter as the former does to psyche" because "no one knows what 'psyche' is, and one knows just as little how far into nature 'psyche' extends" (Jung, 2008: 157).

Social-functional interpretations from the anthropological literature have tended to look at spirits as nothing more than mechanisms for the attainment of social goals. A major exposition of this perspective can be found in I. M. Lewis's book *Ecstatic Religion* (1971). In this book Lewis suggests that spirit possession provides the possessed with the opportunity to protest against social norms in a manner that frees the possessed of responsibility for their actions while in the trance state. Such interpretations, however, fail to take into account the experiences of the possessed, and fundamentally ignore the possibility that the spirit communicators could have any reality that is not the product of delusion or fraud.

Edith Turner, by contrast, is an anthropologist who has opted for a somewhat different standpoint. Following an apparent spirit experience during an *ihamba* healing ceremony amongst the Ndembu in Zambia, Turner's interpretation of both ritual and spirit belief was thoroughly transformed (Turner, 1993; 1998). She realised that for decades anthropologists have been ignoring the claims of their informants to the existence of spirits. She writes:

> Again and again anthropologists witness spirit rituals, and again and again some indigenous exegete tries to explain that spirits are present... and the anthropologist proceeds to interpret them differently (1993: 11).

Turner's solution to this problem is to cast aside the strictures of "positivists' denial" and ultimately learn to *"see what the Natives see"* (ibid.). This approach goes beyond anthropology's traditional position with regard to passing comment on the ontology of the objects of supernatural belief (Hunter, 2010).

An Anthropology of the Spirit-World

Fiona Bowie, an anthropologist at the University of Bristol, has recently established the Afterlife Research Centre (ARC) as a means to promote and disseminate ethnographic approaches to the study of the afterlife and related phenomena. Bowie has proposed a methodology, which she terms "cognitive empathetic engagement" (Bowie, 2010), by which an ethnographic exploration of the afterlife can be achieved. This process involves adopting a frame of mind in which reports of afterlife communication are treated "as if" they were ethnographic documents describing life on the "other side." A similar approach could well be utilised in the study of communications from spirits received via trance mediumship and possession. Bubandt (2009), for example, has argued that spirits can be treated as informants as a means to understand the society in which the possession takes place. Bubandt treats spirits as "methodologically real" rather than "ontologically real" (2009: 298), as Edith Turner (1993) has suggested.

I attempted this, to an extent, with a spirit called Charlie at the Bristol Spirit Lodge. But, rather than using him as an informant to examine the social makeup of the Lodge, I asked him questions about the spirit world and what exactly he was. His answers offered intriguing food for thought. Perhaps most revealing was his assertion that he was not the product of a single source, but was rather a collective manifestation:

> ...there are three sides involved; [the spirit], the conscious host and the subconscious host (Di Nucci & Hunter, 2009: 18).

When in the trance state, Charlie explained, all three components must be "*in a state of common trust.*" Without this blending Charlie would have been unable to manifest. Similarly, séance phenomena were explained as being the product of multiple influential factors including the consciousnesses/energies of the medium, the spirits and the sitters. From this perspective we come to understand a little more fully the nature of the spirits: they depend upon us to make themselves known. They are a sort of collectively created thought-form, while maintaining an element of independent individuality, assisted into being by the focused creative concentration of a group of sitters.

This idea is further reinforced when we look at the actual practices of Lodge. The séances themselves are highly ritualised activities, following a regular pattern. The séances are always conducted in the same building; a purpose-built 12'x10' shed. Entering into this building indicates a moving out of the world of the profane into a sacred (or at least special), liminal, space. At the start of the proceedings a prayer is read to invoke the protection of the "Almighty Father" and the presence of spirits. This serves as a cue to suggest that spirits will be present, thus inducing expectancy in the minds of the sitters. The effect of dimmed lighting and music in the induction of altered states of consciousness (ASCs) has been widely noted (Peters & Price-Williams, 1980: 399; Noll, 1985; Eliade, 1989), as has the tendency to encounter spiritual beings when experiencing ASCs (Devereux, 1997; Strassman, 2001; Luke, 2008). All of these factors, including the potential influence of external spiritual agencies, combine to allow spirit communication to take place.

This is where we see the benefit of the ethnographic approach in trying to understand the manifestation of the paranormal. Inferences are drawn not only from information gathered by talking to informants (incarnate or otherwise), but also from observing behaviours and practices. From this perspective we can potentially understand more fully both the purpose of the ritualised séance procedure and the nature of the spirits it assists in conjuring.

Conclusions

There is, seemingly, considerable reason to treat spirits *as though* they were ontologically real if not *as* ontologically real. Indeed, to my mind, this is our primary route towards ascertaining their ontological status: through conversation. We can gain, from this perspective, sociological insights as well as, potentially, parapsychological insights. We can use spirits as real informants, treating them not as "social facts" but as those who regularly interact with them do – as natural facts.

MEDIUMSHIP, ANIMISM AND ALTERED STATES OF CONSCIOUSNESS

When it comes to examining the many varied phenomena of spirit mediumship two very distinct components quickly become apparent. These two components are the belief in spiritual beings and the use of altered states of consciousness to initiate communication with these beings. Although these are not the only components of mediumship practices (Leacock & Leacock, 1975; Levy *et al*, 1996: 171-172; Kelly & Locke, 2009: 30; Hunter, 2010; Halloy, 2010), which vary hugely cross-culturally (Lewis, 1971; Schmidt & Huskinson, 2010; Dawson, 2011; Hunter & Luke, 2014), they do provide an interesting framework through which to explore mediumship and so will be the main topic of this short article. Throughout the article I will refer to my own fieldwork with the Bristol Spirit Lodge (Hunter, 2009; 2010a; 2010b; 2010c) as well as the writings of other anthropologists who have conducted fieldwork within mediumistic cultures.

Animism

Anthropology, as a disciplined enquiry into the nature of human beings and their cultures and life-ways (Barnard, 2000: 1-14; Eriksen, 2001: 4; Bowie, 2001: 1), has long concerned itself with trying to understand the extremely widespread human belief in the existence of intelligent and invisible agents, commonly referred to in the anthropological literature as "Spirits." Indeed, the man widely regarded as the discipline's founding father, Edward Burnett Tylor, saw the belief in spiritual beings as the minimum, most fundamental, definition of religion (Tylor, 1920: 426) and from this observation developed one of anthropology's first grand theories; a theory which Tylor called "animism" (Harvey, 2005: 5-9). It is the theory of animism in particular that I want to discuss here, as the development of the animism debate can, I believe, shed interesting light on contemporary explorations of spirit mediumship in a general sense.

The term animism derives from the Latin root word "anima" meaning "soul," and in his 1871 book *Primitive Culture,* Tylor established the term as referring to the "belief in supernatural beings," that is the idea that the world is inhabited by a plurality of souls, not all of which are human:

> It is habitually found that the theory of Animism divides into two great dogmas, forming parts of one consistent doctrine; first, concerning souls of individual creatures, capable of continued existence after the death or destruction of the body; second, concerning other spirits, upward to the rank of powerful deities (Tylor, 1920: 426).

Through examining the available ethnographic data (which consisted primarily of the reports of missionaries and explorers), Tylor attacked the assertions of certain of his contemporaries who suggested that there were societies in existence which bore no trace of religious belief (Tylor, 1920: 418-424). He argued that the numerous descriptions of spirits, of all different varieties (from ghosts of the dead to spirits of the weather, and so on), found in the ethnographic literature indicated the existence of, *at the very least,* a concept of spiritual entities in the belief systems that had been documented up to that point. Tylor concluded from this concept the idea that the "doctrine of souls," as he termed it, represented the earliest stage in the development of religious ideas. Indeed, Tylor considered animism to be essentially homologous with religion itself (Harvey, 2010). He wrote:

> Animism is, in fact, the groundwork of the Philosophy of Religion, from that of savages up to that of civilized men. And although it may at first sight seem to afford but a bare and meagre definition of a minimum of religion, it will be found practically sufficient; for where the root is, the branches will generally be produced (Tylor, 1920: 426).

Tylor, however, was not content with simply highlighting the prevalence of animism in global cultures; he had to go one step further through attempting to *explain* this belief. In keeping with the search for grand theories, like Darwin's theory of natural selection as expounded in *On the Origin of Species* (1859), Tylor sought the origin of religion, and he found it in the misinterpretation of experience, and in faulty reasoning. He argued that animistic ideas resulted directly from a misguided attempt to explain the peculiarities of death and the dream state: how, when dreaming, we can seem to travel to distant lands or meet with friends and relatives who live far away. He writes:

> When the sleeper awakens from a dream, he believes he has really somehow been away, or that other people have come to him. As it is well known by experience that men's bodies do not go on these excursions, the natural explanation is that every man's living self or soul is his phantom or image, which can go out of his body and see and be seen itself in dreams (1930: 88).

From the idea that human beings possess souls Tylor further reasoned that primitive people saw, in the various elemental movements of the world around them, hints of the existence of other similarly conscious entities, and in his evolutionary scheme concluded that these perceived entities gradually, over the course of millennia of cultural development, took on the form of omnipresent gods akin to the Judeo-Christian God (Tylor, 1920: 426; Bowker, 1973: 9-10). It seemed that Tylor had achieved his goal of devising a grand scientific theory of religion, and in so doing had demonstrated that the Christian faith, and indeed religion as a whole, was nothing more than a "survival" into the modern-world of a savage and primitive mentality. Later anthropologists, such as Evans-Pritchard (1965), however, argued the case for a not-so-hidden agenda in the writings of Tylor and many of his contemporaries. These early theorists were keen to establish the dominance of positivist scientific rationalism as an advanced world-view over-and-above what they saw as "less developed" systems of understanding. Through suggesting that animistic beliefs (from which religious doctrines were considered to have emerged), were founded on faulty reasoning, and misinterpretations of experiential phenomena, the doctrines of the established religions must also be suspect. He writes:

> They [nineteenth century anthropologists] sought, and found, in primitive religions a weapon which could, they thought, be used with deadly effect against Christianity. If primitive religion could be explained away as an intellectual aberration, as a mirage induced by emotional stress, or by its social function, it was implied that the higher religions could be discredited and disposed of in the same way (1965: 15).

Later anthropologists, therefore, lost interest in Tylor's theory of animism, seeing clearly within it the traits that were so typical of his time (colonial ideas of western intellectual superiority and a tendency towards the arbitrary reduction of complex phenomena), and it wasn't until the 1960s, nearly a century after Tylor's first writings on animism, that the term re-entered anthropological discourse, only this time with some quite different connotations.

In his paper, '*Ojibwa Ontology, Behaviour and World View*' (2002), the ethnographer Irving Hallowell developed the concept of 'other-than-human persons' in his analysis of the Native American Ojibwa wold-view. Hallowell's research reinvigorated the concept of animism and brought it, once again, to prominence in the anthropological discourse. During his fieldwork Hallowell noticed that the Ojibwa notion of personhood referred not only to human persons, but also to other entities, physical and non-physical, as well. The example he employed to highlight this idea, and to show just how ingrained this notion was within Ojibwa thought and culture, was in the use of the term 'grandfather,' which when used in the collective plural, as in 'our grandfathers,' was generally a referent for "spiritual beings who are persons of a category other than human" (Hallowell, 1960: 21). Hallowell noted that that these "other than human" persons were not thought of in abstract terms, but rather were seen as active participants in the social-group in much the same way as a "real" grandfather might. From this observation Hallowell concluded that previous anthropological methods had been somewhat lacking:

> ...if, in the worldview of a people, 'persons' as a class include entities other than human beings, then our objective approach is not adequate for presenting an accurate description of 'the way a man, in a particular society, sees himself in relation to all else.' A different perspective is required for this purpose (2002: 21).

Hallowell realised that previous ethnographers had failed to grasp a central component of the Ojibwa world-view; through ignoring the way in which the Ojibwa spoke about, thought about, and interacted with the world around them earlier ethnographers had completely misunderstood the Ojibwa notion of personhood, as well as their more general ontological scheme. In developing his ideas, based on first-hand fieldwork experience, Hallowell came to an understanding of the Ojibwa concept of personhood as relational: persons were not classified according to whether they were human or physical, but rather according to their capacity to engage in relationships with other persons. Persons, from this perspective, are defined by their capacity to be related to and engaged with, and through this interaction are granted an ontological, as well as a social, status. The only way to approach, and understand, this alternative way of living in the world with its many personified inhabitants is to experience it through intimate participation.

More recently Hallowell's ideas have been used by the anthropologist Nurit Bird-David (1999) in her study of Devaru spirit incorporation in southern India (which I will discuss a little later), and formed the basis of her reformulation of animism as being essentially concerned with relationships between persons. This new shift towards an appreciation of the world-view of the people under study, and the new emphasis on the concepts of personhood and relationality, has led to the development of what is often termed the "new animism." In a similar vein Graham Harvey defines animists as *"people who recognise that the word is full of persons, only some of whom are human, and that life is always lived in relationship with others"* (2005: xi). The new animism aims to redress the deficiencies of Tylor's, and the early anthropologists, theories of animism as the minimum definition of religion through shifting the perspective of observation from the surface appearance of culture and belief to the internal experience of alternative world-views. The primary problem with Tylor's theory of animism is his assertion that the origins of animistic beliefs are to be found in delusions and misinterpretations of experiences. This idea implies a lack of rationality on behalf of traditional epistemologies and ontologies and is clearly representative of significantly outmoded colonial, and ethnocentric, theories. Modern participant observers have revealed not only the internal rationality of different world-views, but also their efficacy as alternative modes of living in, and experiencing, the world.

Altered States of Consciousness

Altered states of consciousness have, for a long time, been recognised as fundamentally intertwined with mediumship traditions. Writing in the 1890s Sir James George Fraser referred to the "abnormal" state in which spirit incorporation usually occurs (Fraser, 1993: 108). More recently, in the 1970s, the anthropologist Erika Bourguignon identified the widespread prevalence of institutionalised altered states of consciousness in human societies throughout the world. Bourguignon estimated that 89% of the world's societies possessed some form of institutionalised altered state of consciousness, and that of these societies 57% associated such altered states with the incorporation of non-physical entities (as cited in Krippner & Friedman, 2009: 93).

The general characteristics of the ASCs associated with mediumship and spirit incorporation practices include "alterations or discontinuity in consciousness, awareness or personality" (Bourguignon, 1976: 8) and amnesia of the period during which the entity was incorporated by the medium. These features have been classed under the heading of "dissociation" in the psychiatric literature (Crabtree, 1988; Levy *et al*, 1996: 18), and consequently are seen as indications of underlying pathological conditions. The psychoanalyst Adam Crabtree (1988) defines Dissociative Identity Disorder (DID) as a "condition in which two or more personalities manifest themselves in one human being." The similarities with mediumistic phenomena, therefore, are striking and psychical researchers have long been aware of the inherent difficulties in attempting to distinguish between the pathological and the potentially paranormal (the psychical researcher David Scott Rogo (1988), for instance, referred to *The Infinite Boundary of Spirit Possession, Madness, and Multiple Personality*).

It is the amnesic component of the medium's trance that is generally considered the feature which differentiates mediumistic ASCs from those associated with shamanistic practices (Eliade, 1989: 6; Winkelman, 2000: 156). Mircea Eliade highlights this distinction when he writes: "the shaman controls his 'spirits' in the sense that he, a human being, is able to communicate with the dead, 'demons,' and 'nature spirits,' without thereby becoming their instrument" (Eliade, 1989: 6). The medium, therefore, is understood to surrender his/her control of the body to an external intelligence, while the shaman remains in complete control during his performance and is able to recall his trance journeys through the spirit worlds.

The anthropologist Morton Klass (2003) attempted to make a further terminological distinction whereby the term "trance" is used solely to describe the more shamanic experience of soul-flight and journeys to other worlds, and suggested that the concept of "Patterned Dissociative Identity" be used to refer to instances of spirit possession in which the personality of the medium is altered or replaced by another in a culturally recognised context (Klass, 2003: 118-119). Although it is useful and easy to make such clear-cut distinctions in theory, however, the real life ethnographic data do not always fit so neatly into rigidly defined categories, and aspects of mediumship and shamanism very often overlap with one another (Jokic, 2008a,b). Mediumship, for example, can often be a technique in the wider repertoire of the shaman, and Euro-American platform, or clairvoyant, mediums do not necessarily lose consciousness or display alterations of personality when receiving and giving messages from the spirit world.

It is clear, therefore, that we are dealing not with a single altered state of consciousness, but rather with a variety of different states which are, despite their differences, utilised for communing with the invisible world of spirits. Indeed, members of the Lodge (with whom I conducted my own fieldwork), as well as many spiritualists in general, are aware of a continuum of different altered states utilised by mediums. The depth of the trance is usually determined according to the degree to which the medium is disconnected from reality – if a medium is still able to perceive his/her surroundings the trance is light; if, on the other hand, the medium is completely senseless to the physical world the trance is considered to be deep. The dislocation of the medium's consciousness from his/her surroundings is often described in terms very similar to the classic description of an out-of-body experience (cf. Blackmore, 1992), as this description from my fieldwork demonstrates:

> Often now, when [the spirits] are talking I'll go back into myself and get a strange sensation of vertigo and being detached from the conversation, not just intellectually but physically as well. As if I'm on the edge of a precipice or inside a vast canyon. It's a sense of scale I think, I feel very small in comparison to something very large [...] (Jon, cited in Hunter, 2009: 74).

My own experience, during my undergraduate fieldwork, of slipping into what the circle leader identified as a trance state, also featured several of the characteristics of an OBE:

> ...this time the physical sensations [...] came on again much faster; my heart rate increased and the tingling in my hands returned. I began to feel myself distancing from my body, and at the point of greatest distance I felt as though there was a space in my body that could easily be filled, it was as though I had made room in my physical body by moving myself out of it (Hunter, 2009: 71).

It is through these altered states that ostensible spirits are apparently able to make their presence known. Altered states of consciousness, particularly dissociative states with their capacity to dislocate the individual's consciousness, seem to open up the space required for alternate personalities to emerge. Establishing whether or not these alternate personalities are products of the unconscious mind which are temporarily allowed to surface, or ontologically distinct spirit individuals, is beyond the scope of this short article (though others have approached the issue, for instance Myers, 1992, and see also Gauld, 1983; Taves, 1999; Braude, 2003; Pearsall, 2004; Blum, 2007; for more general overviews). At this point all that is required is to acknowledge the importance of altered states of consciousness in allowing these other personalities to express themselves as distinct from the medium's normal everyday waking consciousness. The following section will explore the ways in which such personalities are recognized – the culturally recognised patterns in Klass' patterned dissociative identity (Klass, 2002).

Expressions of Personhood at the Lodge and Further Afield

In many non-western societies a particular spirit or deity, when incorporated, is discerned through specific, socially and culturally recognised, characteristics and behaviours. For instance, in the Afro-Brazilian religion of Batuque a medium must act in a certain way if they are to be perceived as genuinely under the influence of an *encantado*. Anthropologists Seth and Ruth Leacock (1975) describe this when they write:

> In order to prove that an encantado is really present, the medium must dance, sing the proper songs, and interact with the other participants in the ceremony in an acceptable manner. The behaviour that is most admired in the accomplished medium is very often the behaviour that appears the least frenzied and the most normal to the outside observer (Leacock & Leacock, 1975: 171-172).

Simply to fall into trance, then, is not necessarily enough to signify the presence of non-physical persons. In order for persons to be discerned, specific, culturally recognised, behaviours are required, and these may take a long time to perfect. In this sense, therefore, the mediumship process may be interpreted as a complex form of performance. Levy et al (1996), for example, write that *"[f]ull possession behaviour is highly skillful"* requiring *"mastery of playing and of subtle, specialized kinds of communally significant communication"* (1996: 18). Performance, therefore, plays a significant role in the expression of the non-physical persons embodied by mediums. In this context, however, the world performance should not be read as an indicator that what the medium does is necessarily fake (Beattie, 1977: 2), rather it should be considered as a specific tool employed to allow ostensibly non-physical entities (whether ontologically distinct or an aspect of the medium's subconscious) to express themselves in a culturally recognised manner.

When a spirit first makes itself known through an entranced medium at the Lodge the communication is often weak, and it may take several development sittings for an individual spirit personality to express itself fully and for this expression to be recognised. Occasionally a personality will show the early signs of emerging but will never reach its full expression as a regular communicator. The strongest, most fully developed, communicators generally form a group called a "spirit team." A medium will regularly channel the members of his/her spirit team, and these communicators will become recognised by sitters as distinct individual personalities. Of the members of the spirit team there is usually one who takes the role of "main spirit guide," "control" or "gate-keeper." This spirit is often the most developed personality of the spirit team and, more often than not, was the first personality to present through the entranced medium in the earliest stages of his/her development.

Because each personality must express itself through a single physical body, the spirits utilise exaggerated body movements and unusual vocal tones to differentiate themselves from one another. Occasionally the presence of a spirit is inferred simply by the physical posturing of the medium's body, and this posturing is recognised as signifying the presence of a distinct personality. In some mediums (a medium referred to as S in particular), more than one spirit may present itself simultaneously through the body of the medium; in such instances, individual presences are inferred from the distinctive movements of certain body parts: for instance, the legs may move in a manner distinctive to one particular personality, while the arms may behave in a completely different manner associated with the personality of another spirit. The exaggerated postures and vocalizations can often give the impression that the individual spirit personalities are caricatures. I would suggest that this is a necessary aspect of the mediumship process, assisting in the development and expression in the social moment of distinctive personalities: the exaggeration of postures and movements serves to signify the presence of a particular spirit-person. Bird-David (1999) describes an analogous process in her analysis of the Devaru performances of the South Indian Nayaka. She writes:

> The devara evoked often improvise on the same repetitive phrases. The saying, the voicing, the gesturing are important. (Bird-David, 1999: 76).

Over time the spirit-teams of the individual mediums will become regular fixtures at the Lodge's weekly séances and are treated in many ways as anyone else who attends regularly. Through this regular interaction the spirit communicators become much more than abstractions; interaction allows them to manifest in a socially real and very tangible way. Similarly, Bird-David (1999) understands the Devaru as relational persons, brought into social existence through interactions, i.e. conversation. She writes that: "[k]eeping the conversation going is important because it keeps the Nayaka devaru interaction and in a sense the devara themselves 'alive.'" Moreover, the form this interaction takes is described as "highly personal, informal, and friendly" and consists of "*joking, teasing,* [and] *bargaining.*" The conversations are said to include "*numerous repetitions or minor variations on a theme*" in which the Nayaka and the devaru "*nag and tease, praise and flatter, blame and cajole each other, expressing and demanding care and concern*" (Bird-David, 1999: 76). The interactions between spirits and sitters at the Lodge could equally be described in this way. Take the following séance transcript for example:

> **Chris** [Circle leader]: Are you there yet Charlie?
> **Charlie** [Spirit]: Of course.
> **Chris:** Is it okay to open the cabinet?
> **Charlie:** If you wish.
> **Chris:** I'll do it slowly [...] How are you?
> **Charlie:** Very well, how are you?
> **Chris:** Fine. We've been sitting in the dark. How was it for you?
> **Charlie:** Wonderful, how was it for you?
> **Chris:** Not too bad actually. I wouldn't say it was the best ever, but not too bad!
> **Charlie:** Some people are never satisfied (Di Nucci & Hunter, 2009: 158-159)

The tone of the interaction is very informal. This sort of quick jokey interchange between the circle leader and the spirit will usually precede the more advanced, philosophical, discussions which form the bulk of the communication. These could be interpreted as a means to build up the personality of the communicator until it is sufficiently formed and able to sustain itself for a more rigorous discourse. The developing personality requires, in Bird-David's terms, "care and concern" (1999: 76) from the sitters. If, as participants and observers in the séance, we do not interact with the developing personality it will not be able to emerge fully. I would argue that the practices of the Bristol Spirit Lodge can be interpreted as a sub-culture, within our dominant western society, of a relational animism. The Lodge has developed specific means of promoting the emergence of spirit personalities through mediums utilising altered states of consciousness, and (sub)culturally specific means of recognising and discerning the presence of spirits in the behaviour of entranced mediums.

Conclusions

The following points are preliminary observations and should not be seen as definitive conclusions, rather, I hope, they can be seen as a springboard for further inquiry. It is the author's hope that these observations and ideas will be of benefit to anthropologists, parapsychologists and psychical researchers engaged in the study of contemporary spirit mediumship in a variety of geographical and cultural contexts:

- Altered states of consciousness and performance allow for the emergence and expression of non-physical persons.
- Discerning the presence of persons in entranced mediums is fundamentally embedded within the cultural matrix within which it occurs; different cultures recognise the presence of persons in different ways.
- Maintaining relationships with these persons enables them to become socially active entities and can grant them an ontological status.
- We cannot understand mediumship practices without an appreciation of the ontological frame-of-reference of the culture (or sub-culture) within which it occurs.

- When we engage with, and participate in, these alternate ontological frameworks unusual experiences may emerge, and these can bring into question the framework from which our investigations began (cf. Long, 1974; Stoller & Olkes, 1987; Turner, 1993, 1998, 2006).

ETHNOGRAPHIC AND PSYCHICAL APPROACHES TO SPIRIT MEDIUMSHIP

The two disciplines of anthropology and psychical research have traditionally approached their subject matter from opposing perspectives. Since the advent of the Society for Psychical Research in 1882, psychical researchers have aimed specifically at the verification or falsification of claims to paranormal experience and phenomena, while ethnographers have been primarily concerned with describing beliefs and experiences without any attempt at assessing the reality, or otherwise, of the objects of these beliefs. This short article will take a comparative look at the methods of ethnography and psychical research with an emphasis on their approaches to the study of spirit mediumship. This will be done with the aim of exploring the potential for a merging of methodologies that might prove fruitful for both disciplines.

A reading of the older psychical research textbooks reveals a very distinct sense of the necessity to prove or disprove empirically the claims of mediums in as rational and scientific a manner as possible. In addition to this endeavour, researchers were also faced with the task of overcoming the ever-present danger of deliberate fraud and trickery perpetrated by the mediums they were investigating. Hans Driesch's book *Psychical Research: The Science of the Super-Normal* (1933), for example, devotes 48 pages to the "Possibility of Deception in Psychical Research" in both spontaneous and controlled investigations. To be duped by a medium was, and likely still is, the worst nightmare of the serious psychical researcher.

In order to achieve an impartial scientific test of the abilities of mediums, psychical researchers developed specific experimental procedures, which could, so they thought, help to insure against trickery. Robert H. Ashby's book *The Guidebook for the Study of Psychical*

Research (1972), suggests "Procedures for Sitting With Mediums" for the "serious student of psi" who wishes to "experience paranormal phenomena personally" (Ashby, 1972: 90). Amongst the methods suggested, Ashby includes: arranging sittings anonymously to insure against the medium's conducting their own background research; refraining from volunteering any information to the medium during the sitting, and recording the sitting on audio tape for later content analysis (Ashby, 1972: 93-95). These precautions apply specifically to the various forms of mental mediumship (clairvoyance, clairaudience, clairsentience and trance mediumship, etc.), and are aimed at preventing information leakage from the sitter to the medium so that any information can be verified as having been received by paranormal means.

In the case of investigating physical mediumship, much more rigorous precautions have traditionally been employed. Driesch (1933) argues that although, at first, it is perfectly reasonable for sitters to adhere to the medium's séance rules, it is the psychical researcher's "imperative duty to free oneself as soon as possible from these conditions" (Driesch, 1933: 23). Driesch suggests that both mediums and sitters "must *a priori* be regarded as 'suspect,'" and that it is essential that physical phenomena be observed in good light. Further suggested precautions include: that the medium's body be "strictly examined" before the séance and that the room be thoroughly investigated before the medium enters. During the séance itself, Driesch suggests: that the sitters form a chain of linked hands; that luminous tabs be placed on the medium's sleeves; that the medium's hands and feet should be controlled by a reliable person, and so on (1933: 26-27). Methods such as these are specifically geared towards the elimination of the possibility for deliberate acts of fraud and trickery.

The approach of psychical research to the study of spirit mediumship is, therefore, proof focused – its aim being to falsify or verify the abilities of mediums and the identities of the spirits they channel. By contrast, the ethnographic method has deliberately avoided the question of the ontological status of the beliefs it studies. Ethnography utilises a primarily descriptive methodology, and seeks to document, in as much detail as possible, the social and cultural conditions in which the ethnographer finds themself. In this regard, therefore, ethnographers are not necessarily concerned with the question of whether the objects of the beliefs of a particular culture are real; instead they are interested in the way in which these beliefs affect and inform the functioning of society, and those who live within it.

In a recent ethnographic account of spirit possession rituals in Indonesia, the anthropologist Nils Bubandt (2009) argued in favour of treating spirits as "methodologically real" informants, as to do so allows the anthropologist to "get on with the business of studying the social and political reality of spirits" (Bubandt, 2009: 298). To treat the spirits as methodologically real does not require the ethnographer to verify or falsify their existence as ontologically distinct entities, nor is it necessary to attempt to prove that the spirits are who they claim to be. Instead, ethnographic accounts of mediumship and spirit possession tend to emphasise the social roles of mediums and the spirits that possess their bodies, and on functional explanations of the act of spirit mediumship itself.

Unlike the psychical researcher investigating physical mediumship, the ethnographer does not insist on modifying the conditions of the mediumship performance to rule out deception and trickery; rather the ethnographer will examine the social and cultural significance of the performance, asking what it means to the people who participate in it. Two illustrative examples of this approach are the social functional theory of spirit possession as a means for subjugated members of society to express their discontent in a socially sanctioned manner (Lewis, 1971), and the view of spirit possession as maintaining social and cultural continuity with the ancestors through regular interaction during possession performances (Stoller, 1994; Lambek, 1998).

How, then, can we fruitfully combine the methods of psychical research and ethnography? To my mind the obvious point of contact is revealed by the deficiencies of each approach. The ethnographer, in refusing to address the question of ontology, is essentially ignoring the native interpretations of the societies they are studying. To take beliefs in spirit possession seriously, and accept the *possibility* that spirits might have an independent ontological existence, is to take a significant step forward methodologically and can only result in a more complete ethnographic description. Conversely, psychical research can benefit from a more thorough appreciation of the role of culture, and of social interactions, in the experience of paranormal phenomena.

THE ISSUE OF FRAUD AND PERFORMANCE IN MEDIUMSHIP

After attending an impressive demonstration of physical mediumship with a medium referred to herein as "medium X" earlier this year, while writing my anthropology dissertation (Hunter, 2009), I began thinking about the way in which we conceive of fraud, performance and trickery, particularly with regard to physical mediumship. There were elements of "medium X's" séance that seemed to me as though they might have been the product of trickery, while there were other aspects that I was very impressed with, as well as yet other elements that I am entirely uncertain of. This article will explore the possibility that our notion of fraud, with its overtly negative connotations and implications of a lack of any validity to the phenomena displayed, is not necessarily applicable to all séance phenomena, even if trickery and deception are utilised in their production. Ethnographic examples will be utilised to shed light on the relationship between performance, trickery and supernatural experience. The article will conclude with the suggestion that the process of physical mediumship is potentially much more complex than we are currently aware of, and that there may be many elements required for the manifestation of paranormal phenomena that do not accord well with our rationalistic framework; for example, some degree of trickery may be a necessary requirement for the creation of paranormal effects in certain circumstances. My approach will be broadly anthropological, drawing on cross-cultural comparisons to illuminate the complexity of the issue.

Physical Mediumship

Before we begin it will be necessary to give a brief introduction to the topic of physical mediumship. Mediumship is defined as a process whereby information is transferred "*from discarnate beings or souls to the living through another human who is sensitive to such information*" (Emmons, 2000: 72). Mediums provide a communication link between the world of the living and the world of the dead; as their title suggests, they are mediators.

Physical mediumship, in addition to claiming to provide a link between discarnate intelligence and the human realm, is also associated with a variety of materialistic phenomena, including: the materialisation of spirit forms via the manipulation of a semi-physical substance referred to as ectoplasm (Pilkington, 2004); dematerialisation of objects, apports (the bringing of physical objects into the séance room by spirit intervention); levitation of the medium and physical objects, direct voice phenomena and so on. John Klimo defines physical mediumship as "*the human ability to channel unknown energies that affect the physical environment in ways that can be directly experienced by persons other than the channel*" (Klimo, 1987: 200), and it is precisely because of the fact that such phenomena are apparently objective occurrences that accusations of fraud have been so commonplace in the history of these unusual practices.

There are two main theoretical stand-points pertaining to the nature of mediumship phenomena within the parapsychological literature: the survivalist, or spiritualistic, interpretation, and the super-psi hypothesis (Sudduth, 2001). The survivalist conception holds that mediumistic phenomena are best explained through the postulated agency of discarnate entities, while the super-psi hypothesis argues that the physical and mental abilities of mediums need not posit the existence of discarnate beings, and instead suggests that they can be explained using theories of ESP between living individuals and psychokinetic processes (PK).

Physical mediumship as it exists today is a product of the 19th century Spiritualist movement, although its roots are probably much earlier; as will be discussed later many aspects of the practice of physical mediumship possess striking similarities with shamanistic practices (Eliade, 1989: 255) and spirit possession cults (Lewis, 1971) from a variety of time periods and geographic regions.

The Spiritualist movement officially dates to 1848 when, in the small town of Hydesville, New York State, two sisters by the name of Kate and Margaret Fox made contact with the spirit of a man believed to have been killed in their home years earlier. The sisters discovered that they could communicate with the spirit by asking it questions to be answered with loud knocks in the room (Doyle, 2006). This was the first widely publicised physical communication with spiritual entities, and was the seed that sprouted an international fascination with spirit communication in the late nineteenth century.

From this point onwards, physical spirit communication became increasingly refined and diversified. Mediums developed different methods for communicating with the spirit world and the phenomena associated with these communications became increasingly fantastical. Physical phenomena developed from simple raps and knocks through planchette and ouija board communications (Kardec, 2006), to full-blown materializations of spirit forms, levitation, spirit lights and ectoplasmic secretions.

Even during this halcyon period for mediumship and spiritualistic endeavours, accusations of fraud, deception and trickery were regularly directed at those reportedly producing physical phenomena, and many mediums were indeed found to be engaged in such practices. Both Margaret and Kate Fox, for example, have been recorded as specifically stating that their own manifestations of physical spirit communication were the product of trickery. Interestingly, however, one year after the sisters' announcement, Margaret Fox reversed her statement saying that it had been made under the influence of money and anti-Spiritualists (Klimo, 1987: 99). It is interesting to note this apparent uncertainty in the minds of mediums about whether the phenomena they produce are the product of their own agency or the agency of discarnate energy-consciousness. This blurring of distinctions is an issue that will be returned to later on in this article.

Today, physical mediumship is relatively rare. This is the result of a trend away from physical manifestations towards more subjective forms of spirit communication, perhaps best exemplified by the modern phenomenon of channelling. So called modern "New Age" channellers do not claim to be able to produce physical phenomena (Spencer, 2001), and the forms of consciousness they channel are not necessarily those of deceased humans but may be anything from angelic and inter-dimensional beings to intergalactic federations of extraterrestrials (Klimo, 1987). This trend has likely developed as a consequence of accusations of fraud filed against mediums claiming to be able to elicit physical manifestations over the course of the last 150 years or so, and the poor treatment they have received while being investigated (Foy, 2007: 226).

The Séance

This séance with "medium X" was not held under rigidly controlled conditions. It was not intended as a scientific investigation, but was a private event that I had been invited to witness. The following discussion, therefore, is primarily concerned with the phenomenology of the mediumistic experience, for both the medium and the observer.

Unlike the séances I had been used to attending over the course of my fieldwork, in which communications would be relatively un-dramatically received through an entranced medium in red light conditions, "medium X's" séance was theatrical. This particular medium tends to work in the traditional manner: the medium was tied, strapped and bound into his chair in front of the audience of nine sitters by myself (see Fig.1 for details of the séance room). He was then gagged and the curtains of the cabinet were pulled shut. The lights were extinguished, which plunged the whole room into pitch darkness, purportedly a necessity as ectoplasm (believed to be a light sensitive substance) was to be utilised. It was requested that we remain silent during the first two pieces of music played on the CD player. As we sat there in the darkness, loud banging sounds and growls began to be heard from within the cabinet. As the music intensified so too did the sense of the uncanny. Soon we were witnessing demonstrations of the impossible – spirit-lights, spirit materialization, dematerialization of physical objects, and trumpet phenomena. Within half an hour, distinct personalities were making themselves known through the entranced medium: we were conversing with the deceased.

These physical phenomena and the sense of the uncanny were not the only factors that prompted me to take seriously what was happening during the séance. In addition to demonstrating physical effects, "medium X" provided a number of apparently personally significant messages to sitters. One message was particularly pertinent to one of the sitters, eliciting a highly emotional response: the communicating voice required only to make itself heard to the sitter, even without saying anything particularly evidential, for her to know that it was the voice of her father. The sitter had never previously met with the medium. Phenomena such as these cannot be ignored.

It was an impressive display and a very peculiar experience. But how do we interpret what happened that evening?

It is the definitively physical reality of the phenomena produced by "medium X" that brings them into question. In some respects, it is easier to accept those paranormal phenomena that seem to exist within the realm of subjective experience than it is to accept an apparently impossible event that multiple witnesses are able to perceive; we assume that it must be an illusion or an elaborate trick. Indeed, we would be naïve not to question them in this way. However, I feel that mediumistic research ought to consider the role that deception might play in the practice of mediumship without assuming that the presence of deceptive techniques inherently denies the existence of genuine paranormal phenomena. Trickery does not negate the paranormal: the two can co-exist, and indeed may be fundamentally interwoven.

Blurring Boundaries

In his book, *The Trickster and the Paranormal* (2001), parapsychologist George P. Hansen discusses the way in which the characteristics of the trickster archetype (including: trickery, liminality, etc.) appear to manifest in those who engage in direct contact with the supernatural or paranormal, whether the approach is mediumistic or investigative. Hansen suggests that the paranormal realm becomes apparent through liminality and that those who are prone to experience and encounter it are often also possessed of liminal and trickster characteristics. Liminal characteristics are those that fundamentally blur distinctions: blurring seemingly incompatible opposites.

The concept of liminality derives from the writings of anthropologist Victor Turner. Liminality arises when binary distinctions break down: when the normal order is inverted. The classic example in the anthropological literature concerns coming of age ceremonies. The ceremony represents a liminal period between childhood and adulthood. During the course of the ritual the initiates are reduced to the same level and must undergo some form of ritual ordeal together. This produces what Victor Turner refers to as communitas: a sense of communion. Following the ceremony, the initiated return to normal society as adults – transformed by their ritual ordeal. Through the blurring of distinctions and a journey through liminal space the social standing of the individual is affirmed (Turner, 1985: 160).

The blurring of distinctions is clear in the annals of mediumistic research. While many eminent researchers in the Victorian era investigated the claims and abilities of Spiritualist mediums and were convinced of the reality of phenomena they were observing, there were other researchers discovering the same mediums engaged in fraud and deception. One such example is the case of the Italian medium Eusapia Palladino. Several serious researchers found her to be actively engaged in blatant attempts at deception and yet, despite such exposures, continued to consider many of her phenomena to be genuine. In the second volume of Arthur Conan-Doyle's *History of Spiritualism* (2006), a whole chapter is devoted to the discussion of this intriguing medium, and particular attention is paid to her trickster nature:

> Many are the crafty tricks she plays, both in the state of trance (unconsciously) and out of it – for example freeing one hand of her two hands, held by the controllers, for the sake of moving objects near her; making touches; slowly lifting the legs of the table by means of one of her knees and one of her feet... (Doyle, 2006, Vol. 2: 9).

Despite such blatant attempts at deception, dedicated researchers continued to take her claims seriously and in a great many situations were convinced of the reality of her abilities and the phenomena she produced. Doyle writes:

> In her visit to America... she was detected in these obvious tricks and offended her sitters to such an extent that they discarded her, but Howard Thurston, the famous conjuror, narrates that he determined to disregard these things and continued the sitting, with the result that he obtained an undoubted materialisation. Another well-known sitter deposed that at the very moment when he was reproaching her for moving some object with her hand, another object, quite out of her reach, moved across the table (ibid).

Despite her evident (and exceedingly blatant) use of deceptive techniques, Palladino was vouched for by such eminent researchers as Sir Oliver Lodge, Sir William Crookes and Hereward Carrington (Doyle, 2006, Vol. 2: 1-11; McCreery, 1973: 43-66). How can this be accounted for?

The character of the medium is a paradox of the genuine and the fake. Hansen suggests that it is this paradox that renders the paranormal so difficult to stomach for the scientific approach; it is inherently irrational. The medium is an embodiment of the trickster archetype. As a mediator between the "spirit world" and the "earth-plane," the living and the dead, the medium occupies a liminal position.

As is perhaps evident, I remain agnostic as to the nature of the physical phenomena produced by "medium X." I simply cannot say one way or the other whether the spirit lights I experienced were genuine or the product of trickery, or indeed whether the numerous communicators were simply the medium acting out roles, or, on the other hand, actual spirit beings. I can accept, however, that some degree of deception was taking place. The uncertainty produced in séance situations is an element of the liminal nature of the paranormal. When we attempt to engage with the paranormal reality we put ourselves in an irrational position; our conceptual boundaries become increasingly blurred (this is likely the reason why objective "scientific" research is required, but also the reason why objective methods may not be entirely appropriate, or even possible).

Having spoken to mediums of different developmental stages, and also engaged to some extent with mediumistic development myself, this uncertainty is also often present even within the medium him/herself, particularly during development.

It is not uncommon – and I have experienced it myself – for developing mediums, whose guides are being spoken to by the circle leader, to feel an intense desire to speak out but of being entirely uncertain as to whether this desire is their own or that of the spirit entity being addressed. The distinction between self and other is entirely blurred; the developing medium finds it very difficult to say whether the communicators they channel are separate from, or one and the same as, their own consciousness. In such circumstances established mediums advise those developing their abilities to ignore this apparent contradiction. It would seem that communication with discarnate entities arises from a cognitive paradox that must be accepted and embraced.

We are seeing, here, a breakdown of structure: the binary opposition of reality; illusion is blurred. Hansen would suggest that this is an inevitable result of the nature of paranormal phenomena in general: they are anti-structural and highly liminal. I would agree with this suggestion.

Performance

Performance has a transcendental capacity to move the attention of human beings away from the "everyday" reality towards something "other" or "higher." The experience of this motion is very real, and, in many cases, far exceeds the original stimulus, rendering the process of attaining the experience much less significant than the outcome. Watching a performance, or looking at a piece of art, can have a profound effect on the viewer: an emotional response as real and significant to the experiencer as any other life situation might inspire (Frijda, 1989: 1546) It is said that we may suspend our disbelief when watching a play or reading a book in order to fully engage ourselves in the situation being presented to us:

> In viewing a movie or play, one does not perceive unreality, but one knowingly abandons oneself to an illusion and within the illusion accepts the events unquestioningly for what they pretend to be (Frijda, 1989: 1546).

This suspension of disbelief is usually created by the performance: if the performance is good the observer will be better able to immerse him/herself in the drama, and may even forget that what they are observing is an act. This is a powerful phenomenon, and its implications for the study of mediumship and related practices are very significant.

Performance often takes a central role in the practices of shamans throughout the world. The types of performance utilised might include: dancing, singing, drumming, illusions/tricks, role playing and fantastic feats of physical ability, alone or in combination with one another. Historian of Religion Mircea Eliade, in his definitive text *Shamanism: Archaic Techniques of Ecstasy* (1989) describes some of the purported phenomena associated with the shamanic healing séance of the Chuckchi:

> The shaman takes off his shirt and, bare to the waist, smokes his pipe and begins to drum and sing... Suddenly the voices of the "spirits" are heard from every direction... A ke'let (spirit) enters the shaman's body, whereupon, moving his head rapidly, the shaman begins to cry out and speak in falsetto, the voice of the spirit. During this time, in the darkness of the tent, all sorts of strange phenomena occur: levitation of objects, the tent shaking, rain of stones and bits of wood, and so on. Through the shaman's voice the spirits of the dead converse with the audience (Eliade, 1989: 255).

Many aspects of such performances feature striking resemblances to both historical and contemporary accounts of physical mediumship séances. Eliade does not address the nature of the phenomena specifically, preferring to leave such investigations to parapsychological researchers, but many other researchers have attempted to reduce such occurrences to explanations of trickery and sleight of hand. Eliade notes, for instance, that the American Baptist preacher Bogoras, who visited Siberia in 1901, felt that he could explain the apparent multiplicity of "spirit voices" produced by the shaman as the product of ventriloquism but admits that his recordings of the séances are very peculiar indeed. Uncertainty is manifested through the shamanic performance.

I would suggest that such performances serve as external cues to induce within the observer a sense of the otherworldly and as proofs to the witness that the shaman is indeed in contact with this other world. Performance serves as verification that the shaman's supernatural abilities are effective, and in so doing have the effect of inducing positive reactions in the observer. Fiona Bowie (2001) writes:

> Whatever sleight of hand or other means used by the shaman to achieve dramatic effects, many observers… were convinced of the séance's therapeutic effects. Sick individuals become, for a while, the focus of attention and their will to live is strengthened. Community tensions can be brought into the open and resolved, and the séance itself acts as a cathartic event (Bowie, 2002: 204).

Performance, then, may serve an integral role in the work of physical mediums; performance may help to induce the necessary atmosphere for paranormal phenomena to occur. This would account for the element of showmanship: the binding of the medium, the use of gags and restraints and so on. The "act" of tying the medium sets up a scenario in which the observer is waiting for something to happen: an element of suspense is manifested.

In addition to this atmosphere of suspense, tricks and illusions can cause the observer to look at reality differently; they can induce in the observer a sense of the impossible and magical. To this end, the element of performance may increase the acceptance of the witness that something is actually happening, which may well be the case. Performance and/or elements of trickery may be a fundamental aspect of the process of inducing something to happen: creating an atmosphere in which things may occur through providing stimulus to suggest the tangible action of the spirit world; through allowing the individual to suspend their disbelief. Once in that frame of mind, an individual will be open to experience on more subtle levels and will be better able to engage willingly with them. Performance is a two-way process: the observer and the observed are engaging with one another.

As an example of the way in which performance opens the way for paranormal experiences, I point you in the direction of Edith Turner's 1993 article *The Reality of Spirits*, in which she recalls the performance of an Umbanda trance ceremony in New York in 1980:

> We enacted the Umbanda trance session which we had observed and studied in one of the slums of Rio de Janeiro. The New York University students duly followed our directions and also accompanied the rites with bongo drumming and songs addressed to the Yoruba gods. During the ritual a woman student named Sharon who was a street theatre director in Jerusalem actually went into trance, there in New York University. We... [were] rather impressed with the way this ritual works out of context (1993: 9).

In this one passage we see the metamorphosis of an 'enactment' into a 'ritual' resulting in contact with the supernatural realm (through trance). The distinction between sacred and secular was immediately blurred during the performance (again an element of liminality). The performance sets up cues to the mind-body and consciousness that something is meant to happen, and consequently it does. On returning from her trance experience Sharon successfully predicted the outcome of a football match. A paranormal effect – precognition – arose from a liminal situation: where secular performance and religious ritual became indistinguishable.

I would suggest that a similar process is in operation during physical mediumship séances.

Blending

Blending is the term utilised by mediums and channellers to describe the interconnectedness of the medium's consciousness with that of the discarnate entity utilising his/her body as a vessel. Hughes (1991) has highlighted the positive connotations and sense of "harmony... between channel and entity" (1991: 166) implied by the term, which clearly distinguishes this mode of spirit incorporation from involuntary possession states.

When an entity is incorporated within the body of a medium it makes itself apparent to the outside world through manipulations of the medium's vocal tonality and physical demeanour.

Umbandaists believe that spirits and saints, known as Orixas, can inhabit the bodies of spirit mediums during trance performances (St. Clair, 1971; Turner, 1985: 129-130). Each Orixa has a favourite rhythm and dance, which is performed by musicians and mediums respectively. During the trance session *the medium's movements are the movements of the Orixa inhabiting his/her body*; at that moment the Orixa and the individual are blended. The medium is the spirit and the spirit is the medium. The dance performance is the physical demonstration of Orixa control over the medium's body.

Similarly, it is understood in many so-called "shamanic" societies that the shaman has the ability to physically embody spirits. According to the Yanomamo Indians of the Orinoco valley in Venezuela the *shapori* (being the Yanomamo shaman) initiation process involves the metamorphosis of the initiate into a *hekura* spirit:

> The shaman is correspondingly perceived by non-initiated Yanomami as something other than a human being; he is a living spirit in the flesh... [The] Yanomami term for shamanic initiation, hekura prai, can be translated as 'the metamorphosis of a human being into a hekura spirit,' or human body into a cosmic body (Jokic, 2008a: 38-39).

While the *shapori* is inhabited by the spirits he carries out specific tasks, such as healing, divination, and other-than-normal behaviours under their direct control and influence. To the outsider this may appear to be an elaborate act, but to the Yanomami it is a blending of the human and spirit worlds. The *shapori* may appear to be acting, but he is not. If anything, it is the incorporating spirit entities that are acting through his body.

Edith Turner (1998) also records a similar blending of an individual with spirit in her account of the *Ihamba* healing ritual; "*in Ihamba the spirit and you may be one, and you may speak to the spirit or speak to the person as the need arises*" (1998: 62). It is clear, then, that we are dealing with an issue that is in no way clear-cut. There is abundant evidence for trans-cultural notions of the blending of an individual with a spirit, both physically and mentally.

Foley (1985) has distinguished between the "dancer" and the "danced" in Indonesian possession performances. She writes:

I define the dancer as the performer who maintains his or her self-awareness while impersonating another, and the danced as those who strive for an altered, trance state and allow themselves to become mediums for another presence – a phenomenon known as possession trance (1985: 29).

We might also consider this to be the case with physical mediums. When in the deep trance state the medium is no longer consciously in control of his/her body; it is now under the influence of the incorporating spirit consciousness: the medium is no longer the "dancer," he/she is the "danced." His/her actions are, in fact, the actions of the entity. The spirit and not the medium might, from this perspective, perpetrate any tricks and deception in such a situation. This is an uncomfortable issue to consider, but is worth the effort.

Following "medium X's" demonstration, regular mediums felt that some form of residual energy had settled in the séance room. This energy was manifesting itself in the form of communications from two of "medium X's" spirit team (Tom and Rachel) through the regular medium. This prompted a discussion about "medium X" while in séance conditions communicating with a spirit called Billy. Billy had this to say about "medium X's" mediumship:

> Billy: …you have to remember it's not him [referring to "medium X"]. It's easy to think just because he's got a name and a physical body that he's doing it: he's not doing anything. He's just sitting there going for a sleep… And that's where a lot of people get upset, because they think it's him, and then they get all angry with him because he's not doing what they think he should be doing, and it causes a bit of an upset really. Because all he's doing is sitting there and getting all the blame […] And then his, the rest of them that are coming through, they're giving their demonstrations and just because they don't demonstrate what people want him to demonstrate then they get angry with the poor chap just sitting there…. It's not his fault is it? And he's got the trust and the faith to let the others come through and do what they want. He doesn't know what they're doing, or anything other than what people tell him afterwards (17/03/09).

It is clearly understood, then, even from the spirit-side, that the process is one of allowing oneself to be controlled, that is of giving yourself over to an external influence.

Why should we be disappointed if the spirit hand we feel is actually the hand of the medium? Certainly, when I was touched by a spirit hand during "medium X's" séance I was aware of the allegations of "fraud" that have been laid upon him, and yet the touch did seem to possess a certain energy. Whether this energy was pure spirit energy, spirit energy projected through the medium's body, or my own imagination my experience cannot be successfully reduced to irrelevance – I can still recall that uncanny sense that something out of the ordinary was going on, and I am confident in its reality, at least within myself. If the séance was a performance, it certainly put me in contact with the strangeness of a transcendent reality. It is for this reason that I question the validity of the term "fraud," with all its overtly negative connotations, and wish to highlight, at the very least, the spiritual efficacy of performance as a means of achieving a transcendent experience. In other words, the experience of the séance is more than its means.

In writing this I am not trying to be an apologist for the use of fraud in the history of physical mediumship, but am rather suggesting that our understanding of such matters is far from complete and that dismissing mediums on the grounds that they have utilised trickery is not necessarily the right move to make. Shamans maintain a high status in their societies for aiding communication with the other world, even if this process involves an element of trickery and deception; the communication with the spirit world and its effects are, nevertheless, still valid in performing an important social function.

Conclusion

Liminality, trickery and blending are combined to produce séance phenomena. It is not possible to distinctly separate these aspects. This is an important point that researchers investigating mediumship and its related phenomena need to address and incorporate into their conclusions. When we observe a séance and its phenomena we are being engaged by a performance. In the suspension of our disbelief we open ourselves up to subtler influences, providing an entry point through which contact with the paranormal realm can be achieved. The opening occurs when boundaries are blurred: when we can no longer distinguish the genuine from the fake, the real from the imaginary, the subject from the object and so on. The paranormal realm is paradoxical: it is irreconcilable with rationalistic thought. The presence of trickery does not equate to the non-reality of the paranormal. In writing this I am not attempting to downplay the necessity for objective investigation, utilising specialist equipment, of the claims of physical mediums; indeed, these are fundamental to gaining a complete understanding of the processes involved in the act of mediumship. The issue is rather that the process may be more complex than it might appear at first glance: *some degree of trickery may be required for the production of paranormal phenomena.* It is for this reason that I question our use of the concept of fraud in the investigation of mediumship (although admittedly there are likely to be individuals who claim to be able to produce paranormal phenomena who are intent only on the acquisition of wealth), as it implies that there is no paranormal reality to the phenomena being manifested: it is not fraud, but may in actuality be a technique, perhaps an irrational and paradoxical technique, but a technique nonetheless, which allows contact with a paranormal reality.

TALKING WITH THE SPIRITS:
ANTHROPOLOGY AND INTERPRETING SPIRIT COMMUNICATIONS

Anthropological approaches to the study of spirit mediumship groups, and related practices, have usually tended to focus on social-functional interpretations, arguing that spirit mediumship groups function as a means to enable female practitioners to protest against their traditional roles as "mothers, wives and sexual partners" in oppressive male-oriented societies (Skultans, 1974; Lewis, 1971; Boddy, 1988). Such approaches, however, have failed to address the experiential core of these groups: members believe that they are able to make direct contact with the world of spirits, whether through communicating with spiritual entities channelled via entranced mediums, witnessing ostensibly paranormal phenomena in the context of séances, or through falling into trance themselves and experiencing direct communion with the "numinous" (Otto, 1958). The experiential element cannot be removed from an analysis of mediumship, as it represents the primary motive for séance attendance as the members themselves perceive it. To ignore it would be to detrimentally reduce the complexity of the phenomenon.

In addition to providing an overview of a variety of anthropological approaches to the issue of spirit possession and mediumship, this paper will detail the experiences of an anthropologist exploring this experiential component while conducting fieldwork for his undergraduate dissertation (Hunter, 2009a). The fieldwork itself was conducted at the Bristol Spirit Lodge, a centre established specifically with the aim to promote and develop trance and physical mediumship. The fieldwork methodology was one of immersive participant observation informed by the work of Edith Turner (1993; 1998; 2006), who has advocated the necessity of complete immersion in ritual if its functions and effects are to be adequately understood. In an attempt to understand the role of experience for the members of the group, participant observation was carried out in séances and mediumship development sessions as a means to gain an appreciation of the types of experience encountered by both sitters and mediums. This paper will present the research findings and describe the experiences of the researcher while engaged in the field.

Introduction

As a discipline concerned specifically with the study of humanity, anthropology has long had to tackle the issue of spirits: entities that seem to follow us, in one form or another, wherever we go. Anthropology, then, has a wealth of theoretical standpoints from which we can interpret the phenomena of spirit mediumship, possession and other forms of communication with the spirit world. Paul Stoller (1994) has suggested that commentators on spirit possession have traditionally tended towards five dominant explanatory frameworks: "functionalist, psychoanalytic, physiological, symbolic (interpretive/textual), and theatrical" (1994: 637). These perspectives, amongst others, will be discussed in the following pages.

My own research into mediumship practices in Bristol (Hunter, 2009a) led me to some interesting questions concerning the way in which anthropologists interpret spirits, both methodologically and ontologically. I was puzzled when I found that the spirits communicated with at the Bristol Spirit Lodge were much more than the abstractions I had anticipated them to be: when communicating through the physical body of the medium, the spirits were essentially the same as any other human being. I realised that, to those who participated regularly in séances, the spirits were clearly thought of in terms of actual, objective, personhood (Hunter, 2010). Before I begin a discussion of this, however, it would be best to give a brief exposition of the various alternative perspectives that have grown out of anthropology's dealings with the world of spirits.

Spirit Mediumship and Spirit Possession

This article will explore both spirit possession and spirit mediumship as related phenomena. It should be noted from the outset, however, that there are distinct differences between these two manifestations of spirit incorporation. Primary amongst these differences is the fact that while possession is usually, although not always, a spontaneous and undesired occurrence often requiring exorcism, mediumship is usually a voluntary practice. It will become clear, when reading this article, that although this distinction has been made, the actual ethnographic facts do not fit so neatly into solid categories. The problems associated with labelling these, and related phenomena, have been widely debated in the anthropological literature (Lewis, 1971; Skultans, 1971; Winkelman, 1986).

Spirit Mediumship and Shamanism

Many writers have sought to explore the link between spirit possession, mediumship and shamanism (Emmons, 2000). Shamanism, as it is used in contemporary discourse, is an exceedingly broad term referring to a wide array of beliefs and practices throughout the world. The historian of religion Mircea Eliade (1989) was keen to stress the need for a strict definition of shamanism so as to distinguish it from a variety of other "individuals possessing magico-religious powers," such as sorcerers, magicians, medicine men, witch-doctors, priests and so on. In order to do this, he highlighted several key characteristics of Siberian and Central Asian forms of shamanism (indeed from where the Tungus term *"šaman"* originates), as examples by which we can judge whether a certain magico-religious practitioner is, strictly speaking, a shaman, or not. Eliade identified these characteristics as specific techniques by which a shaman achieves his/her desired result: for instance, special techniques for healing, ecstasy and so on (1989: 1-5). Although there are clearly similarities between the shaman, the possessed, and the medium, in that all three are concerned with spirits of one form or another, Eliade is quick to make this significant distinction:

> It will be easily seen wherein a shaman differs from a "possessed" person, for example; the shaman controls his "spirits," in the sense that he, a human being, is able to communicate with the dead, "demons," and "nature spirits," without thereby becoming their instrument" (Eliade, 1989: 6).

According to Eliade's strict definition, a shaman does not necessarily have to become possessed to initiate communication with the world of spirits (though he/she often does), while mediums and the possessed must give their bodies over to the spirits: essentially surrendering themselves to spirit control. Jokic (2008b) made some very interesting observations regarding the differences between spirit mediumship and shamanism while studying the state of modern Siberian Buryiat neo-shamanism. He noted that the Buryiat shamanic performances involved the possession of the shamans by spirits, and recognised that, after the event, the shamans claimed to have no memory of the séance proceedings – a trait particularly common in spirit possession and mediumship (Leacock & Leacock, 1975: 206). When he asked the shamans about this they, after an initial defence of their shamanism, replied that at one time their shamans had been able to recall their trance journeys but that this skill had by now been forgotten. Jokic suggests that:

> ...the lack of memory (post-trance amnesia) in contemporary shamanic séances is the result of particular historical circumstances, in this instance discontinuity or decrease of practices during the repressive Soviet era. As a result the shamans could not progress to higher degrees that would enable them to have more lucid out-of-body experiences during their possession trances and consequently to have more continuity of memory (2008b: 43).

Such an example goes a long way towards highlighting the similarities and differences between shamanism, spirit possession and mediumship.

Pioneering Explorations

No account of the development of anthropological approaches to the study of spirits would be complete without acknowledging the work of the early pioneers. Sir E.B. Tylor's contribution has been hugely influential in the history of anthropology's dealings with the spirit world. Tylor proposed that "the belief in spiritual beings" was the minimum definition of religion itself. From this perspective, therefore, spirit beliefs must be considered amongst the oldest of humanity. To refer to this "primitive" ancestor of religion, Tylor devised the term "animism," from the Latin *anima* meaning soul. He then attempted to delve deeper into the notion of an animated universe by trying to develop a theory to explain the origin of the belief itself. His theory suggests that belief in the existence of spirits arises from human observations of the world:

When the sleeper awakens from a dream, he believes he has really somehow been away, or that other people have come to him. As it is well known by experience that men's bodies do not go on these excursions, the natural explanation is that every man's living self or soul is his phantom or image, which can go out of his body and see and be seen itself in dreams (1930: 88).

Tylor then suggests that this idea is expanded upon to apply to other living creatures and features of the environment (plants, animals, rocks), and also to explain the facts of death, which in all outward appearances is much like a long sleep during which the *anima* fails to return to its body. The assumption in this argument, however, is that the conclusions that have been widely drawn from such experiences are based on a complete misinterpretation of the data, Tylor is essentially suggesting that so-called "primitive" humans are somehow less developed in their rationality and so lead themselves into misconceptions about the world. The notion that belief in spirits is a result of faulty logic and misperception has been exceedingly influential and widespread within anthropology.

The theorising of Emile Durkheim, the founding father of modern sociology, has also been particularly influential. Indeed, reiterations of his perspective, although appearing superficially different, are still commonly utilised today. Durkheim developed the notion of "social facts," that is ideas that, while not necessarily existing as facts of physical nature, continue to have a tangible influence on human social life. In his view, therefore, spirits are conceived of as social facts performing a specific social function, in particular the maintenance of social cohesion: "Religious force is the feeling [which] the collectivity inspires in its members, but projected outside and objectified in the minds that feel it" (Durkheim, 2008: 174).

Spirits and the Embodiment of History

Paul Stoller has emphasized the importance of the concept of embodiment in understanding spirit possession: "There can be little doubt that the body is the focus of possession phenomena" (1994: 636). Stoller writes that spirit possession is a "commemorative ritual" utilising "gestures, sounds, postures and movements" (1994: 640). Amongst the Songhay, with whom Stoller conducted his fieldwork, possession involves the bodily incorporation of spirits from six different spirit families, each one representing a particular period of Songhay history.

Similarly, Michael Lambek (1998) has noted the use of spirit possession among the Sakalava of Madagascar as a means to retain their history. Spirits representing different epochs of Sakalava history possess the bodies of mediums to give advice on the decision-making activities of the present. There are many benefits to discussing such issues with the ancestors: for instance, it is possible to produce "historically informed" responses to modern situations in a way that is "pragmatic" while acknowledging the "concerns of earlier generations" (1998: 109).

Interestingly a similar theme appeared in my own dealings with the Bristol Spirit Lodge. On many occasions, during conversation with the circle leader, the idea of using spirit mediumship as an educational tool arose. It was suggested that mediumship provided the ideal means to teach history in that it allows direct communication with spirits who had lived on the earth in bygone times. Even in modern European spirit mediumship it seems that there is a yearning to reconnect with the ancestors: to bring the past back to life and use the wisdom of those who came before us to better inform the decisions we make.

Spirit Mediumship as Theatre

In our modern western culture when we see a theatre performance we do not suppose that the actor has *become* the character he/she portrays; rather we understand that they are *pretending* to be someone else (Foley, 1985: 27). In other societies, however, certain performances are understood in an entirely different way. Foley (1985), for example, explains how, during Javanese trance dance performances, the personalities of the dancers are believed to have been entirely "displaced... by some other being" (ibid). Our interpretations of spirit mediumship performances, being based on our own ethnocentric understanding of what a performance entails metaphysically (i.e. a form of deception and nothing more), are therefore greatly distanced from the interpretations of those practicing and observing such performance in their own culture. Beattie (1977) has pointed out certain assumptions often held by anthropologists considering spirit mediumship as theatre, and has suggested that they lead to a false interpretation of the way in which spirit mediumship is understood in non-western societies. He writes:

The first of these [assumptions] was that a medium had to be *either* in a state of possession, a genuine trance, *or* in a condition of normal everyday awareness. This too sharp disjunction allowed for no intermediate conditions; that there might perhaps be *degrees* of dissociation. And the second false assumption... was that if 'possession' was in some sense and in some degree an 'act' consciously performed, it followed that the whole thing was therefore fraudulent, a mere trick and not to be taken seriously. It did not take me very long to realise that this view was naïve and superficial (Beattie, 1977: 2).

Similarly, I have noted elsewhere the difficulties associated with trying to distinguish between what might be termed "reality," performance and fraud in the context of contemporary physical mediumship practice (Hunter, 2009b). Spirit mediumship may very well be a form of performance, but this does not necessarily detract from the possibility that something more profound is actually taking place. Firth (1967) has suggested that such performances can have a significant therapeutic effect, and McClennon (1993) has argued that shamanic performances operate in a similar fashion, utilising subconscious cues and wondrous events to provide "proofs" of the efficacy of their abilities.

Spirit Possession as Social Protest

I.M. Lewis' (1971) theory of peripheral spirit possession has been especially popular in anthropological explorations of possession and mediumship practices around the world (Giles, 1987: 235). The theory suggests that individuals inhabiting "peripheral situations," for example women in particularly male dominated societies, are at risk of possession from spirits that "play no direct part in upholding the moral code of the societies in which they receive so much attention." Possession cults, from this perspective, are seen as nothing more than "thinly disguised protest movements directed against the dominant sex." Lewis argues that when in the possessed state the protester is "totally blameless" for her actions; "responsibility lies not with them, but with the spirits" (Lewis, 1971: 31-32). Analyses of spirit possession from this social protest perspective have been conducted worldwide: in the Zar possession cult of Northern Sudan (Boddy, 1988), amongst the Digo in Southern Kenya (Gomm, 1975), in the case of spontaneous epidemics of spirit possession in Malaysian factories (Ong, 1988), amongst Spiritualists in Wales (Skultans, 1974) and even in Japanese literature (Bargen, 1988); the list could go on.

Mediumship can, undoubtedly, provide women with significant social benefits. Kilson (1971) has written of the transformation in status that spirit mediumship brings about in Ga society. The Ga consider women to be innately inferior to men, which, combined with illiteracy, unmarried life and, potentially, an inability to conceive children leads to a particularly low social standing. Through becoming a spirit medium, a woman is able to achieve a degree of status that she could not have attained under her normal circumstances. Peter Wilson (1967), however, disagrees with Lewis' hypothesis on the grounds that within so-called "male dominated societies," in which males and females operate in different spheres, it is not clear that women even necessarily feel downtrodden and neglected: "Deprivation surely implies withholding that which is due, but in what traditionally male dominated society is it ever regarded as a woman's due that she be granted access to the man's domain?" (1967: 367) Wilson implies, therefore, that to suggest spirit possession acts as a form of female protest in traditionally male dominated societies leads to a contradiction in terms: what are they protesting against if everything they have is all their society allows? Donovan (2000) has argued that Lewis' hypothesis, although being generally applicable to peripheral possession cults, might not be a complete theory, but rather can be supplemented by other perspectives.

Spirits as Agents and Informants

Bubandt (2009) has pointed to the huge benefits concomitant with treating spirits as informants during ethnographic research. While conducting fieldwork on the island of Ternate in Indonesia, Bubandt treated the spirits he encountered via entranced mediums as "methodologically real" through using them as informants to further his understanding of the political state of the society he was investigating. Through treating the spirits as methodologically real, Bubandt was able to get "on with the business of studying the social and political reality of spirits" and recognized "that the invocation of spirits does make a difference in the field (to both the anthropologist and to the people we study) without opening oneself to accusations of political naivety or cultural solipsism" (2009: 298). Like the spirits in

Madagascar (Lambek, 1998) and amongst the Songhay (Stoller, 1994), the spirits that Bubandt encountered were figures from history brought forward to give advice on issues of modern politics, and, as such, they were key political agents – having a direct effect on the political decision making of the present day.

Is Spirit Possession Pathological?

One of the great debates with regard to both spirit possession and spirit mediumship is concerned with whether or not these phenomena are symptoms of a pathological condition (Emmons, 2001: 72). Possession behaviours are often compared to psychological states such as dissociative identity disorder (DID), which, in terms of outward appearances, bears certain behavioural similarities to both possession and mediumship (Crabtree, 1988). Crabtree defines DID as "a condition in which two or more personalities manifest themselves in one human being" (1988: 60). In the early days of inquiry into these practices, anthropologists were particularly keen to draw the conclusion that they were symptoms of mental illness. Psychoanalytic anthropology has also commented on spirit possession, arguing that the phenomenon is a result of traumatic experiences in the personal life-history of the possessed.

Another medical interpretation of spirit possession that was, until relatively recently, popular in the anthropological literature is the "nutrient deficiency hypothesis," which essentially suggests that instances of spirit possession, particularly in women, occur as a result of malnourishment (Kehoe & Giletti, 1981; Bourguignon, Bellisari & McCabe, 1983: 414). Kehoe & Giletti (1981) write:

> There is a strong correlation between populations [subsisting] on diets poor in calcium, magnesium, niacin, tryptophan, thiamine, and vitamin D, and those practicing spirit possession; conversely, populations reported as having probably adequate intakes of these nutrients generally lack culturally sanctioned spirit possession (1981: 550).

Kehoe & Giletti suggest that spirit possession cults represent "institutionalised recognition of class endemic symptoms of nutrient deficiency" (1980: 551). Naturally, however, the idea has been subject to much criticism as it is easy to see instances where the hypothesis fails to stand up to scrutiny. Bourguignon *et al.* (1983), for instance, have provided several counter arguments against the nutrient deficiency hypothesis. Many other anthropologists have directly questioned the idea that spirit possession is a pathological condition (Budden, 2003; Klass, 2003). Budden (2003) argues that the prevalence of dissociative possession and possession-trance states across the world, and the extent to which such states are "embedded within historical and cultural contexts" (2003: 31), indicates that the phenomenon is far from abnormal; indeed in many societies it may be a desirable state, with those able to incorporate spiritual entities at will being granted higher social status.

Spirit possession is, however, undoubtedly associated with illness in many societies, whether in terms of the illness being caused by an intruding spirit or being healed by a medium in trance (Freed & Freed, 1964; Lewis, 1971). Such societies may be thought of as "externalizing" pathology rather than "internalizing" it, as is the norm in the western scientific view (McClennon, 1993). It would seem reasonable to suggest, then, that spirit possession, dependent upon the context within which is occurs, can be seen as both a cause and cure for illness.

Spirits as Ontologically Real

Traditionally if anthropologists came back from their fieldwork experience, having adopted some of the conceptual perspectives of the people they were studying, they were said to have "gone native." To "go native" has, for a long time, been a great taboo in academic anthropology, being considered an indicator that an ethnographer had lost their objectivity. Edith Turner (1993) is an anthropologist who has been brave enough to breach this taboo in writing about the possibility that the spirit beliefs, and related practices, of so many disparate societies around the world might have some basis in reality. Her radical shift in perspective resulted from her own direct personal experience of an Ndembu healing ceremony in Zambia (Turner, 1998). At the culmination of the *ihamba* ritual, a long and emotional ceremony involving many participants, Turner perceived what she describes as a "spirit-form" being extracted from the back of the afflicted patient:

> ...the traditional doctor bent down amid the singing and drumming to extract the harmful spirit... I saw with my own eyes a large gray blob of something like plasma emerge from the sick woman's back.

Then I knew the Africans were right, there is spirit stuff, there is spirit affliction, it isn't a matter of metaphor and symbol, or even psychology (Turner, 1993: 9).

Turner's personal realisation that there is much more to spirits, and indeed the paranormal in general, than the reductive theories of anthropology have hitherto managed to explain has essentially opened up a whole new arena of anthropological inquiry and understanding.

Approaching the Spirits

It seems necessary at this point to give an insight into my own personal approach to the interpretation of spirits in the fieldwork setting. This is done with the aim to give the reader a great contextual understanding for what follows. When I first started my undergraduate research, I was predominantly interested in trying to understand *why* the belief in spirits is so widespread, and, as such, I was not necessarily interested in their ontological status. As far as I was concerned I was investigating spirits as social constructions, and nothing more (a traditional sociological perspective). I was, nevertheless, entirely open to the possibility of there actually being spirits in an ontologically real sense. It was with this open-minded perspective that I first encountered the Bristol Spirit Lodge.

The Bristol Spirit Lodge

Basing my approach on that advocated by Edith Turner, namely an immersive form of participant observation, I endeavoured to explore contemporary mediumship in Bristol at the Bristol Spirit Lodge, a non-denominational home-circle devoted specifically to the development of trance and physical mediumship. Christine Di Nucci founded the Lodge itself in 2005 after a friend introduced her to the world of physical mediumship séances. After attending a number of séances her newfound interest blossomed into a full-blown fascination. In order to further her interest, she had a 12'x10' wooden shed constructed at the bottom of her garden in which to conduct séances on her own terms. The séances were initially carried out in a small circle of close friends with new members attending occasionally. At the time of my fieldwork, early in 2009, the Lodge had a total of nine regular members, of whom two were developing mediums: Jon and Sandy.

The development process revolved primarily around séances conducted on a twice weekly basis: Tuesday evening sittings were set aside for the development of Jon's mediumship, and Thursday mornings were for Sandy's. Both Jon and Sandy were working towards the development of so-called face transfiguration phenomena, whereby energy around the face of the medium is apparently manipulated by discarnate entities in order to physically manifest facial features other than the medium's to the sitters. In addition to this, both mediums also went into trance in order to allow communications to be received from their respective spirit teams. Neither medium was usually able to recall the events of the séance while entranced.

The séances themselves followed a strict and ritualised format. The proceedings began with the locking of the door to the Lodge so as to avoid any unnecessary distractions. Once the sitters were all comfortably seated around the edges of the séance room, and the medium was positioned inside the cabinet (a curtained off corner of the room used by the medium to induce their trance state), an opening prayer was read primarily as a means to set the proposed intention for the session. For example, the opening prayer might have featured any of the following invitations:

> We invite physical healing for those that spirit feels able to heal
> We invite materialisation phenomena
> We invite spirit's support for our developing mediums
> We invite transfiguration phenomena to be displayed

The opening prayer itself reads as follows:

> Heavenly father and Spirit friends
> We ask that you draw close to us tonight
> We are sitting together in love and light
> And are working only for the highest good
> We invite communication with the spirit world
> That is evidential of continuing life and consciousness
> We invite physical phenomena that may be witnessed by us all
> And be spoken about to others so that they too
> May become open towards belief
> We thank Spirit for their love and protection and

> Ask for a circular canopy to be placed over us all
> Thank you. Amen.

Following the opening prayer, a CD was played while the medium relaxed into his/her trance state. The music served to provide a relaxing and positive atmosphere for the séance proceeding. The séances were generally conducted in red light conditions. The mediums at the Bristol Spirit Lodge were keen to demonstrate that there was no trickery involved in what they did. Full blackout conditions were only occasionally used for special events or when spirit communication suggested that it should be so. The length of the séances was usually between one and two hours. During this time the first hour was generally spent in silence with the music playing while the medium's spirit team attempted to manifest physical séance phenomena: small lights, hazy mists, and face transfiguration. After an hour or so of this, members of the spirit team would come forward to communicate with the sitters. Questions were asked to the communicating entities on a wide range of topics, from metaphysical issues to politics. The communications were generally characterised by lucidity and intelligence (see Di Nucci & Hunter, 2009 for transcripts of séances at the Lodge).

When the ostensible spirits indicated that the session was coming to an end, the "closing music" was played. This music was always the same, providing a reassuring and grounding focus of attention for both the medium and the sitters. When the medium "returned" to normal waking consciousness the closing prayer was read:

> We thank Spirit for their love and protection
> We thank Spirit for all that they have achieved
> We ask for Spirit to close us down now, and to
> Use any excess energy within this room for the purpose of healing
> May love and protection remain with us all
> Until we meet again
> Thank you. Amen.

All séances were recorded using a digital voice recorder, the aim being to upload the recordings to Lodge's website in order to disseminate the spirit wisdom that had been received. When asked whether the séance proceedings were religious in nature, all members responded in the negative. Spirit communications were understood to be a natural fact, regardless of any religious interpretation: séances were treated as experiments. Nevertheless, there was evidently a sense of differentiation between the sacred space of the Lodge and the profane world outside. The Lodge space was treated with great respect; a respect that in many ways resembled religious awe. Even if the Lodge's practices were not considered religious, they certainly partook of at least a semi-religious character (reverential awe, prayers and so on).

Experiencing the Séance

In an attempt to gain a deeper understanding of the experiential component of séance practice at the Bristol Spirit Lodge, I participated fully in séances and mediumship development circles. This mode of inquiry was greatly influenced by the work of the anthropologist Edith Turner, who has written extensively on the necessity for total immersion in the study of spirit beliefs and rituals (Turner, 1993; 1998; 2007). It was important to my investigation that I expose myself to elements of experience that would simply go unnoticed from a purely observational perspective. I wanted to "feel" what it was like to sit in séance.

I participated in numerous séances as a sitter at the Bristol Spirit Lodge, and in this capacity experienced some very interesting visual phenomena: apparent transfiguration of the medium's face and torso, small shining lights, hazes, mists and so on. I found it very difficult to classify these experiences as either objective or subjective. For the most part they seemed so subtle as to be a product of my own mind, and yet, interestingly, other sitters often validated the experiences. One example I recall vividly was when I noticed that the medium's head was now bald and rather stern looking. When discussing the events of the séance afterwards, several of the other sitters independently commented, as I had not mentioned what I had seen, that they had witnessed the transfiguration of the medium's head into that of a bald Chinese man. Moments like this really make you wonder. How can more than one individual witness an apparently subjective phenomenon?

In addition to sitting as a witness, I also engaged in mediumship development and, to my great surprise, underwent some very peculiar sensations. I will now describe in detail the most peculiar, and profoundly affecting, experience I had while developing my own trance mediumship. Because Jon was unable to attend a séance on the evening of 10/3/09, it was decided that the time would best be spent with the intention of development: this involved sitting in red light conditions and relaxing into a guided meditating. Michelle, a regular sitter who had had previous mediumistic experience, was placed in the cabinet, but the intention of opening prayer was for spirit intelligence to make itself known through *any* of the vessels present in the room.

After the prayer was read, the music was put on and we were told to relax "and just see what happens." As I sat there I decided I would meditate and enjoy the relaxing atmosphere. I closed my eyes and focussed my attention onto my breathing. Eventually I felt my hands tingling as they rested on the arms of the chair and my heart rate began to quicken. I started to feel as though I was going to lose control, as though I was verging on fainting. I wasn't afraid of losing consciousness – it didn't feel as though that would occur – but I did feel that I was becoming distanced from my physical body, as though I was somehow sitting just back from my body. It was a very peculiar sensation. At the point when I felt most distanced from my body I heard Christine say that she sensed a presence standing by me. This made me panic, because I, too, was feeling a distinct presence at the time, and her confirmation was shocking. In response to all of this I panicked and opened my eyes. My heart was still racing, and I felt light headed. I had to regain control of myself; to calm down and reassure myself that everything was ok.

When I had regained composure, I decided to begin my meditation again. This time the physical sensations I felt in the first meditation came on again much faster; my heart rate increased and the tingling in my hands returned. I began to feel myself distancing from my body again, and, at the point of greatest distance, I felt as though there was a space in my body which could easily be filled; it was as though I had made room in my physical body by moving myself out of it. I then felt an energy move into my left hand, and my index finger began to rise of its own accord. It felt as though it were being lifted by a cushion of air. My second finger began to move upwards also, and soon my hand was quivering on the arm of the chair. I was aware of the movement, but also of the fact that I was not consciously willing it to happen. I was observing the movement, but not with my eyes. This motion began to become more vigorous and soon my whole arm was vibrating and shaking from side to side. All the while my head felt heavy and was drooped down onto my chest. It wasn't long before my hand began to lower itself; it felt as though the energy was becoming less intense, and, as it did so, my hand's movement also became less intense. Soon it was only my two forefingers that remained up, and then these too had returned to normal. When it had all subsided I had "returned" and was fully in control of my body. I was quite shocked by this experience, and it took quite a while before I was fully calm afterwards.

The second occasion on which this occurred was 19/3/09. Similarly, this was a development sitting due to Jon's absence. I was sitting in the cabinet this time with the intention of conducting a guided meditation. As the meditation progressed it came to a point where the guiding was no longer having any effect. Christine noticed this and decided that she would stop guiding me. Soon after Christine had stopped I once again felt the vibration in my left hand, particularly concentrated on my two forefingers. The sensation was much less intense than on the first occasion but was nevertheless similar in many ways.

Conclusions

It is clear that the phenomena of spirit possession and mediumship are complex and multi-faceted, a fact that is testified by the great many theoretical and methodological interpretations devised for them (Dawson, 2010: 1-22), and, ~~as such~~, require multiple perspectives if they are to be understood. It seems evident that all of the interpretations described in this paper succeed in shedding light on these mysterious phenomena, though no single theory successfully accounts for all of their aspects, particularly, in my opinion, the parapsychological dimension. And yet, if we begin to bring these perspectives together, a much more coherent picture starts to take shape (Giesler, 1984): If we consider dancing, deception and trickery as methods by which mediums can induce altered states of consciousness, both in themselves and in observers, we begin to see the significant role of performance as a tool for spirit contact. We also begin to understand the role of participation in ritual performance, as Edith Turner discovered, in the manifestation of the supernatural world. Through this we start to fathom the significance of the social component in developing social realities, which, in themselves, may facilitate the mediation and experience of genuine spiritual entities and parapsychological phenomena. The experiential ethnographic method essentially bridges the gap between the theoretical interpretations, social and parapsychological components of spirit mediumship – it gives access to the elements that the more traditional approaches miss out on.

CAN SCIENCE SEE SPIRITS?
THE NEUROPHYSIOLOGY OF SPIRIT MEDIUMSHIP

Spirit mediumship is a complex, near universal phenomenon, which, despite over 130 years of investigation from psychical research and the social sciences more generally, continues to evade scholarly attempts to pin it down and neatly explain it. Countless attempts have been made, however, from the debunkers who suggest that all mediumship is a mixture of fraud and delusion, to the social anthropologists who argue that spirit mediumship is a purely social phenomenon, performing specific social functions, and certain parapsychologists who suggest that spirit mediumship offers proof of survival after death. And yet, none of the theories that have been put forward quite seem able to offer a fully satisfying explanation for what is going on.

In this short article I would like to highlight some of the reasons why spirit mediumship is such a difficult phenomenon to get a grip on through outlining some of the research that has been conducted, and pointing out gaps in our understanding of the underlying processes. This article will present an overview of the, really rather sparse, neuroimaging data on spirit mediumship, and will briefly discuss what it does and doesn't tell us about the phenomenon.

Background

It was long suspected that mediums might exhibit unusual neurological activity, and yet, despite countless studies of the neurophysiological correlates of other forms of altered consciousness, such as meditation, very few neurophysiological studies of spirit mediumship have actually been conducted. Altered States researchers Edward F. Kelly and Rafael

Locke have suggested that, despite the potentially fruitful use of EEG and other physiological monitoring devices for classifying and differentiating specific altered states of consciousness and their physiological correlates, there are unfortunate technical and social difficulties associated with attempting such studies in the field. Technological difficulties include the problems associated with trying to monitor and record brain activity naturalistically in the field setting, using cumbersome equipment, while social difficulties include getting spirit mediums, and other practitioners, to agree to participate in such studies. Fortunately, since Kelly & Locke first published their research prospectus in 1981, technological advances have made it possible to measure EEG in the field (see Oohashi *et al.* below), but other forms of neuroimaging still rely on heavy-duty equipment, which is impractical for field studies. Despite these difficulties, however, a small number of studies have been successfully carried out specifically looking at the neurophysiological correlates of mediumistic states of consciousness.

Neurophysiological Speculations

Even before the advent of neuroimaging studies of mediums, American psychologist Julian Jaynes, drawing on his theory of the bicameral mind, predicted the following neurophysiological correlates of spirit possession:

> We must naturally hypothesize that in possession there is some kind of disturbance of normal hemispheric dominance relations, in which the right hemisphere is somewhat more active than in the normal state. In other words, if we could have placed electrodes on the scalp of the Delphic oracle in her frenzy, would we have found a relatively faster EEG (and therefore greater activity) over her right hemisphere, correlating with her possession? And in particular over her right temporal lobe? (Jaynes, 1976: 342-343).

Based on neurophysiological studies of other altered states of consciousness, such as on the many varieties of meditative states, anthropologist Michael Winkelman has argued that a wide variety of trance induction techniques lead to similar neurophysiological states, specifically involving a 'parasympathetic dominance in which the frontal cortex is dominated by slow wave patterns.'

Owing to apparent similarities between trance mediumship and dissociative identity disorder (DID), psychical researchers Bryan Williams and William Roll (2007) speculated that mediumship and DID would share similar underlying neurophysiological correlates, specifically postulating the involvement of the temporal lobe. Based upon their overviews of the neurophysiological research on dissociative identity disorder, and the few EEG studies of mediumship, they offer the prediction that future fMRI studies of mediumship will reveal 'activation of the angular gyrus and the areas around the temporal-parietal junction when a medium senses the presence of his or her spirit control.'

Mesulam (1981): Dissociative Identity Disorder and Spirit Possession

Neurologist M. Marsel Mesulam suggested that there might be common underlying neurophysiological activity in both spirit possession and DID, noting that EEG recordings taken from twelve subjects, seven with DID and five with symptoms of spirit possession, revealed unusual spikes of activity in the temporal lobe (except for in two unclear recordings), very similar to the activity associated with epileptic seizures. The implication here is that epileptic seizures in the temporal lobe are responsible for both spirit possession experiences and dissociative identity disorder.

Hughes & Melville (1990): Channelers in Los Angeles

Anthropologist Dureen J. Hughes and Norbert T. Melville conducted an early EEG study on ten trance channelers, five male and five female, in Los Angeles. The channelers were monitored both in and out of trance, and during the trance state their possessing entities were asked a series of questions, so as to create as naturalistic a setting as possible. Based upon their EEG recordings, Hughes and Melville concluded that the channeling state is 'characterized by large, statistically significant increases in amount and percentage of beta, alpha and theta brainwave activity,' which appears to represent a distinctive psychophysiological state that can be differentiated from other altered states of consciousness (e.g. forms of meditation and hypnosis), as well as from pathological states such as temporal lobe epilepsy and schizophrenia.

Oohashi *et al.* (2002): Possession Trance in Bali

One of the first studies to use EEG to investigate traditional spirit possession performances in the field was conducted by a team of Japanese researchers, using a newly developed portable EEG device to measure the electrical activity of the brain in an individual performing a ritual possession drama in Bali. The team found that the possessed individual exhibited enhanced power in the theta and alpha frequency bands, again suggestive that the possession trance represents a psychophysiological state distinct from pathological states such as epilepsy, dissociative identity disorder (DID), and schizophrenia.

Peres *et al.* (2012): Psychography in Brazil

Recent neuroimaging research conducted by Julio Fernando Peres and colleagues, employed single photon emission computed tomography (SPECT) to scan the brain activity of ten automatic writers (five experienced, five less experienced), while in trance. The research findings have been summarised as follows:

> The researchers found that the experienced psychographers showed lower levels of activity in the left hippocampus (limbic system), right superior temporal gyrus, and the frontal lobe regions of the left anterior cingulate and right precentral gyrus during psychography compared to their normal (non-trance) writing. The frontal lobe areas are associated with reasoning, planning, generating language, movement, and problem solving, perhaps reflecting an absence of focus, self-awareness and consciousness during psychography, the researchers hypothesize. Less expert psychographers showed just the opposite – increased levels of CBF in the same frontal areas during psychography compared to normal writing. The difference was significant compared to the experienced mediums (Thomas Jefferson University, 2012).

The implication here is that during the trance states of the experienced automatic writers, activity is reduced in the areas of the brain usually associated with reasoning, planning, language, movement and problem solving, suggesting that the medium's dissociative experience during trance is far from delusional or fraudulent. Furthermore, the researchers conducted an analysis of the complexity of the writing and found that, contrary to what would normally be expected, the complexity increased as the activity in the areas of the brain usually associated with such complex behaviours was reduced. This raises the question of how, if the brain's functioning was reduced, such complex writing was possible. The spiritist interpretation suggests that it was spirits doing the writing while the medium's consciousness was absent, and the data could indeed be read in this way. More cautiously, however, Andrew Newberg has suggested that this research 'reveals some exciting data to improve our understanding of the mind and its relationship with the brain' and calls for further research in this area.

Delorme *et al.* (2013): Mental Mediumship in the USA

Mental mediumship differs from the types of mediumship discussed so far, which might best be labelled as forms of *trance* mediumship. The mediums investigated in this study did not enter into a trance state during which they surrendered the control of their bodies to discarnate entities. Instead these mediums experience communication with discarnate entities while in a waking state of consciousness. Because of this difference the results aren't directly comparable with the results of the previous studies; they are, however, still interesting. EEG recordings with mental mediums revealed a predominance of activity in the gamma frequency band, which is also characteristic of certain meditative states. Perhaps the most interesting finding from this research project was the correlation between the accuracy of the mediumship reading and specific alterations in electrocortical activity. fMRI scans revealed increased activity in the frontal areas of the brain, similar to fMRI readings for other spiritual states. Decreased frontal midline theta rhythms were also noted, and it was suggested that this might be 'consistent with a medium accessing a receptive mental state.' Again, the authors conclude that 'the experience of communicating with the deceased may be a distinct mental state that is not consistent with brain activity during ordinary thinking or imagination.'

But we still don't know what is actually going on...

At the very least, the neuroimaging work that has been conducted on mediumship appears to support the idea that there is more to mediumship than simply fraud and delusion – something, whatever that something might be, is definitely going on here. But the data are by no means *conclusive* of anything more than that. The research does seem to indicate a predominance of alpha, beta and theta waves in trance channeling and possession states, and gamma frequencies in mental mediumship. It is unclear, however, how these EEG readings relate to the findings of other studies that suggest a decrease in brain function during mediumistic trances. There is also a considerable discrepancy between studies that suggest similarities with pathological conditions such as DID and temporal lobe epilepsy, and those that seem to indicate that mediumship is a distinctive psychophysiological state.

The truth of the matter is that there are significant difficulties associated with the interpretation of any neuroimaging data. Such studies are, for example, subject to the classic problem of distinguishing between cause and correlation – are these data suggesting that the mediumship experience is caused by alterations in brain physiology, or do they show us what happens to the brain when mediumship takes place? Do they explain mediumship, or do they show us the processes of mediumship? These are important questions that only further research can resolve. Psychologist Joan Hageman and colleagues list other problems inherent in the interpretation of neuroimaging data. They warn against the following tendencies in neurophysiological research:

1. Naively [accepting] materialist monism (mind as brain product) as an obvious fact, and [rejecting] a fair consideration of other hypotheses for the mind-brain relationship.
2. [Basing] work on secondhand descriptions of original findings or writings.
3. [Focusing] only on one side of psychophysiological parallelism, i.e. changes in brain function modify mental states.
4. [Assuming] that experiences based on superficial similarities are identical.
5. [Identifying] a brain region involved with some spiritual experience and [concluding] that this region is the ultimate cause of that experience.
6. [Ignoring] the complexity of the body and [refuse] to take a holistic perspective.
7. [Focusing] studies on beginners or participants who have not had a full-blown spiritual experience (Hageman *et al.*, 2010: 87-89).

Only further careful research, taking into account the difficulties inherent in the interpretation of neurophysiological studies, will help to resolve questions about what is happening in the brain during mediumistic trance states. For the time being, however, the research indicates that something unusual is going on, whatever that something might ultimately turn out to be, which demands more attention.

EXPRESSIONS OF SPIRITHOOD:
PERFORMANCE AND THE MANIFESTATION OF SPIRITS

Spirit possession is an extremely complex phenomenon, with social, cultural, psychological and, potentially, parapsychological components, all of which interact and coalesce to produce something that is very difficult to compact into a single reductive scheme (Gauld 1983; Levy *et al.* 1996:18; van de Port 2011: 28). In this article, however, I am going to do just that by focusing only on the behavioural aspects of this unusual phenomenon, and, in particular, the central role that performance plays in the mediumship process. This is not to suggest that spirit possession can easily be reduced, but, rather, is an introduction to one facet of an exceedingly complex phenomenon. This approach could be called an 'ethology' of spirit possession because it will be concerned only with observable behaviours, bracketing out, for the time being, internal processes and experiences. Such an approach is inspired by the work of an anthropologist by the name of Ray Birdwhistell, who developed the notion of 'kinemes,' which he defined as culturally specific non-verbal bodily behaviours used by human beings to express themselves (Argyle 1987).

To begin, then, we'll start from first principles. Human beings are embodied entities. We exist in three-dimensional physical space, and have bodies which act as our interface with the world around us. We are also social creatures in that we gather together in groups and communicate with one another, and this communication usually takes place via physical means, generally mediated through the body (Goffman 1990). We have, therefore, developed specific ways of using the body to communicate our internal psychological states (emotions/moods), and distinct personalities, both verbally and non-verbally. We have an extremely large lexicon of facial features, bodily postures and gestures, as well as different tonalities of voice, that enable us to express ourselves as individual personalities with subjective psychological states (Argyle 1987). From the very outset, then, our bodies are the mediums through which our individual consciousness and personality are expressed.

A standard definition of the notion of 'personality,' taken from the *Oxford Dictionary of Psychology*, suggests that personality is 'the *sum total* of the *behavioural and mental* characteristics that are distinctive of an individual' (Colman 2009). We recognise the personality of an individual by drawing general conclusions from observations of their behaviour and characteristics. By comparing the behaviour of an individual against the behaviour which we have come to expect from that individual, we are able to determine that they are the same person. In a sense, then, personality and bodily behaviours are intimately connected, as we cannot know an individual's personality without the mediation of the physical body.

The body can also be used in different ways to express not only the individual's personality but also the personalities of other people. Actors, for example, manipulate their bodies in such a way as to give the impression that they are a different person. Character actors are good examples of people capable of using their bodies in many ways to express different personalities. In order to successfully express a different personality, and to distinguish it from the actor's own personality, it is necessary to display physical characteristics that differentiate the personality they are attempting to convey from their own. Such physical alterations are usually supplemented by manipulation of vocal tonality. The body and the voice, as we have already seen, are the main means by which personality is expressed, and so are also the means by which alterations, or changes, of personality are expressed. Bodily transformations can also be augmented with make-up and 'props,' such as masks and other ritual objects that serve to differentiate the portrayed from the portrayer. These are the basic methods employed in the expression of alternate personalities.

We are now ready to move on to considering the main subject of this article, the manifestation of spirits through practices commonly referred to as 'spirit possession' and/or 'trance mediumship.' Broadly speaking, spirit possession can be split into two distinct categories, the first being spontaneous, or involuntary possession, whereby an intruding spirit takes control of an individual's body without that person's consent, and the second being voluntary possession, often referred to as trance mediumship, whereby the possessed deliberately invokes a state of possession and wilfully surrenders control of his/her body to an external intelligence.

Trance mediumship can be defined simply as a practice employing altered states of consciousness (trance) and performance for the expression of ostensible spiritual entities. The trance medium will generally enter into an altered state of consciousness, often referred to as a dissociative state, during which their personality is allegedly replaced by another, often claiming to be the spirit of a deceased individual. While the medium is entranced their physical behaviours and vocalisations are thought to be those of the spirit occupying their body, so that when the medium's original personality returns they have no, or limited, recollection of what took place in the preceding interval. For the time-being we will bracket out questions relating to the ontological status of the spirits (though I do consider these issues to be of great importance for anthropologists), and focus specifically on the way in which spirits, whether 'real' or otherwise, are discerned and recognised through the body in different cultural contexts in which spirit mediumship is practised.

One of the first issues that needs to be addressed is how, from just observing physical behaviours, it is possible to infer that an individual is experiencing an altered state of consciousness. Altered states of consciousness are near universally associated with spirit possession, and, more specifically, dissociative altered states designated by the term 'trance.' Recognising the trance state, as distinct from the normal everyday waking state of the individual, is the first step in determining whether or not they are possessed by a spiritual being. The behaviours associated with altered states of consciousness would appear to be fairly standard across cultures and through time. Take, for example, the behaviours of individuals possessed by spirits in Voodoo and Candomble, the glossolalia of Pentecostal Christian faith healers, the trance performances of the Manchu shaman from China, the serene face of Maharishi Mahesh Yogi (the populariser of transcendental meditation), a Yanomami *shapori* from Venezuela experiencing the spirit-world through the hallucinogenic snuff *Yopo*, the Sufi dervish dancer, Saint Theresa D'Avila's ecstatic rapture and Daryl Anka channeling his spirit guide Bashar. Although all of these examples come from different cultural traditions, the physical behaviours associated with their altered states are very similar, even if the underlying neurophysiological and experiential states are ultimately different. The closed eyes seem to be a near universal bodily symbol for altered states of consciousness, perhaps because of its association with sleep and the dream state, maybe indicating that the individual is no longer concerned with the physical world, but is now looking beyond it.

Another possible explanation for this cross-cultural commonality is the use of sensory deprivation in the induction of altered states of consciousness: for example as employed in the Hmong shamanic tradition and the parapsychological Ganzfeld experiment. The closing of the eyes can be thought of as *both* a behaviour associated with altered states of consciousness, and a technique for inducing them. Recognising altered states of consciousness, however, is not the same as recognising the presence of ostensible spirit entities; it is only the first step.

Once the trance state has been recognised, the next step is to watch for signs that a spirit, deity, or other supernatural being, is using, or attempting to use, the body of the medium to communicate, and this is where possession differs from other altered states of consciousness. In my own research with trance mediums in Bristol, the earliest signs of a spirit's attempts at communicating through an entranced medium may include twitching of the hands and legs, or gurgling sounds and coughing. Indeed, on one occasion as I sat for mediumship development myself, I experienced an unusual altered state of consciousness in which I felt myself becoming distanced from my body (dissociation). At the point of greatest distance, I felt my left hand moving of its own accord, and, though I was aware of the movement, I was completely unable to stop it. The movement of my hand was interpreted by the circle leader as indicative of the fact that a spirit was attempting to communicate through my body (Hunter 2009; 2010), and it certainly felt as if this was the case. Subsequent research has revealed that this is not an uncommon occurrence amongst those in the early stages of trance mediumship development:

> Although in the early moments of the trance there may be some uncontrolled movements, the medium must quickly gain control if his or her activity is to be interpreted as representing possession by a supernatural being. It is certainly not enough to fall on the floor and thrash around, or stagger about, or make incoherent sounds, or give other evidence of having some kind of unusual psychological experience. The meaning of this kind of behaviour is ambiguous in Batuque beliefs [...] In order to prove that an encantado is really present, the medium must dance, sing the proper songs, and interact with the other participants in the ceremony in an acceptable manner. The behaviour that is most admired in the accomplished medium is very often the behaviour that appears the least frenzied and the most normal to the outside observer (Leacock & Leacock 1975:171-172).

Similarly, in Balinese sanghyang performances the trance performer is expected to perform specific dances while being 'ridden' by the spirits. The dancers are first ritually 'smoked.' The smoke is not psychoactive but induces the trance state in which the spirits must perform their dance, while the 'performer' is dissociated from his/her actions (Schechner 1988:175-176). The masquerades of the Nigerian Kalabari people also provide a good example. Young men must practice the Okolokurukuru performance, with its elaborate costumes, so that when the time comes for them to be possessed they are able to dance the correct dances.

In my own fieldwork with trance mediums in Bristol (Hunter, 2009; 2010; 2011; 2012), I have also noticed the use of specific bodily symbols to indicate the presence of spiritual entities, which the circle-leader and sitters must learn to recognise. One particular medium, for example, incorporated a group entity, consisting of several members of her spirit team. As we have seen, her closed eyes indicated an altered state of consciousness, while her unusual hand gestures suggested the presence of an external entity, as such gestures are not common to the medium in her normal waking consciousness.

Similarly, bodily postures can be used to signify the presence of other personalities. In the case of another of this medium's spirit team, for instance, the medium's shoulders appeared particularly broad, and were indicative of the presence of a character by the name of Graham, a burly nineteenth century undertaker.

All of this brings up the issue of 'unconscious performance,' or, potentially, 'extra-conscious performance,' which might be defined as performance directed by a conscious agent other than that of the 'performer.' As an example from my own field work, a medium by the name of Sandy describes her own experience of unconsciously assuming the mannerisms of her spirit controls:

> Sometimes, in the earliest days, they used to come through, and they'd come through presenting differently, and some of my movements changed. And depending on which spirit comes through depends on what I do with my hands, or, the one where I was dragging my leg, I just couldn't not drag my leg as I walked in (Interview with Sandy 23/03/2011).

The voice, as well as the body, is also used to differentiate between the personality of the medium and the spirit or deity communicating through them. Amongst Pentecostal Christian groups, for example, sporadic utterances, often referred to as 'speaking in tongues' or 'glossolalia,' are taken as indicative of the presence of the Holy Ghost. Although such groups would not consider glossolalia to be a form of spirit possession, the practice does bear striking resemblances to spirit possession performances in that the act of speaking in tongues implies the immanent presence of the Holy Ghost.

Another good example of the use of the voice in expressing the distinction between the personality of the medium and that of the spirit communicator comes from the now infamous 1977 Enfield Poltergeist case. Here, Janet Hodgson, an 11-year-old girl, was occasionally possessed by a spirit who referred to himself as 'Bill' and who was assumed to be the agent behind the poltergeist activity that was plaguing the Hodgson family. The effect can be quite uncanny and often startling, with Bill's voice bearing no resemblance to Janet's and thus clearly indicating a separate, and distinct, personality. This particular case, however, does not fit quite so neatly into the category of dissociative performance, as Janet did not appear to be in an altered state of consciousness while Bill spoke through her.

Anthropologist Nurit Bird-David describes a similar process of gestural expression of spirits in her analysis of the *devaru* performances of the South Indian Nayaka. She writes:

> These [principal] aspects of their behaviour are, in Bateson's term (1979), meta-communication, namely, communicating that devaru are communicating, because the *devaru* are present as they move, talk, make gestures, etc. They are present as they communicate and socially interact with Nayaka (Bird-David, 1999:76).

Exaggerated behaviours and vocalisations, then, can be thought of as a form of 'meta-communication,' signifying the presence of distinct personalities and serving as a means to allow them to be communicated with as individuals.

So, to conclude this short essay, what does it mean to say that spirit mediumship is a performance? Firstly, I think it is important to make the point that just because something is a performance does not necessarily mean that it is fraudulent (Firth, 1967; Beattie, 1977: 2; Schechner, 1988:175). I use the term 'performance' in a fairly loose sense to refer to the use of the body for the public expression of internal states. To say that spirit mediumship is a performance does not, therefore, deny the importance of the cognitive (Cohen 2008) and neurophysiological processes that underlie the trance state (Oohashi, 2002; Krippner & Friedman, 2010), nor does it deny the importance of the medium's subjective experiences while in the trance state. Indeed, the phenomenon is so complex that reduction to any single aspect will significantly detract from our understanding of it (Boddy, 1988:4; Halloy, 2012). Furthermore, I do not think that describing mediumship as a performance detracts from the possibility that there might be some genuine parapsychological processes and/or entities involved in the mediumship process. Performance is an essential part of the process of mediumship, and indeed a central part of living as an embodied being. Without performance there would be no way for human beings to communicate with one another, let alone for ostensible discarnate spirit entities to communicate. Performance is the means by which the medium is transformed into the spirit so that the spirit may communicate. The medium becomes the manifestation of the spirit.

How, then, can we fruitfully apply this insight in mediumship research? This emphasis on somatic performance allows us to approach the issue of the mind-body relationship, and to explore the fundamental interconnectedness of consciousness and the body. We also come to appreciate the significant role of culture in shaping the form of interactions between consciousness and the body, and begin to understand in more detail the ways in which ostensibly independent spiritual entities could potentially interface, and so manifest, in the physical world. It would appear, based upon the ethnographic literature, that dissociative states of consciousness and bodily performance are essential components in this process.

ECTOPLASM, SOMATISATION AND STIGMATA:
SPECULATIONS ON PHYSICAL MEDIUMSHIP, STIGMATA AND THE DEVELOPMENT OF EXTRAORDINARY MIND-BODY STATES

In the spirit of open-minded Fortean speculation, this article will explore the *possibility* that the unusual phenomena associated with physical mediumship and stigmata might be understood as extraordinary mind-body states.

Physical mediums have traditionally sought to produce directly observable manifestations that demonstrate the reality of the spiritual realm, usually in the context of the séance room. Physical mediumship thus ostensibly renders the invisible world tangible to onlookers, referred to in Spiritualist circles as 'sitters.'

At the Bristol Spirit Lodge (a small non-denominational home-circle where I conducted my research fieldwork), mediums were working towards the production of ectoplasm (a classic of nineteenth and early twentieth century Spiritualist séances), the transfiguration of facial features, the movement of physical objects, and unusual bodily phenomena, such as levitation, for example, or the disappearance of limbs. Although mediums at the Lodge were not necessarily able to produce such phenomena, the mediumistic development sessions were nevertheless geared towards their production, and it was hoped that through regular, patient, practice and training they *would* be able to manifest them during séances.

This article suggests the possibility that physical mediumship is a psychosomatic phenomenon, and that séances may function as a form of culturally specific biofeedback training. To reach this point we will explore some speculative links between physical mediumship and other psychosomatic phenomena, including conversion and somatoform disorders (which appear to manifest physiological symptoms with no organic cause), psychoneuroimmunology (which emphasises the role of psychological states in physiological healing), the 'placebo effect,' and the religious phenomenon known as 'stigmata,' which shares some interesting similarities with physical mediumship.

Before we proceed, I feel it is important to point out that the approach taken in this article should not be considered an attempt at explaining away paranormal phenomena; rather it ought to be seen as an exploration of some of the possible psychophysiological mechanisms underlying them.

Weird Symptoms: Hysteria and Somatoform Disorders

We will begin with a brief discussion of hysteria. In the nineteenth century, pioneering neurologists like Jean-Martin Charcot (1825-1893) at the infamous Salpêtrière hospital in Paris, carefully documented the symptoms of hysterics, often through the pioneering use of medical drawing and photography. The symptoms of hysteria manifested in a wide variety of ways, including 'amnesia, blindness, anaesthesia, hallucinations, excited and inappropriate behaviour, together with fits and paralyses' (Littlewood, 1995:154), amongst others.

Dermatography was just one of many strange hysterical phenomena documented at the Salpêtrière. In dermatographic experiments, words would be lightly drawn onto the bodies of hysterical patients using only the tip of the finger, or some other blunt object, so as not to leave any trace of what was written. Later, these words would emerge from the skin in relief. Hysteria was literally written onto the bodies of patients at the Salpêtrière hospital.

Such phenomena seemed to suggest that hysteria's underlying causes were psychological, rather than physiological. Later, one of Charcot's students, Sigmund Freud, would come to develop his own approach to hysteria with his colleague Josef Breuer. Freud and Breuer adopted the term 'conversion' to refer to the manifestation of somatic symptoms with psychological origins. As the term 'conversion' suggests, Freud essentially posited that psychological distress was actually converted into physical symptoms as a means of releasing and expressing repressed emotions and unconscious trauma.

More recently, conversion disorders, and other somatic symptoms of what was once known as hysteria, as well as other physical symptoms caused by stress, anxiety, and so on, were categorised under the heading of 'somatoform disorders,' primarily as a means to escape from the limitations and associations of Freudian theory and terminology.

Even more recently, somatoform disorders have been re-labelled as 'somatic symptom disorders,' defined in the DSM-V as 'characterized by somatic symptoms that are either very distressing or result in significant disruption of functioning, as well as excessive and disproportionate thoughts, feelings and behaviors regarding those symptoms.'

As often happens with unusual and anomalous phenomena, the nomenclature used to describe them is constantly shifting and evolving, though it is clear that the labels all point towards the same thing. Whether labelled hysteria, conversion, somatoform or somatic symptom disorder, such conditions appear to suggest that physical disorders can have psychological causes. The possible influence of thoughts, ideas, and consciousness more generally, in shaping somatic symptoms is particularly difficult to reconcile with the standard materialistic philosophy of Western science, which suggests that consciousness is an epiphenomenon, or by-product of physiological processes, and thus cannot possess causative powers. These cases seem to suggest otherwise.

Psychogenic Illnesses and Cultural Influence

Medical historian Edward Shorter sums up this idea with the term 'psychogenic illness,' which he defines as follows:

> Psychogenic illness is *any illness in which physical symptoms [are] produced by the action of the unconscious mind* [...] This process of somatization comes in two forms. In one no physical lesion of any kind exists and the symptoms are literally psychogenic: that is to say they arise in the mind. In the second an organic lesion does exist, but the patient's response to it – his or her illness behavior – is exaggerated or inappropriate. *Culture intervenes in both forms, legislating what is legitimate, and mandating what constitutes an appropriate response to disease* (Shorter, 1992: X)

In his book *Crazy Like Us: The Globalization of the Western Mind* (2011), journalist Ethan Watters further explains the concept of symptom pools:

People at a given moment in history in need of expressing their psychological suffering have a limited number of symptoms to choose from [...]. When someone unconsciously latches on to a behaviour in the symptom pool, he or she is doing so for a specific reason: the person is taking troubling emotions and internal conflicts that are often indistinct or frustratingly beyond expression and distilling them into a symptom or behaviour that is a culturally recognised signal of suffering (Watters, 2011: 34).

There are, as a consequence, many so-called 'culture-bound disorders' (Kiev, 1972: 78-108), with symptoms that occur only within particular cultural contexts. A classic example of such a culture-bound disorder is an unusual Malaysian ailment known as koro, which refers to a particular disorder, recognised in the DSM-IV as a culture-bound illness, whereby a man becomes convinced that his genitals are shrinking, or retracting into his body. Koro is a specific culturally recognised symptom of underlying mental distress. The mind can, therefore, seemingly produce often-extreme physiological changes in the body, and the types of change that are produced are influenced by cultural expectations. We will now move on to look at some other interesting mind-body phenomena before exploring the more extreme phenomena of stigmata and physical mediumship.

Psychoneuroimmunology and Biofeedback Training

Freud and Breuer recognised the important role played by altered states of consciousness in the manifestation of hysterical symptoms. Indeed, researchers such as Freud's mentor Jean-Martin Charcot, had used hypnotic states of consciousness to induce hysterical symptoms in his patients. But hypnotic and other altered states of consciousness can also cure certain types of somatic disorder. Most famously, hypnosis has been used as a cure for warts, and for repairing scar tissue – all of which is reminiscent of the efficacy of shamanic, and other forms of psychic, healing.

Michael Winkelman (2000: 207-209) has suggested the possibility that shamanic healing makes use of what Western science has come to call *psychoneuroimmunology*, which, broadly defined, refers to the study of the ways in which psychological states (such as stress), influence and affect the physical body through the mediation of the nervous and immune systems. For example, clinical research suggests that stress plays a significant role in the manifestation of pathological symptoms, decreasing the activity of white blood cells, and reducing the healing time of wounds (Littrell, 2008). Winkelman writes:

> Psychoneuroimmunology requires a simultaneous consideration of the biophysiological and the psychosocial bases of human experience and functioning, the context of the relationship between the cellular level of organismic functions and the psychosocial environment of the organism (2000: 209).

Psychoneuroimmunology suggests, therefore, a complex interrelationship between mental, or psychological, states, bodily health and social and cultural influences. The mind and body are intimately wedded together, with causative efficacy flowing from mind-to-body and body-to-mind. This concept becomes even more intriguing when we learn that we can exert our own conscious control over physiological processes through training.

Biofeedback training is a process of developing mental control over physiological functions, including 'muscle activity, skin temperature, electrodermal activity (sweat gland activity), respiration, heart rate, heart rate variability, blood pressure, brain electrical activity, and blood flow' (Moss & Andrasik, 2008:iii). Biofeedback techniques employ physiological monitoring equipment, such as electroencephalograph (EEG), electromyograph (EMG), electrodermograph (EDG) and others, to feed back data on physiological processes to the individual, who is then able voluntarily to alter their physiological processes by focussing on affecting the patterns of data being fed back to them. Biofeedback training is used as a highly effective treatment for a range of physiological and neurological disorders. Biofeedback training presents a strong case for the efficacy of mind over matter, suggesting that mind plays an active, rather than passive, role in the body.

Mediumship Development

Physical mediumship development sittings may, then, function as a form of physiological monitoring for the medium in trance, with data about external manifestations being fed back to the medium via the circle leader and sitters, and thus reinforcing the manifestation of particular phenomena. Take, for example, this section of dialogue from a session with Emily, a developing physical medium. The medium is sitting entranced in the cabinet, and the spirits are attempting to produce ectoplasm from the medium's mouth:

> **Emily:** [gurgling]
> **Christine:** You're doing well.
> **Emily:** [gurgling]
> **Christine:** I can see it within the mouth.
> **Nicky:** Yeah, I see it.
> **Gareth:** Yeah.
> **Emily:** [gurgling]
> **Christine:** I can see it all around the mouth [...] I can see it from the chin, but I'm closer.
> **Gareth:** I can see something inside the mouth.
> **Paul:** I'm not sure, it's her tongue isn't it?
> **Christine:** I can see it fill the mouth a little bit. In which case it's more than a tongue.
> **Gareth:** Yeah, it's definitely more than a tongue. I can see it.
> **Christine:** Yep.
> **Gareth:** It's really moving.
> (DEVELOPMENT SESSION, JANUARY 10, 2014).

Stigmata

So now we'll move on to look at the similarities between some of the phenomena associated with stigmata and physical mediumship. Drawing on some of the ideas discussed in the previous paragraphs, these kinds of phenomena might be understood as highly culturally specific symptoms, or symbolic manifestations. Selected from culturally recognised symptom pools. In the case of stigmata – the symptoms associated with Christ's crucifixion, and in the case of physical mediumship, which emerged during a complex period often referred to as a 'crisis of faith' – ectoplasm, a half-way substance between the physical and the spiritual – a mediating substance that might bring the spiritual into the scientific laboratory.

Stigmata and physical mediumship share many similarities, despite the very obvious surface differences between the two occurrences.

Altered States of Consciousness

Both stigmatics and physical mediums produce their phenomena while in deep altered states of consciousness. Ian Wilson writes of stigmatics:

> [...] a recurring feature among stigmatics is the variety of altered states of mind that may be broadly labelled dissociated consciousness. These may take the form of trances, hysterical catalepsies, loss of sensation in parts of the body, blindness, loss of hearing, paralysis, and other dissociated states, particularly seeing visions, hearing voices and receiving other hallucinatory impressions (Wilson, 1986: 126).

Alleged Bodily Secretions

Perhaps the most obvious similarity between stigmata and physical mediumship is the production of anomalous bodily secretions: in the case of stigmata it is large amounts of blood that are produced – accounts have even described boiling hot blood – and ectoplasm in the context of physical mediumship. Blood flow can be consciously affected through biofeedback, so perhaps there is some connection here.

Weird Body Phenomena

The Sixteenth century Italian stigmatic Blessed Stefana Quinzani's arm is reported to have elongated while she was reliving the crucifixion. St. Catherine of Genoa's arm was said to have grown 'more than half a palm longer than it was by nature.' And in 1880 the stigmatic Marie-Julie Jahenny reportedly underwent a wide range of bodily distortions and contortions. Ian Wilson writes:

> [...] her head seemed to shrink into her body to just above the level of her shoulders; her whole frame shriveled into a sort of ball, each of her shoulders seemed to protrude at right angles to her collar bone, the right side of her body enlarged while the left shrank to virtually nothing, and [...] her tongue swelled to enormous proportions (Wilson, 1986: 111).

Such accounts are remarkably similar to the descriptions of the bodily contortions produced by the nineteenth century medium

Daniel Dunglas Home, who was said to be able to elongate his body considerably, even under the controlled experimental conditions of physicist Sir William Crookes. These kinds of effects are also reported today, in fact, as we see here, Shannon Taggart has a particularly interesting photograph of the physical medium Gordon Garforth, that seems to fall quite easily into this category of phenomena – his hand is visibly larger than normal.

Early Life Trauma

Early life trauma, and high levels of life stress, appear to have had a role in the development of many stigmatics, and are also apparent in the lives of classical physical mediums, hysterics, and sufferers of somatoform disorders. Eusapia Palladino, again, provides a good example. Palladino's mother is said to have died at birth, and her father was murdered (Alvarado, 2011: 80). When she was young, she had a fall and injured her head, leaving a dent over which her hair was said to have grown white. She is also reported to have suffered from diabetes. Trauma is also, of course, a hallmark of shamanic initiations throughout the world.

Fraud

Both stigmatics and physical mediums, in certain cases, share an apparent intermingling of seemingly genuine phenomena and obviously fake phenomena. Padre Pio, it has been claimed, used acid to supplement his stigmatic wounds (Colborn, 2011: 255). Eusapia Palladino is the usually cited example of a physical medium displaying this characteristic. Although she was caught deliberately cheating on several occasions, there were other times when the phenomena she produced could not be explained in any normal terms – many of her investigators remained convinced that Palladino's abilities were genuine.

Occasional fraud does not, therefore, rule out genuine phenomena. Indeed, the psychical researcher Kenneth Batcheldor found that introducing what he called 'artifacts' into his PK experiments could actually lead to the manifestation of genuine PK events because they increased participants' belief that something *could* happen. Batcheldor writes of his research on the role of belief in the induction of psychokinesis:

What seems to matter is the balance of belief over doubt at the very instant when a PK event is about to occur, rather than the long-term attitude of belief or doubt that exists before the sitting commences. Thus, it is a far cry from a vague general belief in the paranormal to believing that the table in front of you is going to levitate right now (Batcheldor, 1984).

And this, of course, makes perfect sense in the context of stigmata, which usually occurs in people with very high levels of belief.

Ideoplasm

The German psychical researcher Baron Albert von Schrenck-Notzing coined the term 'ideoplasm' to refer to the ectoplasmic materialisations that he observed in his laboratory with the medium Eva C. The term implies that ectoplasmic materialisations are influenced in some way by the active power of the imagination. For example, he accounted for the apparent similarities between certain of Eva C's materialisation and photographs from newspapers by arguing that the materialisations were externalised memories of things the medium had previously seen.

Stephen Braude reports the case of 'Katie' who was apparently able to manifest golden foil, which would appear to materialise on her skin. Further investigation revealed that the foil actually consisted of brass, and Braude suggests that this might have served a symbolic function for Katie. As with the stigmatics and hysterics, Katie's materialisations seemed to be physical symptoms of psychological distress. Braude writes:

> Symbolically, the brass foil satisfies Tom's demand for something valuable. But at the same time Katie needn't run the risk of being the goose that lays the golden egg. After all, the pressure of being a psychic subject is weighty enough as it is (Braude, 2007: 14).

Cultural Biology

In his study of Brazilian psychic surgery, anthropologist Sidney Greenfield developed the concept of cultural biology to account for the seemingly miraculous healings experienced by patients of psychic surgeons. He writes of this concept:

I suggest that culture, as information, often held implicitly in a group's sacred understandings but made explicit during religious rituals, could function analogously to a therapist's suggestions made to a patient in a hypnotically induced trance. Furthermore, under the right circumstances, this information could be transduced to become part of the communication flow within an individual organism, turning on or off immediate-early genes and physiological systems that contribute to healing (Greenfield, 2008: 201).

Drawing in the Threads: Mechanisms for the Paranormal

Of course, although this kind of approach may be interpreted as an attempt to reduce seemingly 'paranormal' occurrences to mechanistic, 'natural,' processes, I would like to stress the idea that these are precisely the kinds of psycho-physiological processes we might expect to see in operation if a spirit really were being incorporated into the body of a medium, or if ectoplasm really was being manifested during a séance, or if an immaterial deity were manifesting symbolic marks through the body of a devout believer. After all, where else, other than the interface between mind and body, might we look for possible connecting points between physical and non-physical worlds?

The ideas outlined here are, therefore, possible mechanisms (for want of a better word) for what is going on, and may point us in further interesting directions in exploring the nature of consciousness and its relationship with the physical world, as well as other questions relating to the possibility of survival after death, or of the existence of non-physical entities.

ENGAGING THE ANOMALOUS:
REFLECTIONS FROM THE ANTHROPOLOGY OF THE PARANORMAL

I was very excited to hear that a special issue of the *European Journal of Psychotherapy and Counselling* on the paranormal was being put together, and I was particularly honoured to have been invited to contribute a short reflection on its contents. For several years, I have been actively involved in trying to initiate a similar dialogue in the context of my own discipline: anthropology. Indeed, there is a long and distinguished lineage to anthropology's engagement with the paranormal as a facet of human experience that goes right back to the discipline's nineteenth-century founders, though standard anthropology textbooks might not give any hint of this. Sir E.B. Tylor (1832–1917), for example, famous for his explanatory theory of 'animism' (the belief in spiritual beings as the most basic expression of religion), had investigated some of the leading Spiritualist mediums of his day. In spite of his clear interest in Spiritualism, however, Tylor never published accounts of his experiences, which included séances with the Reverend Stainton Moses (1839–1892), D.D. Home (1833–1896) and Kate Fox (1837–1892). Tylor's experiences only came to light following the researches of the historian of anthropology George W. Stocking Jr (1928–2013). In his private diaries, so Stocking discovered, Tylor admitted his bafflement at the strange things he had seen with these mediums, and came to the striking conclusion that there is a '*prima facie* case on evidence' for the abilities of certain mediums, and that 'there may be a psychic force causing raps, movements, levitations, etc.' (Stocking, 1971: 92–100).

It is interesting to speculate on why Tylor decided against making his suspicions public, and a clue might be found in his own theory for the origin of animism. For Tylor, the belief in spirits arose out of misinterpretation, and, in particular, from mistaking dreams for reality. According to Tylor, who operated within a broadly evolutionist framework, so-called 'primitive' people developed the notion of spirits through failing to understand that the people they encountered in their dreams were not real, and, from this misunderstanding, they went on to infer the existence of a non-physical part of the human that could leave the physical body under certain conditions, such as in trance, or in death (Tylor, 1930: 87). Belief in spirits, then, represented what Tylor called a 'survival,' something akin to a fossil of an outdated way of thinking, already superseded by rational and scientific modes of understanding the world. Tylor was a modern, rational, Victorian scholar, but he, too, had had unusual experiences in the presence of spirit mediums: experiences for which he could find no rational explanation. We might suggest, therefore, that Tylor's reluctance to publish his own paranormal experiences was, at least in part, due to the fact that to do so would be to admit that even the most distinguished, rational members of modern European societies can also have paranormal experiences. This admission would have been a direct challenge to the prevailing social-evolutionist paradigm of the time. It is also likely that Tylor was worried that an admission of even the possibility of a 'psychic force' could be detrimental to the status of the emerging field of anthropology as a scientific discipline.

Tylor's example serves to illustrate two key points in discussions of the paranormal. Firstly, it highlights the fact that supernatural beliefs and paranormal experiences are not restricted to 'primitive' cultures, nor to non-Western societies. Indeed, they are surprisingly common within modern, post-industrial, Euro-American societies (Castro, Burrows, & Wooffitt, 2014). Secondly, it illustrates the problem that Euro-American academia (maybe even Euro-American culture as a whole) has with the so-called paranormal: it is taboo, not to be discussed or taken seriously. This is a problem that anthropology has long had to deal with, especially when anthropologists have been confronted with the belief systems and extraordinary claims of their fieldwork informants. The standard approach, following the lead of E.E. Evans-Pritchard (1902–1973), has since become a form of ontological bracketing. In his book *Theories of Primitive Religion* (1965), Evans-Pritchard writes:

> As I understand the matter, there is no possibility of knowing whether the spiritual beings of primitive religions or of any others have any existence or not, and since that is the case [the anthropologist] cannot take the question into consideration (Evans-Pritchard, 1965: 17).

This kind of approach has been immensely practical for anthropology, allowing it to document and describe a broad swathe of the world's cultures, and religious, magical and shamanistic belief systems, without the need to enter into debates about the reality status of the objects of such beliefs – this question is simply bracketed out. Things become a little less clear-cut, however, when anthropologists themselves begin to have experiences that seem to support the belief systems of their informants. How should such experiences be understood, and should they be included in ethnographic texts? Evans-Pritchard himself had such an experience while he conducted fieldwork amongst the Azande in Sudan. One night, while out for a walk, the anthropologist observed a mysterious light floating past his hut, seemingly on route to a nearby village. When he told his informants about the experience the next day, they immediately identified the light as 'witchcraft substance' on a murderous errand, and when a report arrived that an individual in the next village had died during the night, it further supported the Azande interpretation. In spite of this, however, Evans-Pritchard transforms the story into a joke in his monograph on Azande witchcraft beliefs, offering the suggestion that it was 'probably a handful of grass lit by someone on his way to defecate' (Evans-Pritchard, 1976: 11). Although clearly an advance of Tylor's approach to the paranormal, Evans-Pritchard still seems uncomfortable with admitting the possible reality of the paranormal.

A complete account of the development of transpersonal anthropology and the anthropology of consciousness exceeds the limitations of this short chapter, but suffice to say at this juncture that it would be another forty or so years before anthropologists finally began to take heed of their own anomalous experiences in the field as potentially valuable research data, without attempting to reduce the complexity of the experience. In the 1970s, two conferences specifically concerned with the implications of parapsychological research for anthropology were held in Mexico City and London, resulting in two ground-breaking publications (Angoff & Barth, 1974; Long, 1977). It was these conferences that ultimately paved the way for the emergence of the Society for the Anthropology of Consciousness, which is still very active today and has the stated aim of investigating 'psychic phenomena, reincarnation, near-near-death experiences, mediumistic communication, divination,' amongst other things (http://www.sacaaa.org/).

One of the leading lights in the anthropology of consciousness over the last twenty years has been Edith Turner, whose experience during the *Ihamba* healing ceremony of the Ndembu in Zambia was a major catalyst for her work on the experiential aspects of ritual healing (Turner, 1993). At the peak of the ritual, Turner witnessed the extraction of an amorphic, plasma-like, grey blob from the back of an afflicted patient, she writes: 'a large gray blob about six inches across, a deep gray opaque thing emerging as a sphere. I was amazed – delighted. I still laugh with glee at the realisation of having seen it, the ihamba, and so big!' (Turner, 1998: 149). It was this sighting, amongst other experiences, that prompted Turner to conclude that anthropologists must learn to 'see as the Native sees' in order to understand ritual, and in doing so must:

> [...] endorse the experiences of spirits as veracious aspects of the life-world of the peoples with whom we work; that we faithfully attend to our own experiences in order to judge their veracity; that we are not reducing the phenomena of spirits or other extraordinary beings to something more abstract and distant in meaning; and that we accept the fact that spirits are ontologically real for those whom we study (Turner, 2010: 224).

Turner's approach has been particularly influential in the anthropology of consciousness and the anthropology of religion in recent years, perhaps most notably in the work of Fiona Bowie, whose methodology of 'cognitive empathetic engagement' might be understood as a means of learning to 'see what the Native sees' in order to get at the underlying experiential core of religious, spiritual and paranormal belief and practice. Bowie explains how cognitive empathetic engagement requires the ethnographer to adopt 'the categories of his or her informants,' and to 'use this knowledge to interpret the world by means of those categories' as an 'effort of will and imagination.' Above all, the method requires 'an active engagement with another way of thinking, seeing and living' (Bowie, 2012: 105–106).

Although much of this may seem tangential to the overall theme of this issue, in actuality, I think there are some rather striking correspondences. The case of E.B. Tylor, as well as the wider lineage of anthropology's involvement with the paranormal since its inception in the mid-nineteenth century, reveals a story similar to that outlined by Andreas Sommer in his paper 'Are You Afraid of the Dark?' (2016), namely a contradictory fascination with the anomalous, paranormal and the occult in the development of modern science, coupled with an almost dogmatic desire to disenchant Euro-American academia, and to rid it of any hint of the magical. These same taboos are still in action today, ultimately resulting in a cultural fear of the anomalous, and an automatic association (and reduction) of anomalous experience to pathology. Examples from anthropology can show that this particular cultural framework is not the only one available for understanding and working with anomalous experiences, and may prove useful for psychotherapists faced with clients reporting anomalous experiences.

E.B. Tylor's experience, and his unwillingness to talk about it in his published papers, also echoes Roxburgh and Evenden's article, 'They daren't tell people,' where we learn that those who have anomalous experiences often feel that they cannot talk about them for fear of 'being labelled with a mental disorder if they did' (Roxburgh & Evenden, 2016). Thankfully, things have changed since Tylor's day, and (some) anthropologists are now comfortable with owning up to their own anomalous experiences, encountered during their fieldwork, and are willing to explore their implications for ethnographic writing and theory formation. The same might also be said of psychotherapy and psychotherapists. The wonderful book *Being Changed by Cross-Cultural Encounters* (1994) is a testament to this gradual shift in anthropology. It also hints at a breakdown of the usually assumed distinction between the observer and the observed. The anthropologist (perhaps also the psychotherapist) can no longer be thought of as somehow separate from the system they are investigating: they are also participants and their experiences matter, too. Perhaps the anomalous experiences encountered by both anthropologists and psychotherapists can reveal insights into the life worlds of fieldwork informants and clients, respectively. See, as an example, Jokic's (2008) insights into Yanomamo cosmology revealed through his participation in shamanic ceremonies involving the psychoactive snuff *Yopo*.

Rose Cameron's paper 'The Paranormal: An Unhelpful Concept in Psychotherapy and Counselling Research' (2016) also ties into all of this on two distinct fronts. Firstly, the author's conclusion that phenomenological bracketing represents the most fruitful means by which psychotherapists can accommodate the anomalous experiences of their clients seems to fall in line with Evans-Pritchard's approach of opting out of considering ontological questions, which is also the standard approach in disciplines such as anthropology and religious studies. Secondly, the author's own anomalous experience of something resembling an 'elongated (and wriggly) jellybean: translucent, yet somehow also encased in a slightly opaque shell' (Cameron, 2016), accords remarkably well with Edith Turner's experience during the

Ihamba ceremony. This convergence potentially signals the centrality of anomalous experiences in the therapeutic setting (Turner's experience was, after all, also in the context of a healing ritual), and, as Cameron suggests, may indicate a need for psychotherapists to have an awareness of the research that has been conducted on anomalous experiences as part of their training. This might also include an overview of the cross-cultural and ethnographic research on anomalous experiences and their role in traditional forms of shamanic healing (McClenon, 2001).

Samuel Kimbles argues that the concept of the 'Phantom Narrative,' as outlined in the paper 'Phantom Narratives and the Uncanny in Cultural Life,' 'operates in what Victor Turner… has defined as a liminal space, which we might here speak of as a place between accepted cultural narrative' (Kimbles, 2016). Turner's notion of the liminal, derived from the earlier research of Arnold Van Gennep (1873–1957) on the structure of rituals, specifically in the context of rites of passage, has in recent years become a central focus in the anthropology of the paranormal. This emphasis has emerged largely from the work of the parapsychologist George Hansen, whose ground-breaking book *The Trickster and the Paranormal* (2001) suggests that paranormal manifestations are, by their very nature, liminal events. Hansen explains the central theme of his book:

> …psi, the paranormal, and the supernatural are fundamentally linked to destructuring, change, transition, disorder, marginality, the ephemeral, fluidity, ambiguity, and the blurring of boundaries (Hansen, 2001: 22).

From this perspective, then, the association between the paranormal and the psychotherapeutic process makes perfect sense. The psychotherapeutic process, like the shamanic healing ceremony, is a ritual, itself taking place within a liminal space separated from the outside world. It is also clear how, from this perspective, anomalous experiences might arise in individuals whose routine has been 'destructured,' who are in 'transition' or who feel 'marginalised.' The psychotherapeutic encounter, like the shamanic ritual, can help bring back order for the patient, help them make sense of their anomalous experiences, and eventually re-integrate themselves into society as part of the ritual structure.

To conclude, then, the special issue on the paranormal in psychotherapy is a welcome contribution to the widening scholarly engagement with the anomalous, and I hope that some of the convergences I have highlighted, as preliminary as they are, might point to some interesting directions for future research. I am sure that anthropologists of the paranormal stand to learn a lot from the experiences of psychotherapists and their clients, and I am certain that the anthropological literature – particularly in the context of the anthropology of consciousness, transpersonal anthropology and paranthropology – contains valuable tools to help psychotherapists better make sense of anomalous experiences in their own practice.

REFLECTIONS ON A 'DAMNED' CHAPTER

The following chapter was originally written for inclusion in an edited volume on the supernatural in history, society and culture that I was invited to contribute to. The chapter is essentially an overview of the ethnographic and parapsychological literature on spirit mediumship and possession, and argues that from the perspective of this much wider context there is still quite a lot we don't know about the phenomenon, so that the standard reductive explanations of fraud and trickery are certainly not always sufficient. This was intended as a nudge for the social sciences to consider possibilities that extend beyond the limits of its standard materialist underpinnings: to push past purely social and psychological explanations into new ontological possibilities.

On completion of the first draft, I submitted it to the editors for review. After a couple of weeks, I received a response to my chapter, along with a short list of recommended changes and suggestions for tweaks to make it clearer, and my argument stronger. This is normal practice in academia – a process of *peer-review* to ensure the highest standards of scholarship. I completed the suggested changes and sent the chapter back to the editors so that they could send the finished manuscript on to the publishers. They enjoyed the chapter, were happy with the changes I had made to it and thought it made a valuable contribution to the scope of their volume. All good.

Several weeks later, however, after having signed a publishing agreement for the book, I received an e-mail from the editors with some bad news. My chapter had to be removed from the final manuscript because a certain member of the publishing board had objected to it, primarily on the grounds that I – not even the chapter specifically – have presented information that supports claims to the reality of the paranormal in the past. The editors tried their best to keep my chapter in the book, but ultimately – and unfortunately – failed to convince the publisher that it was suitable for inclusion. The following are extracts from the e-mail the editors sent to me following the board's decision:

> Initially all members of the board voted in favor – all except one. Instead of going with the majority vote, that one highly aggressive board member demanded that the book be tabled for a later meeting. This one individual did extensive background research on authors in this volume and, at this later meeting, he managed to convince enough of the other board members that your status as a scholar should be called into question because of publications and associations in which you present information that supports claims to the ontological reality of supernatural phenomena. In the eyes of these board members, such public statements by an author may be damaging to the reputation of [the publishers], and therefore they see the inclusion of your chapter as a liability (Personal Correspondence)

The editors went on to explain how they:

> [...] spent a great deal of time developing a set of edits and revisions that we thought would make your chapter better fit the board's vision of the book. This was difficult because there were no major stated objections to the actual content of what you wrote (again, a very frustrating situation for us). Nonetheless, we felt the contribution your chapter made to the volume was important, and hoped that with some edits and revisions the board would agree. Even after we provided the board with an extensive set of edits and revisions as well as a rationale for why the chapter should remain, the board rejected our changes and drew a firm line in the sand. The word from them is clear: they are unwilling to publish the book if you are a chapter author, regardless of the content of your chapter (Personal Correspondence)

In addition to being a particularly potent illustration of the taboo against taking the paranormal seriously as a *possibility* in academia (even in the context of a book on the supernatural in history, society and culture!), this incident also raises a couple of other interesting issues in the sociology and philosophy of the social sciences that I would *very* briefly like to raise here.

Firstly, there is the issue of a board of scholars rejecting a publication not due to the content of the chapter in question, but rather because the author's *personal beliefs and opinions* do not accord with those of the social-scientific orthodoxy. In what way is this different from rejecting a chapter because the author is a committed Christian/ Muslim/ Hindu/ Buddhist/ Atheist? Should the personal beliefs of the author really trump the content and scholarly contribution of the chapter? Furthermore, in this instance, I also feel it is important to point out that I do not necessarily consider myself to be a 'believer' in *anything*, but rather think of myself as an *entertainer of alternative ontological possibilities*. My approach is more akin to that of the collector of anomalies Charles Fort, and his philosophy of intermediatism, or Robert Anton Wilson's notion of 'model agnosticism' (Hunter, 2015; 2016).

Secondly, this incident raises some important questions about the status of indigenous knowledge and understanding in Western social-scientific scholarship. If I *were* a committed believer in the reality of the paranormal (which I'm equally not saying I'm not), do my *emic* perspectives on the dominant *etic* scholarly theories have no value or significance? Is there really nothing that the *insider* can offer to help clarify the *outsider's* view? These are important issues to unpack, but this is not quite the right place to do so. Suffice to say, here, that I am very grateful to the editors of the volume for sticking up for my chapter, but was overall disappointed that it had to be removed from the collection in this rather unpleasant way. Anyway, here it is. What do you think?

RETHINKING THE SÉANCE:
MEDIUMSHIP IN A CROSS-CULTURAL CONTEXT

It is tempting, when discussing spirit mediumship, to think only of the types of mediumship that are most familiar to us. In the Western, Euro-American world, the form of mediumship we are most familiar with is Spiritualist mediumship. The origins of the Spiritualist movement can be traced back to March 31, 1848, to the small town of Hydesville, New York State, where the Fox sisters – Leah, Margaret, and Kate – initiated contact with the spirit of a deceased peddler by the name of Charles B. Rosma (often also referred to as Mr. Splitfoot by the sisters). Through a simple code of knocks – one for "yes" and two for "no" – the mysterious Mr. Splitfoot allegedly revealed the location of his skeleton in the Fox family basement, claiming that he had been murdered in the house some years before they moved in (Gauld, 1983). The events at Hydesville propelled the Fox sisters to national and international celebrity status and, before long, they were touring the US giving public demonstrations of their mediumistic abilities to audiences in packed music halls. Their careers were by no means straightforward, however. There was intense pressure on the sisters to produce dramatic physical phenomena during their séances, and they were often accused of fraud by debunkers and skeptics, who argued that the raps and knocks alleged to be produced by discarnate spirits were, in fact, the result of cracking the knuckles in their toes (Blum, 2006). The strains of their newfound celebrity, and constant critique of their demonstrations, became so severe that the sisters turned to alcohol and had bitter disagreements. It is interesting to note that in 1888 Kate and Margaret publicly confessed that the dramatic phenomena that had propelled them to fame were the result of deliberate tricks, but a year later Margaret recanted her confession, claiming that the phenomena were genuine. Such toing-and-froing would forever damage the reputation of the sisters, as well as the Spiritualist movement as a whole, and they all died in relative poverty within three years of 1890 (Lehmann, 2009).

The ups and downs of the Fox sisters' tumultuous mediumistic career notwithstanding, by 1853 the mediumship craze they had humbly initiated in Hydesville had progressed from paranormal parlor games (such as the popular fad for table tipping), to become a semi-organized religion, with the first Spiritualist Church established in the North Yorkshire town of Keighley in the UK (Nelson, 1969). Spiritualism, then, is a particularly interesting case study in the "domestication" of the supernatural, from the wild and unpredictable spirit rappings in Hydesville to the relatively stable, semi-liturgical demonstrations of mediums in Spiritualist Churches across the US and UK.

News of the Fox sisters' apparent interdimensional communication spread rapidly across the USA, taking full advantage of recent technological advances – especially in the form of railways, telegraphy, photography, and newspapers – and soon afterwards word spread across the Atlantic to Britain and Europe (Nelson, 1969). As news spread, mediumship became a craze, and many people began to experiment themselves as they attempted to make contact with those beyond the threshold of death. As more and more people began to experiment with mediumship, different forms started to emerge. Mental mediumship, including 'clairvoyant' (mental imagery), 'clairaudient' (inner voices), and 'clairsentient' (feelings and emotions) varieties were, and continue to be, particularly popular. These varieties of mediumship usually involve symbolic communication between the medium and the deceased, where the spirit might present the medium with emotionally significant objects or ideas, and often required the medium to serve as an interpreter for the client. Another form of mental mediumship known as trance mediumship involves the medium's body being completely "possessed" by an external spirit, who uses the medium as a vessel, or channel, for communicating with the living. Of the different varieties of mental mediumship, trance mediumship makes use of the deepest dissociative states of consciousness – for the duration of the trance state the medium claims to be completely unaware of what is going on in the room around them, and very often claims to have no memory of the preceding interval while spirit personalities were communicating through their bodies.

Physical mediumship, with its enigmatic physical phenomena – raps, knocks, apports, levitations, and so on – was one of the most popular and dramatic forms of mediumship in the early days of the

Spiritualist movement, and eventually culminated with the alleged full-form materialization of spirits through the strange semi-physical substance known as "ectoplasm" (Moreman, 2010). Owing to its exotic and outlandish phenomena, physical mediumship became especially popular with psychical researchers and debunkers. Numerous exposures of fraudulent activity in physical mediumship séances, most notably by the likes of the famed magician and escapologist Harry Houdini (1874-1926), ultimately led to a decline in the practice in the early-to-mid twentieth century. However, the practice has seen something of a renaissance since the 1990s with the establishment of new physical mediumship development circles in the UK and Europe (Hunter, 2012).

Today, the most common form of mediumship is of the clairvoyant variety, frequently seen at Spiritualist Churches and mediumship demonstrations across the UK and USA. Although the more elaborate forms of trance and physical mediumship do persist, primarily in private home-circles (Hunter, 2010), they are much less commonly practised and are often skeptically associated with notions of fraud and trickery, even amongst some Spiritualists. Indeed, for many outside of the Spiritualist subculture, these are the default attitudes towards mediumship in general, regardless of the specific variety of mediumship being practised.

Discussions of Spiritualist mediumship, however, often neglect to place the practice in a wider cross-cultural context, and generally see the Spiritualist movement as a fairly isolated, historically contingent phenomenon – when the topic comes up in conversation, for example, our minds are likely to conjure up gloomy images of Victorian séances in grand manor houses. In fact, mediumistic practices are remarkably common around the world; in virtually all historical and cultural contexts there are people who have claimed, and continue to claim, the special ability to facilitate communication between the physical and spiritual realms (see Hunter & Luke. 2014; Schmidt & Huskinson, 2010). An awareness of this wider context can serve to enhance our understanding of mediumship as a ritualized practice that performs important social functions in our own and other cultures. To this end, this chapter provides an overview of mediumship practices in the Euro-American world and beyond. This presentation of a range of mediumistic traditions illuminates core features of mediumship that persist across cultures, such as its social and psychological functions, the ritual and performative dimensions of mediumistic séances, and the role of altered states of consciousness in initiating contact between the world of the living and that of the dead. My review is not exhaustive, but should, nevertheless, suffice in demonstrating that there are other ways of understanding mediumship that are often overlooked in the contemporary scholarly discourse on the subject. Additionally, not only do these apparent core features hint at a universal, or at least near-universal, human experience, they also point us in some interesting ontological directions that ultimately exceed the limitations of this chapter. The very fact that there appear to be core functions of mediumistic practices across history and culture – that the same (or similar) performative aspects are recurrent features in the manifestation of spirits through both time and space, and that most mediumship traditions employ alterations of consciousness to initiate contact between the visible and invisible worlds – is suggestive that we *may* be dealing with a phenomenon that has an existence independent of culture and individual psychology; that the ability to communicate with, and embody, spirits might be a universal human capacity relating to some underlying spiritual reality, a possibility that should not be ruled out in our analysis of mediumship practices (Bowie, 2013; Hunter, 2015; Turner, 1993).

Social and Psychological Functions of Mediumship

Much scholarly research has focused on the social and psychological functions of spirit mediumship. Anthropologist I.M. Lewis (1971), for example, famously put forward the suggestion that spirit mediumship cults serve the social function of providing socially acceptable forms of protest for individuals, usually females in male dominated societies (although it could equally be any other socially marginalized group). Lewis' theory rests on the assumption that during the medium's trance state they are no longer in control of their actions, which are now under the influence of the possessing entity (this is the *emic* understanding). In this possessed state, then, the individual is able to express their discontent without being directly responsible for their controversial opinions (this is Lewis' *etic* understanding).

From this functionalist perspective, the medium can also be said to enhance their social status through their capacity to incorporate spiritual beings. In societies where women are traditionally subordinate, for example, spirit mediumship may offer a route towards improved social standing – it provides women with a special magico-religious social role that may imbue them with supernatural authority, where other means of attaining authority might not be available. Lewis gives examples from the Somali Zar possession cults, where Zar spirits "demand luxurious clothes, perfume, and exotic dainties [...] voiced in no uncertain fashion by the spirits [...] with an authority which their passive receptacles can rarely achieve themselves" (1971: 76). With this notion in mind, then, it is perhaps unsurprising to note similarities in the Western context of Spiritualist mediumship (see Skultans, 1974). Indeed, many of those involved in the Spiritualist movement of the mid-nineteenth and early-twentieth centuries were also deeply involved in Women's Suffrage and other progressive social reform movements of the time (Braude, 2001) – just as with the Zar spirits in Somalia, the supernatural authority of the spirits in nineteenth century America served to legitimise new progressive attitudes towards women in wider society.

Another example of a functionalist account of mediumship can be found in the more recent work of Danish anthropologist Nils Bubandt (2009). Bubandt's research focused on the political functions of mediumship and possession in North Maluku, an Island province in Indonesia. Here, mediumship is used as a political tool when mediums incorporate the spirits of deceased chiefs, politicians, and military leaders to give their advice and guidance on the decision-making processes of still-living politicians. In North Maluku, mediumship plays a very significant role in contemporary politics; a fact which has led Bubandt to re-interpret spirits as "methodologically real," if not ontologically real (Bubandt, 2009: 298), in that they clearly have important implications for social scientific analysis of contemporary politics in the region – to ignore them would be to dismiss an essential component of social and political life in Maluku.

Recent psychological research has also taken a functionalist turn in suggesting that mediumship facilitates important psychological functions for both mediums and their clients. Rates of mental illness, as well as dependence on pharmaceutical drugs, have been found to be significantly reduced among Brazilian practitioners of mediumship compared with baseline samples of non-practitioners (Moreira-Almeida *et al.*, 2008), which perhaps indicates that mediumship can serve important therapeutic functions for the mediums themselves. It is also becoming clear that mediumship may very well assist in alleviating the pain and distress of the bereaved clients of mediums through enabling a continuation of bonds between the living and the dead (Beischel, 2014; Osborne & Bacon, 2015).

Of course, the functionalist perspective on mediumship essentially implies that mediumship is little more than a social performance aimed at legitimising dissent, rendering protest socially acceptable, enhancing social status of mediums, and providing therapeutic relief for both mediums and clients. In that respect, mediumship is something that can be *used* to achieve specific goals. This, however, raises the question of what exactly mediumship consists of – is it simply a form of "pretending" to achieve specific goals, a careful and deliberate use of fraud, trickery and role-play to bring about change in society? The social functionalist perspective certainly seems to suggest such a dismissive attitude. The functionalist perspective focusses on the phenomenon as performing a single, easy to understand, social function and, consequently, ignores the experiential depth of the phenomenon (as well as apparent veridical evidence from the parapsychological literature), which would seem to imply that there is something more going on. Similarly, the psychological functionalist approach does not *need* to understand mediumship as "real," that is involving *real* discarnate spirits, because what is most important is the *function* that the "belief that it is real" performs for the individual.

So, we can already say that, far from being pure fraud and trickery (as the early debunkers would have had us believe), mediumship may well perform important social and psychological functions in the societies where it is practised, including in the Euro-American context. Mediumship may be used for social protest, to gain social status, as a political tool, or as psychological defence against the pain and distress of bereavement. Nevertheless, it should be noted that the fact that mediumship performs such social and psychological functions does not mean that there is nothing more going on here – there *are* other dimensions to the phenomenon. Already we are beginning to see that what we are dealing with is something that cannot, and should not, be lightly brushed aside or explained away in reductionist and dismissive terms. Mediumship is far more complex than one might initially assume.

Ritual and Performance of Mediumship

From a cross-cultural perspective, spirit mediumship is a rich and varied phenomenon with numerous expressions across the globe. Each cultural system has its own mediumship traditions and each tradition is couched in its own culturally specific symbolism. Indeed, most mediumship traditions rely on specific culturally recognized ritual behaviors, which are used as indicators of when a spirit is incorporated in the body of the medium, and when it is not. Such behaviors range from subtle bodily gestures and movements (e.g., twitches, spasms, ticks), which indicate the onset of possession, to elaborate dances, performances and rituals employing lavish costumes and props to show when a particular spirit is present.

Spiritualism also features very strong ritual and performative aspects (Lehmann, 2009). For example, in my own fieldwork with trance and physical mediums in suburban Bristol, UK, the presence of individual spirit personalities during séances is indicated by subtle (and sometimes not so subtle) transformations in the medium's physical demeanor – they may begin to move in a very specific way, they may exhibit a characteristic tick, move with a distinctive limp, and, more often than not, will talk with a completely different vocal tonality. These are the primary indicators that the medium is now incorporating a particular spirit being, with its own personality and backstory as distinct from that of the medium, and are essential in order for a dialogue to be initiated and sustained during séances (Hunter, 2013).

Amongst the Kel Ewey Tuareg, on the other hand, possession is indicated by increasingly vigorous head movements known as *asul* (Rasmussen, 1994), while in Afro-Brazilian traditions like Candomble and Batuque, the presence of particular *Orishas* or *Encantados* respectively is indicated only when the medium performs particular dance movements to rhythms associated with the possessing spirit. If the performance is not right, then the possession is not complete or genuine:

> In order to prove that an *encantado* is really present, the mediums must dance, sing the proper song, and interact with the other participants in the ceremony in an acceptable manner. The behavior that is most admired in the accomplished medium is very often the behavior that appears the least frenzied and the most normal to the outside observer (Leacock & Leacock, 1975: 172).

Similarly, in Taiwanese spirit mediumship, possession by underworld spirits is demonstrated during gory rituals of self-mortification, where the medium, under the influence of a deity, cuts and pierces his body with swordfish blades and metal skewers, or douses himself with boiling oil. While under the control of a deity the medium feels no pain. If they are unable to perform these acts of self-mutilation, then the possession is not deemed to be genuine (Graham, 2014). These rituals are social performances that indicate the presence, in the medium's body, of incorporated underworld spirits, and the extraordinary physical abilities of the possessed medium's body are evidence that this is more than just role-play – they suggest that a real change has taken place.

In the Western world, our conception of performance is intimately bound up with notions of "pretending," "imitating" and "playing" (Foley, 1985: 27). When we see an actor on the stage, or in a movie, we do not assume that the actor actually *is* the character they are playing (even if we suspend our disbelief for the duration of the play or film). We implicitly assume that the actor *portrays* a role. A cross-cultural perspective, however, reveals that there are other ways of interpreting and understanding performance, which may provide alternative means for interpreting Western mediumship practices. For example, when in Candomble the medium "performs" as the *Orisha*, the movements are no longer understood to be under the medium's direction; if this were not the case then the possession would not be a true possession. In fact, for the duration of the performance, the medium's body *is* the body of the *Orisha*. Here performance is an actual *transformation* – not a simple role-play (Schechner, 1988). Similarly, for the Yanomamo Indians of the Venezuelan Orinoco Valley, when the Shaman incorporates the forest *Hekura* spirits, his body is *transformed* into a "cosmic body – the body is no longer under the control of the shaman's consciousness but now the body of the *Hekura* spirit itself (Jokic, 2008). There is an understanding, therefore, that the body can be *both* a physical object *and* the locus of spiritual activity. In other words, the body is the point of contact between the physical and spiritual realms, and bodily performance is the means of expression for non-physical beings, just as Erving Goffman (1959: 253) suggests that the body is not only a "peg" on which a person's self is "hung for a time" but also a primary means of self-expression for living human beings.

In what ways, then, might an alternative approach to performance influence our interpretation of Western mediumship traditions? From the outset, the *possibility* that mediumistic performances might be understood as a *transformation*, rather than as role play, may present a challenge to those skeptics who seek to explain mediumship away merely as a fraudulent and disingenuous activity. Anthropologist John Beattie, writing on Bunyoro possession performances in Uganda, has suggested the need to avoid such assumptions in our analyses of mediumistic performances:

[...] the second false assumption [...] was that if "possession" was in some sense and in some degree an "act" consciously performed, it followed that the whole thing was therefore fraudulent, a mere trick and not to be taken seriously. It did not take me very long to realize that this view was naïve and superficial (1977: 2).

What if, for example, the debunking of mediums during the early-twentieth century, where psychical researchers would reach out to grab at the materialized arms of spirits in the séance room only to discover that the arm belonged to the medium, totally missed the point of the séance ritual? What if, in the Spiritualist séance, the medium's body itself is the primary means of expression for the disembodied spirits they incorporate? What if it is not a disingenuous act on behalf of the medium, what if they are not pretending – what if mediumship is best understood as a *transformation* of body and consciousness?

At the very least, an appreciation of alternative modes of interpreting performance could help us more closely to engage with the practices of spirit mediums and to understand them in more empathetic terms, rather than simply dismiss them as fraudulent. All of this may be seen as an effort towards what anthropologist Fiona Bowie calls "cognitive empathetic engagement;" a process of attempting to investigate the supernatural, the transpersonal and the religious with a "[c]uriosity to push the boundaries of human knowledge… and courage to document and then to draw conclusions from these data, whether or not they transgress the largely materialist *Weltanshauung* of Western academic culture" (Bowie, 2013: 703).

Mediumship and Altered States of Consciousness

Another core feature of spirit mediumship traditions is their association with altered states of consciousness. To illustrate the widespread nature of this connection, Erika Bourguignon (2007) conducted a cross-cultural survey of 488 societies and determined that 90% of her sample societies utilised some form of institutionalised altered states of consciousness (439 societies), and that of these societies 70% associated altered states of consciousness with the belief that the body can be possessed temporarily by an external spiritual being. Altered states of consciousness, often termed "trance" in the context of the literature on spirit possession and mediumship traditions, appear to be necessary conditions for communication between the physical and spiritual worlds. However, mediumistic traditions employ many different types of altered states. Trance, for example, can refer to psychological states ranging from a light shift of attention away from the external world towards the inner world (most common in mental forms of mediumship), to a full dissociation of consciousness during which the medium's consciousness is completely displaced by another intelligence, as in trance mediumship, possession, and often physical mediumship as well (Klimo, 1987).

Neurophysiological research has only begun to scratch the surface in understanding the neural correlates of mediumistic states of consciousness, but the research that has been done so far already suggests some interesting correlations. To date, neurophysiological research indicates that mediumistic states of consciousness are distinct from psychopathological conditions, such as epilepsy, dissociative identity disorder, and schizophrenia (Hughes & Melville, 1990; Oohashi *et al.*, 2002), as well as from other non-pathological states of consciousness, such as meditation (Delorme *et al.*, 2013). EEG research suggests a predominance of *alpha*, *beta* and *theta* waves in trance channeling and possession states, and *gamma* frequencies in mental (clairvoyant) mediumship (see Hunter, 2014 for a more complete overview of these studies). Interesting research by Peres *et al.* (2012) with psychographers (automatic writers) in Brazil, reveals a deactivation of certain brain regions during the mediumistic state, perhaps suggestive of the so-called "filter theory of consciousness," whereby the brain acts as a receiver and filter for consciousness, rather than as a producer (Kelly *et al.*, 2009). The fascinating possibilities for research in this area are endless. Suffice to say at this juncture, however, that the research so far is indicative that "something" is going on when mediums enter their altered states of consciousness to allow spirits access to their bodies. There are detectable neurophysiological changes in brain function, which lends support to the subjective trance experiences reported by mediums – clearly more than just role-play or pretending.

Another interesting observation that the cross-cultural literature reveals is that in the mediumistic séance the altered states of the witnesses are very often just as important in establishing a dialogue with the spirits as the trance state of the medium. Indeed, it could be argued that the séance itself is a ritualized orchestration of consciousness: that the séance is specially designed to produce altered states in participants to enable this communication to take place. It is not uncommon, for example, for observers of Umbanda ceremonies to spontaneously fall into trance themselves while seemingly objectively observing Umbanda rituals. Similarly, Sidney Greenfield found in his study of Brazilian mediumistic healing that the altered state of the client was fundamental to the healing process:

> All displayed the same "body language," regardless of age, gender, or social status. They were perfectly calm, almost motionless unless instructed to move, with faces whose expressions can be described as placid, perhaps even serene. This demeanor did not change when they were stabbed, sliced, or punctured during a treatment procedure (Greenfield, 2008:89).

The realization of the centrality of the altered states of the clients, or sitters, during séances essentially breaks down our usually assumed model of objective observation. The séance is participatory – not a spectator event. To observe a séance is to participate in a séance. With this in mind, then, the subjective experiences of the sitter are just as important as those of the medium, and part of the reason that people attend séances in the first place – they want to have anomalous and extraordinary experiences.

At this juncture I will now turn to some of my own ethnographic observations of Spiritualist mediumship in the UK to illustrate the dissolution of objectivity during the séance and the role of altered states in the experience of the sitter. Indeed, I will go right back to my very first experience of mediumship in the field. It was as an undergraduate student, in the final year of my degree, that I first attended a séance as part of my dissertation research. The séance took place on a bright and snowy morning in January 2009, in a specially constructed wooden shed at the bottom of a neat suburban garden in Bristol, referred to as the Bristol Spirit Lodge.

There were three of us observing the séance, sitting in a circle with blankets on our laps to keep us warm, and the medium, a 49-year-old female nutritional therapist, sat in a high-backed chair in a curtained-off corner of the room known as the "cabinet," a hangover from the early Spiritualist séances of the Victorian era. Once we were all seated comfortably the circle leader switched on a red light, read a prayer to commence the proceedings, and the medium shut her eyes to begin her trance induction process. Her eyes remained tightly shut throughout the séance, her hands and legs made sudden seemingly uncontrolled jerky movements, and when distinctive spirit personalities eventually began to speak through her body, her entire physical and behavioral demeanor was transformed to match their characteristics.

Then, in the gloom of the red light, I saw small flashes of white and blue flickering in front of my eyes and in the darkness surrounding the medium in the cabinet. I thought that I saw the face of the entranced medium morph and transform to resemble someone else entirely. Her head occasionally seemed to disappear completely as she sat motionless in the darkened cabinet, and a glowing green grimacing face seemed to appear over the top of her own, and eerily slid down before disappearing. I made a mental note of this, but decided against mentioning it to the other sitters. It seemed too subjective, similar to a hallucination. It was only later, after the séance when we had a debrief over a cup of tea and some cake, that the others told me they had seen something similar – a strange validation of what I had assumed was a purely subjective experience.

The séance was, then, an eventful one, but not necessarily in the way I had expected it to be. The strange phenomena I observed (flashes of light, disappearing heads, and green faces), seemed to be as much a part of my own creation as anything else. Yes, the medium was entranced for the majority of the séance, while individual spirits talked to us through her body, but we as sitters also seemed to be in our own altered states, and the experiences we reported appeared to correlate with those documented in the Spiritualist literature. The flashes of light, for example, are often referred to as "spirit lights," and the strange luminous face that we all apparently perceived was an example of what Spiritualists call "overshadowing" or "transfiguration."

Perhaps, then, the weird and enigmatic phenomena documented in the Spiritualist literature from the Victorian period onwards are not so much the product of the medium alone (presumably as the skeptics and debunkers had initially assumed), but rather are best understood as more subtle phenomena arising from a combination of interacting factors affecting consciousness. We know, for example, of the effects of mindset and setting in the modulation of psychedelic experiences – a religious setting, for instance, may lead to a more 'spiritual' experience while under the influence of a psychedelic substance, just as a positive mindset can lead to a more positive trip and a negative mindset to a bad trip (Sessa, 2008). So, it is not inconceivable to imagine the séance as providing the set and setting required to modulate the altered states of mediums and sitters towards spiritual experiences. We also know that music and low-level lighting are effective tools for the induction of altered states of consciousness, and are employed in a wide variety of magico-religious and shamanistic contexts across the globe for just this purpose (Noll, 1985). Altered states of consciousness, then, appear to be fundamental to mediumship traditions – both for the medium and the sitter, and an appreciation of their phenomenology can shed new light on the beliefs and practices of the Spiritualist movement. The belief in spirits, spirit lights, and transfiguration, which may at first seem irrational from a materialistic scientific perspective, make much more sense once they have been experienced.

Conclusions

An awareness of the cross-cultural context can be revealing of dimensions of Western mediumship traditions that are often neglected in the scholarly discourse. This neglect is surprising given the vast anthropological literature on non-Western mediumship traditions and the care and detail that has gone into describing such practices. The discourse on mediumship in the Western context has been bound up with cultural associations of fraud and trickery that are largely the legacy of Victorian and Edwardian debunkers, but are also informed by the skepticism of the popular contemporary New Atheist movement (Dawkins, 2006), and Western academia's preferred materialist metaphysics (Sheldrake, 2012). What if we reframed our analysis of Spiritualist mediumship in terms that ethnographers have applied to Non-Western traditions? If so, we could begin to ask different questions. For example, questions about what mediumship does socially and psychologically, how the body is used during mediumistic performances to indicate the presence of discarnate spirits, or about the phenomenology of trance and other mediumistic altered states of consciousness. These are questions that have been asked of spirit possession cults across the globe, but rarely have they been asked of Western mediumship traditions. Perhaps it is time for a fresh look.

Furthermore, an awareness of the cross-cultural context can offer alternative modes of interpretation and understanding. Performance, for instance, does not necessarily equate to fraudulence. With this in mind, perhaps we could begin to rethink the physical mediumship séances of the Victorian era (as well as those of our own era). For example, perhaps performance is a part of the process of manifesting spiritual beings. Finally, an awareness of the cross-cultural context can lead us to question our own ontological assumptions. The tendency of Western scholarship to strive for objectivity, for example, is challenged by mediumistic séances, where participation is key and the observer is just as likely to be in an altered state of consciousness as the medium. What is needed, then, is an engaged participatory approach to further our research in this intriguing area, to attempt, in the words of the late Edith Turner (1993: 11), to learn to "see what the Natives see."

MAGIC, SCIENCE AND RELIGION:
A CONVERSATION WITH EUGENE BURGER

Jack Hunter: In addition to performing and writing about stage magic, you have stated that the study of religion is one of your main interests, and you have taught college courses on comparative religion. What is it about magic and religion that interests you?

Eugene Burger: First, I believe there was a time when magic, religion and science were not seen as separate areas, as they are today. My friend, Dr. Ricardo Rosenkranz says that magic and medicine share a common DNA. The same is true with magic and religion. There was a time when they were not seen as completely separate activities. What appeals to me about them? It is definitely the sense of Mystery that each brings to us. Magic and religion both point us to the capital "M" Mystery of life.

Jack Hunter: When you use the term 'magic' are you referring specifically to stage magic, or are you referring to traditional beliefs? Do you see a connection between stage magic and traditional magical beliefs?

Eugene Burger: I am referring to theatrical magic primarily rather than what I will call (for lack of a better phrase) ceremonial magic. But I believe ceremonial magic stands behind stage or theatrical magic. Put another way, stage magic points to ceremonial magic for part of its meaning. You might find it interesting that I would follow my friend Bob Neale who believes that behind both ceremonial and theatrical magic is what he calls "life magic." Bob gives two examples of life magic. First, imagine the baby begins crying at 5 am in the morning. What do you do? Well, you pick up the baby and hold it and say, "It's all right." But, honestly, it isn't all right! It is 5 in the morning and you have to go to work and the baby is crying! But you say, "It's all right," and eventually the baby quiets down. Metaphorically, we might say that the magic words have worked; they have been successful. Second, Bob worked with dying patients during his last years in the academic world, teaching Psychiatry and Religion at Union Theological Seminary in New York City. With many dying patients, who might be afraid, or even barely conscious, what do we do? We take their hand and say, "It's all right." Again, this is life magic – using the word or touch to achieve real world ends.

Jack Hunter: So, would I be right in saying that your view on ceremonial magic, and presumably also religion, is that it serves an essentially psychological function in allowing people to think that "It's All Right" even when it isn't? Do you think this is a sufficient explanation, or could there be something more to it?

Eugene Burger: No, I do not think that magic or religion serve an "essentially psychological function." This may be part of what both do but it is surely not the entire story. Magic and religion also serve sociological functions (finding a group in which one feels safe and honoured, etc.) As I said, I think theatrical magic points us to the fact that we are living in the middle of an immense Mystery. I think this metaphorical or symbolic function is at the core of both magic and religion.

Jack Hunter: I agree. Psychological and sociological functions are almost certainly factors, but are not complete explanations in themselves. There is something else going on, something more profound. I wonder whether we can explore this Mystery a little deeper. Could you describe how, in your opinion, theatrical magic points us towards the immense Mystery? What is it about performing illusions that reveals the Mystery?

Eugene Burger: Words are difficult here, speaking about mystery. My use of the word "points," of course, is a metaphor. I might have used other words or phrases such as "suggests" or "reminds us of." The use of such words is to communicate the idea that the little mystery of the magic trick can have some connection in the mind with the larger, capital "M" Mystery of the Universe. Part, but not all, of this larger Mystery can be expressed with questions such as, "Why is there something and not nothing? Why is there anything at all?" And, I might add, I do not believe this happens very often for audiences or for everyone in an audience. In the same way, being deeply moved by a painting or a play, deeply moved in our very existence, probably is also rare. If we are rushing through the art gallery, for example, we probably won't be deeply moved by too many paintings. All art seems to require an openness on our part if there is to be a deep engagement at all.

Jack Hunter: I wonder now whether we can talk a little about the smaller, but no less intriguing, mysteries of the so-called paranormal. What is your opinion on the phenomena labeled as "psi" by parapsychologists (including, for example, telepathy, psychokinesis, and so on)? Do you think there is evidence for these phenomena?

Eugene Burger: I am open to psi phenomena but I neither affirm nor deny it. I think that I am a skeptic who does not have the answers. So many so-called skeptics are, in my view, really debunkers. They have already come to a definite decision. Sometimes I think of them as being fundamentalists turned inside out.

Jack Hunter: Do you think that a knowledge of stage magic can help us to understand the nature of ostensible psi phenomena?

Eugene Burger: I'm not sure theatrical magic tells us much about the nature of ostensible psi phenomena. A good deal of theatrical magic, of course, seeks to create the illusion of various psi phenomena. Theatrical magic creates the illusion of telepathy or telekinesis and so I do think that a knowledge of theatrical magic is certainly of use to investigators if they are going to be successful at catching psi cheaters.

Jack Hunter: I have been thinking quite a lot, in the context of my research into trance mediumship practices, about the role of performance in mediumship, not in the sense of "mediumship is a performance therefore it is fraudulent," but in a more open-ended manner whereby performance is seen as a particular technique for the 'manifestation of spirits.' Similarly, there seems to be a performative aspect to traditional forms of shamanism, employing sleight of hand and so on, which were important factors in bringing about genuine cures for illnesses. The parapsychologist Kenneth Batcheldor found, in his experiments with table-tipping, that if he introduced 'artefacts' (fake levitations) early on in the experiment, 'genuine' levitations would be more likely to occur later on. He put this down to the idea that it is the 'instant belief' of the experimental participants that is necessary for the manifestation of psi, and that seeing apparently paranormal phenomena increased this instant belief, thus leading to stronger manifestations. It seems to me that there might be a deep connection between performance, belief and manifestations of psi phenomena.

Eugene Burger: And a connection with healing generally. What is the relation between one's belief state and being healed? Expectation is a powerful tool. In theatrical magic, I want to awaken your inner sense of expectation and use it to my advantage in deceiving you. And, yes, I think it is important that we do not begin our investigations with the assumption that all psi phenomena must be fraudulent. That, as I said earlier, is fundamentalism turned inside out. It has no place in the academy and yet this view seems deeply entrenched there. Why wouldn't experiencing the Shaking Tent, or some other shamanistic demonstration, lead one to have more trust in the shaman's pronouncements – Including pronouncements about one's health and healing? At the same time, I really believe that for many people in the group these demonstrations involving sleight-of-hand or other trickery were seen in a totally naturalistic way: they were seen as theatrical demonstrations to impress and teach the young of the group and not supernatural events at all. Many might even have reached the critical stage where they compared last year's Shaking Tent with this year's – and found this year's performance a bit lacking! We must not assume that everyone who witnessed them interpreted these demonstrations in the same way.

Biography

Eugene Burger was an American magician. He was born in 1939 and was based in Chicago, Illinois. He was reputed for his close-up skills and his work in mentalism and bizarre magic. He was also a philosopher and a historian of religion.

INTERVIEW WITH ROBERT DICKINS
FOR PSYCHEDELIC PRESS UK

Robert Dickins: Hi, Jack. Thank you very much for your contribution to *PsypressUK 2013 Vol.2*, and for agreeing to answer a few of our questions. In your two-part article, *Beyond Castaneda*, you look at the history of anthropological research with psychedelics. Obviously, the author Carlos Castaneda has been panned academically, while still retaining a popular following for his texts on Yaqui sorcery. What kind of impact do you think he has had on researchers working today?

Jack Hunter: Carlos Castaneda has undoubtedly had a huge impact on many researchers investigating the traditional use of psychedelic substances. Of course, there has been a great deal of controversy over Castaneda's books, with critics questioning the veracity of his claims, but, regardless of whether his books are works of fiction or accurate ethnographic description, they have inspired people to take an experiential approach to investigating the use of psychoactive substances. In many ways, Castaneda's books represent a turning point in anthropology: a movement towards a more reflexive ethnographic method that takes not only the experiences of informants seriously, but also the ethnographer's own experiences. It's interesting that you ask this question, as I recently discussed this matter with Dr. Alberto Groisman at Breaking Convention at the University of Greenwich (where I presented a version of my paper). Groisman queried the title of my paper ('Beyond Castaneda'), and told me that he wanted to start a campaign for the academic rehabilitation of Castaneda, and, to an extent, I agree with him. Castaneda's writing points towards an interesting ethnographic method that merges subjective and objective observations to present a participatory picture of a particular world-view.

Robert Dickins: Your e-book *Why People Believe in Spirits, Gods and Magic* has recently been published. Could you tell us a little bit about this work, and why you think it is a necessary time to examine people's belief in such discarnate entities?

Jack Hunter: *Why People Believe in Spirits, Gods and Magic* is basically a beginner's introduction to the anthropology of the supernatural. The introductory chapters give an overview of general anthropological theories of the supernatural from the nineteenth century to the present day, from the intellectualist theories of E.B. Tylor and J.G. Frazer, through the functionalist approaches of Emile Durkheim, A.R. Radcliffe-Brown and Bronislaw Malinowski, the cognitive theories of Stuart Guthrie and Pascal Boyer, to the more experientially oriented approaches of scholars like Edith Turner, David J. Hufford and Fiona Bowie. The chapters that follow on from it then look at specific phenomena, including Shamanism and Spirit Possession, Witchcraft and Magic, and Ghosts, Spirits, and Gods, looking at different ethnographic examples and the various anthropological theories developed to account for them. The final two chapters explore the paranormal experiences of ethnographers themselves while engaged in fieldwork, and the intersections between anthropology and parapsychology. Rather than presenting a unified explanation, the book aims to present a variety of different perspectives, all of which shed interesting light on these often-confusing topics. Through emphasising this kind of pluralistic approach, and above all taking people's experiences of the 'paranormal' seriously, the book seeks to foster an open-minded, and respectful, approach to the study of systems of supernatural belief. It is this respectful approach that I think is particularly important at this time.

Robert Dickins: Psychedelics and the paranormal appear to have a long, entwined history, especially in regard to the visions people purportedly have. Also, the visionary aspect usually appears to be quite culturally-contingent – depending on the period and culture one examines – to what extent, do you think, is the study of the perceived symbology examining either the culture in which they are perceived, or a universal phenomenon contingent to the experience itself?

Jack Hunter: This is an interesting question, and it's one that has been pondered by anthropologists, folklorists, and others, for many years. David J. Hufford's book *The Terror that Comes in the Night*

(1982) explored these themes in the context of the old-hag tradition of Newfoundland, and more widely in beliefs about nocturnal encounters with malicious entities during episodes of sleep paralysis around the world. Hufford came to the conclusion that the global spread of old-hag beliefs is best understood using what he called 'the experiential source hypothesis,' which suggests that certain supernatural beliefs arise from specific types of experience that occur cross-culturally. This conclusion ran counter to the usually accepted 'cultural source hypothesis' which holds that the cross-cultural similarities arise from a combination of cultural diffusion and cultural expectation on the behalf of the experiencer. I think the truth of the matter is more complicated than either the cultural source hypothesis or experiential source hypothesis alone. Cultural expectation undoubtedly has an influence on the way we interpret experiences, but I also feel that there are specific types of experience that suggest particular interpretations across the board. Many people report, for example, encounters with a feminine presence with *Salvia Divinorum* and Ayahuasca, and there is something about the sleep paralysis experience that frequently suggests a malicious presence.

Robert Dickins: You're currently working towards gaining your PhD. Can you tell us about what your research is concerned with? And perhaps offer any advice to people who may wish to conduct such research themselves?

Jack Hunter: The research for my PhD takes the form of ethnographic participant observation at a contemporary non-denominational spiritualist home-circle called the Bristol Spirit Lodge. The Lodge was established in 2006 specifically for the development of trance and physical mediumship, and I have been investigating the group since 2009. The main focus of my research is on personhood (exploring the way in which experiences with mediumship inform the way that members of the Lodge think about the nature of the person, consciousness and its relation to the body), performance (examining the way in which the body is used to experience and express the presence of non-physical spirits), and anomalous experience (exploring how anomalous experiences are interpreted and incorporated into the worldview of Lodge members). The best route for people who want to pursue such research in academia is to find a supervisor who is interested in similar topics and get in touch with them to discuss possibilities.

Robert Dickins: Finally, you run the journal *Paranthropology: Journal of Anthropological Approaches to the Paranormal*. In today's academic climate, what are the difficulties in concentrating on such an area? And do you find that wider academia is accepting of these approaches?

Jack Hunter: The paranormal might seem like a fringe subject area from the perspective of mainstream academia, but, for a great many people, paranormal experiences are important aspects of everyday life, and, as such, it is surely incumbent upon scholars to take the paranormal seriously. Indeed, there is a growing community of academics interested in taking the paranormal seriously and subjecting it to the same rigorous standards as any other area of academic inquiry. Along with well-established research societies like the Society for Psychical Research and the Association for the Scientific Study of Anomalous Phenomena (ASSAP) in the UK, and the Parapsychological Association, Parapsychology Foundation and Society for the Anthropology of Consciousness in the US, new groups such as Exploring the Extraordinary (based in York), and the Afterlife Research Centre (based at the University of Bristol) are making it easier for scholars interested in studying the paranormal to connect with one another. Paranthropology serves a similar purpose through providing a platform for researchers with overlapping interests to share ideas. There is, then, a large community of academics interested in these issues, and in developing different modes of investigating them.

IN AN OPEN-MINDED WAY:
AN INTERVIEW WITH DAVID METCALFE ON AN ETHNOGRAPHY OF ANOMALOUS PHENOMENA

David Metcalfe: What got you into all this?

Jack Hunter: I have always been interested in the paranormal, and when I went to university to study archaeology & anthropology I came to the realization that anthropological and, more specifically, ethnographic methodologies provide an ideal means to investigate the paranormal in an open-minded way.

David Metcalfe: How can the study of anomalous phenomena help our understanding of human experience?

Jack Hunter: I think the best answer to this question was given by the psychologist William James in the nineteenth century when he wrote that "no account of the universe in its totality can be final which leaves these other forms of consciousness quite disregarded." James stressed the fact that our understanding of reality will be limited, and hence fundamentally flawed, if we fail to take into account all aspects of existence – no matter how weird and unusual they are. To ignore these "anomalous" phenomena and experiences is to arbitrarily neglect a facet of the human condition and of reality as a whole.

David Metcalfe: Did being directly involved in learning mediumistic techniques change your perspective on the phenomenon?

Jack Hunter: Through participating in mediumship development sessions I was able to directly access personal experiences that would otherwise have gone unnoticed. The few experiences that I did have while developing in this way have enabled me to appreciate, to a greater extent, the fact there is an experiential reality (at the very least) underlying the beliefs and practices of contemporary mediums. This opened up new avenues of inquiry and new possibilities for study. It became clear to me that the experiential component is key to understanding the sort of group I am investigating, and that no account of the group would be complete without addressing the experiences of its members (again echoing William James).

David Metcalfe: How do you think your perspective would change without those experiences in the field?

Jack Hunter: If I hadn't had the strange experiences associated with the mediumship development experience, I doubt whether I would have been able to appreciate the experiential component of mediumship traditions.

David Metcalfe: In studying mediumship in the UK, have you been able to develop an understanding of the differences and similarities between spiritualist mediumship, and trance work in, say, Afro-Carribean traditions, North African traditions, Asian shamanism, etc.? What are some of those differences and similarities?

Jack Hunter: Not having conducted fieldwork with Afro-Cuban and African spirit mediums, or Asian shamans, I am not really in the position to definitively state that they are doing precisely the same thing as Euro-American spiritualist mediums. But, based on my own field research, and my reading of the ethnographic literature pertaining to spirit possession practices around the world, it seems to me that there are similar processes involved across the board. Chief amongst these are alterations of consciousness in the mediums/possessed and the use of bodily performance in the manifestation of spiritual beings. When I talk about performance I am not implying that what trance mediums do is necessarily fake, but rather that performance is a means by which non-physical entities can be expressed in the physical world. I have discussed this is greater detail in my MLitt dissertation *Talking With Spirits*.

David Metcalfe: Did you encounter the "trickster" phenomenon that George Hansen explores in his work?

Jack Hunter: I would say so. The trickster really rears its head when it comes to trying to pinpoint precisely what is going on in physical mediumship demonstrations. In the gloom of the séance room it isn't easy to tell what is going on: an air of uncertainty is generated. I have come to view this, however, as an essential component in the paranormal experience. As Hansen suggests, drawing on the ideas of Arnold Van Gennep and Victor Turner, séances are periods of liminality and anti-structure in which clear-cut distinctions break down. As an observer it becomes very difficult to distinguish between reality and what might be termed trickery: our usual modes of interpretation cease to be adequate. I think this, whether conscious or unconscious, is a deliberate aim of the séance – to develop a social situation in which such distinctions break down, which, in turn, may lead to alterations of consciousness in the participants and to "paranormal" experiences.

David Metcalfe: After studying the phenomenon of spirit possession in the field, do you have further insights into how/why lab work with anomalous phenomenon and abilities has been difficult?

Jack Hunter: This is an interesting question and brings to the fore, I believe, a really significant issue for paranormal research – the role of emotion and participation. When we look at first-hand accounts of paranormal experiences, including many of the experiences reported by ethnographers in the field, we see that such experiences, more often than not (though of course there are always going to be exceptions), occur during periods of emotional arousal. For instance, the classic example of a paranormal experience – the crisis apparition – is often associated with the intensely emotional period immediately preceding the death of a loved one. Poltergeist cases are usually associated with the emotional turbulence of puberty, or with individuals experiencing some form social liminality. The most elaborate paranormal experiences recorded by ethnographic anthropologists often take place at the climax of emotionally intense rituals (see for example the descriptions on pages 12 through 15 of the October 2010 issue of *Paranthropology*). Emotional intensity of one form or another, therefore, would appear to be a fairly recursive element of many different forms of paranormal experience. Now, when we come to look at the lab-based experiments of parapsychology, particularly after the development of J.B. Rhine's methodologies, we find none of this; in fact we find quite the opposite: a deliberate attempt to generate a sterile, controlled and unemotional environment in which to verify the existence of psi phenomena. When we look at it from this perspective it is remarkable that modern parapsychological experiments achieve positive results at all (this could perhaps be considered testament to the strength of psi phenomena: that psi can even make itself known in conditions entirely removed from the environment in which it naturally manifests). I'm not the first person to notice this by any stretch of the imagination. Ernesto de Martino, an Italian philosopher and historian of religion, described just this disconnect between the traditional, spontaneous, paranormal experience and the phenomena produced in the laboratory when he wrote in 1968 that "in the laboratory, the drama of the dying man who appears... to a relative or friend, is reduced to an oft repeated experiment – one that tries to transmit to the mind of a subject the image of a playing card, chosen at random," this, he suggests, represents "an almost complete reduction of the historical stimulus that is at work in the purely spontaneous occurrence of such phenomena." In other words; the drama of real life is ignored in the laboratory experiment. This is where ethnographic approaches are able to shed light on the paranormal, through documenting its occurrence in the midst of the social drama, which allows it to manifest in its most elaborate forms.

David Metcalfe: How has working with the Paranthropology journal changed your perspective on the field of anomaly studies?

Jack Hunter: Paranthropology was set up as a means to encourage greater, and more open, dialogue amongst anthropologists on issues of the paranormal. Many anthropologists have encountered "anomalous phenomena" in the field but have been unable to express their experiences in the professional academic journals for fear of ridicule. A field anthropologist recently told me that university colleagues had warned him against publishing an article on seemingly paranormal phenomena because it was "threatening" to the "basis of scientific rationalism." Paranthropology aims to provide a platform for anthropologists to discuss these issues openly. It also aims to develop an interdisciplinary dialogue between anthropology and other disciplines including folklore and parapsychology so that a more holistic understanding of the paranormal can be developed. Working on the journal has proven to me that *interdisciplinarity* is the route towards gaining an understanding of the anomalous.

David Metcalfe: Do you have any other projects you are working on in the field?

Jack Hunter: I am involved in a group – the Afterlife Research Centre, based at the University of Bristol – that aims to promote ethnographic approaches to the study of the afterlife through a method that we have termed "cognitive empathetic engagement" (see the website for a more details exploration of what we mean by this). Members of the group are researching afterlife beliefs, primarily in the context of mediumship traditions, in a variety of different cultural settings. We have organized a conference at the University of Bristol and are aiming to publish a book on the ethnography of spirit mediumship.

INTERVIEW WITH SHARON ANN ROWLAND
FOR ODDITIES NEWSLETTER

Sharon Rowland: In your own words, what do you see as the main difference between an Anthropologist and a Para-anthropologist (or Paranthropologist)?

Jack Hunter: In essence, there is no difference between an anthropologist and a paranthropologist. As I see it, paranthropology is basically an anthropological approach to the paranormal, employing the methodologies and techniques of social anthropology in the study of paranormal beliefs and experiences. Some of these key methods include the use of participant observation as a means to investigate human social and cultural life in the field as it is lived and experienced by those who are native to it, and cross-cultural comparison as a means to explore broader aspects of human life beyond the confines of a particular culture. Where paranthropology might differ, however, is in its initial assumptions about the nature of paranormal/supernatural beliefs and experiences. While the dominant approach to such beliefs has tended towards the position that paranormal phenomena (such as telepathy, psychokinesis, out-of-body experiences and so on), do not exist, and that experiences associated with spirit possession, witchcraft and shamanism are essentially illusory, paranthropology begins its investigation from the perspective of those who believe (that is the culture under investigation) and proceeds from there. This approach is influenced by the writings of anthropologist Edith Turner, who has called for anthropologists to 'learn to see what the native sees' in order to develop a fuller appreciation of the role of such paranormal experiences and beliefs in everyday life. Paranthropology can also be seen as an offshoot of what Charles Laughlin calls 'Transpersonal Anthropology,' being the anthropology of transpersonal experience. For Laughlin the transpersonal anthropologist must be able to experience, as far as is reasonably possible, the kinds of experience that are important to the culture under investigation, and this means getting involved in a particular culture's ritual activities.

Sharon Rowland: Did you begin life as a sceptical person (prior to university)? If so, how and when did your belief system open up to other (unknown/untested) possibilities?

Jack Hunter: I have always been fascinated by the paranormal, but have gone through many different phases in my thinking about these issues. When I was much younger I remember priding myself on being an atheist, but now my position would probably best be defined as agnostic. I have had a few experiences (not particularly dramatic ones) that have opened me up to the possibility of a far weirder reality than the standard materialist models usually imply. Experiences with psychedelics, in hypnagogic and hypnopompic states, and, during fieldwork in a spiritualist home-circle, all seem to have given me tantalising glimpses of this underlying weirdness.

Sharon Rowland: Would you please share with my readers an experience you have had in the field? One that has changed the way you think and/ or feel about our world.

Jack Hunter: One of the strangest experiences I've had while in the field (my fieldwork looks at a contemporary trance and physical mediumship circle in Bristol), occurred when one of the mediums wasn't able to attend. It was decided that those of us who were there would sit for an open development session whereby spirits would be invited to make themselves known to the group, in whatever way, as we sat in quiet meditation. As I sat there meditating I felt my heart rate increase, and a tingling sensation in my hands. I felt myself sort of sliding away from my body, and could feel my left hand beginning to move. I was able to observe the movement of my hand, but from a slight distance behind my body, and at the furthest distance from my body I heard the circle leader announce that she felt a presence with me. This freaked me out, so I snapped myself out of my semi-trance state. It took me a few minutes to compose myself before I tried the meditation again. I relaxed, felt my heart rate increase and felt my left arm shaking erratically before gradually stopping. It was a weird feeling, but it gave me an interesting perspective on the experiences of those developing trance mediumship: the strange feeling of detachment and of 'something else' controlling the body. This convinced me that, at the very least, there is an experiential reality to spirit mediumship that deserves further investigation. I have also experienced a couple of instances of apparently subjective hallucinations being observed by multiple people during séances, which, again, seems to suggest that something more than simple misperception and illusion is going on.

Sharon Rowland: Some inside the scientific community would label Paranthropology as a pseudoscience, something to be dismissed due to a lack of evidence/results etc. Have you ever felt pressure to discontinue your research into this fascinating area?

Jack Hunter: As I have already said, I don't consider paranthropology to be substantially any different from anthropology, except (perhaps) for its unwillingness to take the dominant materialist perspective as the benchmark against which to judge paranormal beliefs and experiences. I wouldn't consider this to be a pseudoscientific perspective. As a discipline, anthropology is concerned with understanding and interpreting human life as it is experienced by real-life people. The truth of the matter is that, for a great many people, the paranormal plays a central part in everyday life. A paranthropological approach attempts to understand this social reality from a perspective that does not immediately assume that such experiences and beliefs are delusional or illusory. Like any other phenomenon (physical or social), the paranormal can be investigated scientifically in a number of different ways, including experientially.

Sharon Rowland: Has there been a particular academic, friend, author, family member and/or mentor that has influenced your Anthropological career toward the study of the paranormal?

Jack Hunter: I have been influenced by many different thinkers and researchers whose approaches have sought to be inclusive and respectful of unusual experiences. The work of Edith Turner has been particularly influential, as have the writings of earlier pioneers in the anthropological investigation of the paranormal, such as the nineteenth century folklorist Andrew Lang. Joseph K. Long, the editor of the book *Extrasensory Ecology: Parapsychology and Anthropology*, has also been an influence, as has Charles D. Laughlin's 'transpersonal anthropology.' In many ways I would consider the Paranthropology project as an extension of the work these anthropologists did in the 1970s. Other researchers [whom] I hold in high regard include my supervisor Dr. Fiona Bowie, who has been very supportive of this exploratory approach, and Dr. David Luke, whose concept of 'first-person parapsychology' I find very appealing. There are a great many others as well, many of whom are on the editorial board of the Paranthropology journal.

Sharon Rowland: Professor William A. Tiller, Ph.D. states that 'Psychoenergetic Science' involves the expansion of traditional science to include human consciousness and human intention as capable of significantly affecting both the properties of materials (non-living and living) and what we call 'physical reality.' Are you a fan of the Professor and his beliefs?

Jack Hunter: If I'm honest, I'm not familiar with Prof. Tiller's work, but I would certainly agree that in order to progress, science will – at one point or another – have to face up to the realities of human consciousness and intention as *active processes* in nature.

Sharon Rowland: And lastly, if you had the opportunity to share an irrational truth with the world, what would it be? And where did you learn it?

Jack Hunter: Weird things *do* happen.

INTERVIEW WITH ALEX TSAKIRIS
FOR SKEPTIKO

Alex Tsakiris: Today we welcome Jack Hunter to *Skeptiko*. Jack is a doctoral candidate in the Department of Archaeology and Anthropology at the University of Bristol in the UK. He's the author of a very, very interesting book called *Talking With The Spirits*, and you may know him from through his publication, his online journal, that he's done for several years now, which is called *Paranthropology*. Jack, it's been very interesting diving into your work. I've kind of heard about you for a couple years and I always thought it was such great, great work that you're doing, and I'm certainly happy to have you on *Skeptiko*. So, thanks for joining me.

Jack Hunter: Thank you very much.

Alex Tsakiris: You know, as we were just chatting about really briefly there, what I thought we might do is start with some of the basics. First off, tell us a little bit more about your background, about your PhD work there at Bristol, and your work in the Department of Archaeology and Anthropology, and then certainly some background on this very groundbreaking, brave-to-publish journal that you have – *Paranthropology*. So, do you want to kind of kick us off with some background stuff?

Jack Hunter: Yeah, OK, so I first really became active in this kind of paranormal stuff when I finished my first university degree at the University of Bristol. As my dissertation for that degree I wrote about a group of spirit mediums in Bristol and really became interested in the kinds of experiences they were having. Then, once I had finished my degree, I kind of wanted to carry on working with this group to delve into it a little deeper. So, I applied to do a PhD look into it further.

Fortunately, I was given the opportunity to do it, but it's all been self-funded. I haven't had any major grants from anthropology research funders; in fact most of my funding has come from Parapsychology research organisations. Then the paranthropology journal kind of came out of that. At the time my supervisor Fiona Bowie was setting up this group called the *Afterlife Research Centre*, based in Bristol, and the group was specifically concerned with thinking about the afterlife in the cross-cultural context. We were interested in looking at afterlife beliefs in different cultures, and there was quite a heavy emphasis on spirit-mediumship and shamanism. At [an] early meeting of the *Afterlife Research Center*, we started to talk about the need for a journal in the UK that dealt with these kinds of issues. I mean, in the U.S. there is the journal of the *Society for the Anthropology of Consciousness*, which deals with similar themes, but there's not much in the UK. So, I just thought I'd go ahead and do it.

Alex Tsakiris: Great… you know the other thing I wanted to kind of use as a starting point is for you to tell us about Anthropology… I guess we all know it as we kind of walk through the museum, and we say, "Oh, this is Anthropology, this is what anthropologists do." But, in talking to a couple of anthropologists, I get the sense that I'm not really connected with, I guess, the mindset, because I think there's a very cool, progressive… expansive mindset, at least amongst some anthropologists. I guess not all. But… what is it really about? What do you guys do? What is the fieldwork like? What is the science behind it? And what is the scientific status of it within the University? What do other people think about Anthropology?

Jack Hunter: OK, well, very basically Anthropology is the study of human beings, so I take that in quite a broad way. Obviously, all of my research into the paranormal and things like that comes under the banner of human life, because humans do these things regardless of whether they are real or not. So, for an anthropologist, studying human beings, there are specific ways that we can approach it. The chief methodology that anthropologists use is Ethnography, which is basically going into the field, living with people, and trying to immerse yourself in their life as deeply as possible, then writing it up. From this kind of ethnographic writing grander theories may be developed that can be applied more broadly to human cultures and societies in different contexts. That's kind of Anthropology in a nutshell. For me, though, my fieldwork has been based with this group of spirit-mediums in an urban context. So, you hear about anthropologists going off to Africa or the Middle East, or anywhere in the world basically, but you can also do Anthropology at home, and that's kind of what I've done. One of the interesting things about spirit mediumship is that Anthropology has had a really long history of investigating it, going right back to the very early days of the discipline, but it's always been in far-off distant lands, and actually very little research has been done on spirit-mediums at home, within a Western context. It's almost as though Anthropology hasn't really wanted to face up to the fact that these things aren't just *out there* – they're also at home as well. So, my research has tried to do that a little bit.

Alex Tsakiris: How does that sit with the rest of the college there? The rest of the disciplines? I mean, how do they view Anthropology? Kind of like these quirky guys who are OK as long as they stay out there with the aborigines and the others… but what is it like? Especially when you bring it back home like that.

Jack Hunter: Well… I haven't had any negative experiences with it… in terms of my involvement in the department; I'm not really there very often. I live in Wales, which is quite a ways away from Bristol.

Alex Tsakiris: But I do sense, and again I'm just kind of wading into the waters here so I might be totally off base, but… some of the stuff that comes through from even more mainstream Anthropology does seem to kind of bump up against some sacred cows; just in terms of experience for example. In one of your essays that I found, you mention "taking experience seriously: What are the consequences?" It's one of those little parts of this whole thing that on one hand seems so basic. I think… if you just asked the man on the street this kind of deep philosophy of science kinda question that we really have to wrestle with, I think people would just be stunned. What do you mean we have to take experience seriously? Of course we take experience seriously!

Jack Hunter: Yeah, well what I mean by taking experience seriously is in Anthropology: anthropologists going out into the field always come across people who have completely disparate kinds of experiences to what the anthropologist is used to, and anthropologists have traditionally written about these experiences, but in a kind of distanced, and often dismissive way. So, for instance, *experiences* of spirit mediumship (as distinct from practices), might be mentioned, but they certainly won't be delved into. It's not like they want to find out what these experiences actually *are*, because this goes against the remit of what anthropologists do. They can see that people do have experiences that are unusual, for instance, but they're not genuinely willing to take that extra step and analyze the experience in itself – to take a deep phenomenological approach to experience. That's something I'm particularly interested in, because when you do come across these strange experiences in mediumship, and all the kinds of shamanism and out-of-body experiences and so on, those experiences seem to suggest something that the dominant worldview of our own academic culture is dismissive of, and actively kind-of ignores. So yeah, I think taking those experiences seriously is an important step for Anthropology to take.

Alex Tsakiris: It's a huge step because really when you talk about our culture, you're talking about *science-as-we-know-it*. You're talking about the established scientific paradigm that is pervasive throughout every University, and that says we should not take these experiences seriously, particularly when they go into these areas that you're talking about, which contradict this idea of consciousness being this product of the brain that we can measure very precisely and all the rest of that. I guess what I'm saying is, it seems to me Anthropology is open in some ways because, just being progressive in nature, it's kind of moved away from that outdated idea that we can all look at, and say "Gee, of course, we have to be more accepting of other cultures." We've seen that throughout history, the whole cultural bias that we can place in terms of saying "The Primitives" – these "primitive" people, with "primitive" ideas. I think Anthropology is a discipline that's helped us rise above that and see in a more culturally inclusive way that we can't do that, and I think your work is just a natural extension of that. That's what I get the sense of, that Anthropology is in a unique position to be more receptive to jumping the chasm and saying "well, if I'm taking these other experiences of their culture, of their society seriously, well then of course I should consider taking these paranormal experiences seriously," at least from an experiential basis; from the fact they said they've had it. Am I wrong there? Is Anthropology maybe in a better position to explore some of these anomalies than, let's say, neuroscience is, because they're not totally wed to this idea that mind-equals-brain?

Jack Hunter: Yeah, I really think that is the case. Anthropology, because of its very nature as a discipline that's involved with real-life human beings who have real-life experiences, *has to be* open to those aspects of other peoples' whole worldview. There's no way we can escape from having to deal with it, which is actually what anthropologists have tended to try and do – to not worry about what the implications of those kinds of experiences really are. So yeah, I think that my work is really an extension of that idea – towards taking these experiences that people have seriously and not dismissing them.

Alex Tsakiris: Tell us some more about your work specifically – your fieldwork with your mediumship development group there in the UK, because I think people will find it fascinating – the actual nuts-and-bolts, and what you've discovered, and some of the experiences you've shared in doing that work.

Jack Hunter: Well, the group I've been working with was founded, I think, in about 2006 by a lady who had been invited to attend a physical mediumship séance, which involves ectoplasm and all those kinds of things – floating objects and stuff, and she basically had her mind blown by the experience. When she got home she decided that she wanted to delve into this a little bit deeper, and try to find out what exactly it was that she experienced in the séance room. To do this she decided she would set up her own spirit lodge, and invite people in who would go on to develop as mediums. She basically wanted to take things into her own hands and develop the mediums herself from scratch, and record all of her experiences and the experiences of the developing mediums along the way. So, when I came to write my undergraduate dissertation I was interested in trying to work out the reason why so many people believe in spirits, just out of my own interest, and I wanted to find some way of exploring that idea through Ethnography. I had visited a few spiritualist churches and things like that, but I wasn't able to really get the kind of deep participation I wanted to get into there. I don't know why that is, I think it might be because these Spiritualist churches have got a constantly fluctuating attendance: if I didn't turn up the next day it didn't really matter because that's just what people do in those kinds of churches. So, I found this group, which just happened to be, by some sort of weird synchronicity, about a twenty-minute walk down the road from where I was living at the time. They had this interesting website and a blog that was full of all of these accounts of weird things that they'd seen, and these communications from their "spirit teams." I thought this seemed like the perfect opportunity to talk to people who actually communicate with spirits on a regular basis. So, I went along and it was very interesting (laughing). The very first séance I went to was on a really cold winter's morning; I think it was in January, and I had to trek through the snow to get there. Instantly it broke down my preconceived ideas about what a séance is, because it was in the morning. I had assumed it would be at night, in the dark. We went out into the shed in their back garden; literally like a small wooden shed. Inside it was all done up with a circle on the floor, and a cabinet in the corner, and chairs all around the edge of the room. The medium came in and sat down in the cabinet and went into this kind of trance. Her body was twitching and all of these things. It was really amazing to see because I had never seen anything like it before. Then they switched the red lights on, and I saw these little flashes of light and things like that, which, at the very least, made me think there are certain experiences you can have in these kinds of situations, regardless of what their ultimate ontological status is. So that was kind of my impetus to keep researching the group, because, from the very first séance I went to, I myself had had strange anomalous experiences.

Alex Tsakiris: Yeah, absolutely. So, as an anthropologist you're walking into this séance – what are you thinking and specifically what methodologies, what tools are you using, how are you thinking you're going to approach this as an anthropologist? And then, if you could – you said this sort of shattered your preconceived ideas about mediumship. It sounds like it might have shattered some of your preconceived [ideas] about reality and consciousness as well. How do you deal with that, given your discipline?

Jack Hunter: Well, for Anthropology in general and Ethnography in particular, the whole point is to go into the situation in as open-minded a position as you possibly can…

Alex Tsakiris: Right, but how do you do that? I mean, that's impossible, right? So, you're trying to hold to that, but how does that really play out?

Jack Hunter: I don't know if it is impossible…

Alex Tsakiris: When I say it's impossible, it's impossible because we know from the basics of psychology that we only see what we are conditioned to see. So, I mean, I think it's important – I'm not trying to challenge you on this – I think it's an important discipline and to be trained and try and pull back your biases like a police detective or something like that. But we can never totally distance ourselves from our past and our conditioning and all the rest. What happens when your whole world is turned upside down when you see something that's totally outside your belief system? You're the perfect guy to do it, because you've been trained to do it, but it still has to be somewhat of a trippy experience.

Jack Hunter: Yeah, it is a strange experience! The whole process is kind of like an active process. It's not like you go in there passive and you just let it all wash over you. If you see something that you might not believe (whatever that means), like seeing something levitate in the room and you don't believe it, you've got to actively try to kind of suppress your disbelief, and just go with the flow of what's happening. Then, with Ethnography, what you do at the end is you write it all up. Then you can kind of explore some of the ideas. You can explore the way the people who were involved in it experienced it, and also how you yourself experienced and understood it; but do that afterwards! When you're there, you should be as engaged as you possibly can and, yes, suspending your disbelief. That's definitely what I did anyway. My supervisor came up with this interesting methodology. She calls it "cognitive empathetic engagement." Basically, you have to read her papers to really get the full grounded picture of what she means, but it is this concerted effort to see the world as other people see it. So, not dismissing it, not ignoring these aspects of experience, and trying to understand how these kinds of experience then go on to influence the worldview of the people you're studying. I think, basically, that's what my research has done, or has tried to do overall.

Alex Tsakiris: Yeah, that's fascinating, and again, maybe this is a little bit off topic, but I don't think it is because I see that Dr. Julie Beischel has written a nice review of one of your books – so you're obviously familiar with her work. What is the feedback loop, if you will, like in these areas of Anthropology, Paranthropology – which we kind of have to break apart that word and talk about what we really mean, because "Para" is such a pejorative term sometimes – you attach it to anything and it immediately undervalues it – but let's leave that aside for a second. What is the feedback loop between these strange anomalous phenomena that you're encountering, and a more straightforward, scientific analysis of whether those phenomenon [sic] are "real," or some kind of illusion, or trick-of-the-brain that we hear about so much from our friends in anomalistic psychology – the reality of it or non-reality of it. I mean on one hand I hear you saying it doesn't really matter, it's what the people are experiencing or think they're experiencing, but on another level, *hell yes* it matters (laughing)...

Jack Hunter: It does matter, yeah. I think that is one of the strange things about my kind of perspective on it. Because, on the one hand, I am very interested in whether it's real or not (the ontological question), and that's where my interest in parapsychology comes into all of this. Then the other end of the spectrum is my kind of social science side that's more interested in how the people experience and incorporate these experiences into their lives and understanding of reality. In fact, I feel that both of these aspects are fundamentally interlinked, and ignoring one aspect will hinder our understanding of the other. One of the things I wanted to do with *Paranthropology*, the journal, was to make a space where both anthropologists and parapsychologists could come together and sort of share ideas on what's going on in these situations. There are anthropologists who have done parapsychological experiments in the field as well, which is quite an interesting area of overlap. An anthropologist named Patric Giesler, for instance, has done fascinating work with PK experiments in the field – in the Amazon – with some positive results as well. That kind of crossover is what I'm really interested in.

Alex Tsakiris: Indeed, and Jack, you have some really interesting thoughts in terms of how maybe parapsychology could move forward quicker, better even, by incorporating some of the sensibility that you've gained through this kind of anthropological approach to these phenomena. Do you want to expound on that?

Jack Hunter: Yeah. I think what I've written about previously is the way that parapsychological experiments take these experiences, which are usually spontaneous experiences, and parapsychologists have tried to reduce them down to phenomena that are really easy to investigate in the lab. Obviously, it's an important thing to do, because that's how you get solid proof of things, but, through looking at the social processes that are involved in these kinds of experiences, which is what anthropologists do, parapsychologists could for instance learn ways of making their experiments more true to real life. Does that make sense? Do you know what I mean?

Alex Tsakiris: Actually, I think there are two interesting ways to pull that apart. One is what I've heard from parapsychologists; in particular I remember Dean Radin saying this, which I thought was very appropriate – he's a super smart guy and I respect him a lot. He said look, one of the benefits you get in bringing it into the lab is understanding the nature of the phenomenon in terms of whether it's an innate quality, an innate ability in humans, or whether it is particular to certain human-beings or certain cultures and all the rest of that, and that's an important question, and the only way you can answer that is through that kind of approach. But, I think what you're pointing out, and I totally agree with, is that once you answer that question, you check that check-box, then you might want to circle back around and raise a couple of other questions. One is, does this ability manifest itself more in some people than in others? (And obviously we know it does), but particularly what I think you bring that I had never thought of, and I think is interesting to grind on is, is that it is more prevalent in certain cultures. Is it more prevalent in certain social situations with certain combinations of events, people, rituals, practices, all those things? I just think that's mind blowing! That opens it up in so many different ways. Am I in the right direction, and what are your thoughts on that specifically in terms of what might be the directions that folks might want to go to find this phenomenon manifesting itself more frequently, more measurably, all the rest of that stuff.

Jack Hunter: That's exactly what I'm talking about! When you look at the anthropological literature, all the ethnographic literature, and look at the kinds of experiences that people have reported to anthropologists in the field all over the world, you find these kinds of common characteristics. For instance, like you said, ritual is a very important process for people to go through in order to have these sorts of experiences, and I think that the parapsychological community has missed out on that. They could, for instance, use ritualized procedures in the laboratory. That's one example. Or, take the laboratory out to the rituals. The only problem is trying to maintain the kind of natural quality that a real ritual would have. Those are the kinds of areas where I think more research needs to be done. What is actually, parapsychologically speaking, going on in rituals? Is PK being used? All of those kinds of questions. But, the other useful thing about the Anthropological and Ethnographic approach is seeing the kind of social processes that give rise to paranormal experiences in the naturalistic setting. So what kinds of social, cultural and psychological prerequisites are there for the manifestation of [a] robust parapsychological phenomenon?

Alex Tsakiris: Fascinating. What are your intuitive hunches in terms of what we might find out if we go down those paths?

Jack Hunter: I think the obvious will be found (laughing): that rituals have evolved or developed over thousands of years because they are efficacious, or possibly efficacious. So, rituals, for instance divination, have developed because they do actually work. So, it'd be interesting to do parapsychological experiments on these traditional divination rituals to find out if it's the same kind of phenomenon that seems to be occurring in parapsychological experiments in the lab – to find out if it is psi they're tapping into. I think that's something an anthropologist named Michael Winkelman was getting at in an article he published, I think in 1982, in which he basically challenged anthropologists to take seriously the evidence from Parapsychology which certainly seems to suggest that there is some kind of psi process going on. To think about what that kind of data implies for anthropological theorizing on magic.

Alex Tsakiris: How about what that data implies for Parapsychology, or just science? We can't really go there because science totally ignores all this stuff. But, what does it mean in terms of what's really going on? I guess I could jump in two different directions. I could see some sort of Morphic Field, Rupert Sheldrake kind of thing, where repeating a pattern or repeating a ritual somehow creates some kind of synergy with an existing field that then makes something more possible. Or, I could see something on a more extended human consciousness perspective, there being other dimensions of consciousness that we can only even speculate about. Having some order in some reality that we have to tap into in some different ways to make these things happen. Do you care to even speculate in terms of what direction this could possibly take us?

Jack Hunter: That's a tough question that one. For me, personally, I think it's too early to really come up with any kind of solid, definitive model of what's going on. However, I do think that whatever it is that's going on, it's going to be way more complicated than we're even aware of at the moment. It seems as though, from the evidence of parapsychological experiments, there really is some sort of psi phenomenon, some kind of processes that human beings can tap into. But, as for the wider kind of cosmic scale, I really don't know – but it's probably going to be very weird!

Alex Tsakiris: "Probably going to be very weird" (laughing). I bet you're right. But, how do you balance the speaking to and within the existing paradigm, which we have to be kind of careful to honor and respect because it is the dominant paradigm. I don't have to, but you have to (laughing), because you're a senior PhD. You're trying to succeed in an academic world that has certain constructs. I mean, where do you draw the line? I noticed in one of your papers [that] you're agnostic regarding the mind-brain identity theory; mind-equals-brain as we refer to it. I don't believe for a second that you're agnostic about it, but I think you have to maintain that you're agnostic about it. I mean can we really go forward within the existing paradigm? Playing this little game over this little side game over here, hoping no one notices, but at the same time wanting everyone to notice. How do we play out that dynamic?

Jack Hunter: It's, again, another very tricky question. The paradigm that we've got at the moment, either needs to be completely overhauled and replaced, or it needs some kind of expansion; like an expansion pack added on to it, but I'm not sure how, with this current paradigm, we really can move on. There's going to have to be some kind of change. Either that or we all just give up researching this stuff (laughing), but I don't think that's going to happen.

Alex Tsakiris: I don't think it should happen...

Jack Hunter: No, it shouldn't happen. It's interesting actually, the next issue of *Paranthropology*, which should be coming out at the end of this month, has been guest-edited by Dr. Mark A. Schroll, and he's given the issue the title of "Hypotheses in Search of a Paradigm," and I think probably you'll find that issue particularly interesting. It's got lots of contributions from Stanley Krippner in it. But, yeah, I think that kind of sums up the situation at the moment. We've got all these hypotheses about psi and things like that, but there's no paradigm to kind of tie it all together. So yeah, we definitely need some kind of new paradigm I think, but what that new paradigm is, I don't know.

Alex Tsakiris: OK Jack, while we have you here, tell folks a little bit more about your book *Talking With The Spirits*, because, to be honest with you, I hadn't really discovered it until a couple days ago, so I haven't had a chance to read it. I've just dipped into it. I heard a really fascinating interview you gave about the book, though. It sounds really, really interesting. Tell folks a little bit about what they're going to find if they pick that up?

Jack Hunter: OK. The book is called *Talking with the Spirits: Ethnographies from Between the Worlds*. Basically, it's a cross-cultural survey of spirit mediumship and spirit possession practices around the world. It's got twelve different chapters from various different cultural contexts. So, the first chapter, for instance, is a more general overview on the role of skepticism in ethnography from Fiona Bowie; then we've got a few chapters on mediumship in the Western context – chapters on mediumship in Great Britain and Montreal in Canada. The book even includes a chapter on mediumship on the internet – cyber-psychics in online spaces. Then it goes on to discuss spirit-possession in East Africa, before heading off to Cuba and Brazil, where mediumship is massive, and then finally it goes over to Asia where Charles Emmons looks at spirit-mediums in Hong Kong, and another anthropologist Fabian Graham looked at mediumship in Singapore and Taiwan. So, it's got quite a lot of varied content in there, and I think one of the main aims of the book was to show that mediumship isn't just what we see in the Western context. There's a lot more to mediumship than ectoplasm and table-tipping and platform mediums. It's a really broad, near-universal, human phenomenon.

Alex Tsakiris: And what do you make of that diversity? I guess that gets right back to the huge question we were talking about, that we can't really fully penetrate, but just at the most basic level what's your biggest take away from the broad diversity of these experiences that all fit pretty nicely within the context of what we think about in terms of mediumship.

Jack Hunter: The broad take-away message, I think, is that there seems to be something going on (laughing). There's something that human beings are tapping into, or at least trying to tap into, which suggests, again, that there's *something* going on. I don't know what that something ultimately will be, but people have been doing these things as far back as you care to look, and as far abroad as you care to look as well; even right here, now, in our own back gardens and garden sheds. It's all there; it's all happening. Very interesting!

Alex Tsakiris: Just to underline a point that you made earlier about going in your own backyard, I think if there maybe is a blind-spot, traditionally, in Anthropology it's to see the "Others" as being somehow different than we are, and I think that's been a specific aim of your work to kind of take a different perspective. Is that correct?

Jack Hunter: Yeah, that's correct.

Alex Tsakiris: And I guess I'd just like to add one more thing to what you said. It's happening I guess, is one of the takeaways, and maybe another takeaway is anyone who attempts to pin it down and say, "It's this. It's happening because it's this. Because it's Satan, or through the Bible as described in verse, chapter, this," – that doesn't really fit. Or, people who want to say it's some kind of New Age consciousness-changing, UFO-related – not to put down UFOs – but it's very difficult to say it's this. It's difficult to say it's not this, but it's also difficult to say it is this, right?

Jack Hunter: Yes, it is. That's one of the reasons, again, why I think that anthropologists taking note of what's been going on in Parapsychology and the study of mediums for the last 130 years is so important. Because over and over again anthropologists come to the conclusion that spirit-mediumship either serves a purely social function, or it's a product of cognitive processes in the brain, or whatever, but none of these grand models that have been developed really – when you look at it and how it's played out in the field – actually explains what's going on. Parapsychology has taken that bold step of tackling the ontological questions about what's really real, and I think that's a particularly interesting avenue for anthropology to explore as well. Because it's got huge implications for the rest of science, and the dominant paradigm, as you said.

INTERVIEW WITH CHRISTOPHER LAURSEN
FOR THE EXTRAORDINARIUM

Christopher Laursen: Could you tell me a bit about "paranthropology" – what is it and how did it come about?

Jack Hunter: "Paranthropology" is essentially an anthropological approach to the study of paranormal beliefs, experiences and phenomena. It's not a particularly new approach, as anthropology has, since its inception in the nineteenth century, traditionally concerned itself with studying magic, ritual, religion, belief and the like – all of which intersect with the paranormal in one way or another. Where paranthropology (as I use the term) may differ from other more traditional approaches in the anthropology of religion, is in the fact that it doesn't preclude the possibility of genuine paranormal phenomena – in fact it openly explores the possibility that the beliefs and experiences of fieldwork informants might hint at something more than the usual anthropological models of social and psychological functionalism can account for. This approach draws inspiration from parapsychology, which critically examines experiences and phenomena that seem to go beyond the limits of standard psychological models, and the work of anthropologists whose writings have pushed at the boundaries of standard ethnographic theory – anthropologists such as Joseph K. Long, Edith Turner, Patric Giesler, Charles D. Laughlin and others. Paranthropology might also be considered a sub-set of transpersonal anthropology and the anthropology of consciousness, with their emphasis on experiencing culturally significant states of consciousness first-hand.

Christopher Laursen: How did "paranthropology" transform into *Paranthropology: Journal of Anthropological Approaches to the Paranormal* in 2010, and how has the journal been coming along since?

Jack Hunter: The journal developed as a platform for anthropologists (as well as scholars from others disciplines), who were interested in these issues to share and discuss ideas that might not normally get published. It had a huge amount of support from the outset. I was surprised to find that there are so many people in academia, with an interest in these subjects, who were simply waiting for an appropriate venue for publishing. One of the things I was most interested in doing with the journal was to provide a place for ethnographers to discuss their own anomalous experiences while engaged in fieldwork, as these experiences constitute a particularly interesting body of data. The journal also seeks to foster an open-minded interdisciplinary dialogue on these issues. So far it has been a very successful project, with each issue attracting over 1,000 reads.

Christopher Laursen: You've just recently returned from California where you co-organised a symposium on the anthropology of the paranormal. Could you tell me how that came about, who attended, and what you discussed?

Jack Hunter: At the tail-end of 2012, Jeff Kripal and David Hufford got in touch to ask whether I would be interested in helping them put together a private symposium at the Esalen Institute on the theme of anthropology and the paranormal – inspired by the topics covered in Paranthropology. The symposium was an offshoot of a long-running series of symposia hosted by Esalen's Centre for Theory and Research (CTR), called SURSEM (Survival Seminar), dealing with the question of whether consciousness might survive the death of the physical body. The epic anthology *Irreducible Mind*, edited by Edward F. Kelly *et al.*, was a product of the SURSEM group's meetings. David, Jeff and the SURSEM group came to the conclusion that anthropology is a promising discipline for moving forward in thinking about the paranormal in terms that are neither reductive nor dismissive. Naturally I wanted to be a part of this, and so was asked to help select and invite participants. Together we invited fifteen scholars from anthropology, sociology, religious studies and psychology, including anthropologists Paul Stoller, Edith Turner, Tanya Luhrmann, Fiona Bowie, Geoffrey Samuel, Susan Greenwood, Antonia Mills and Rafael Locke; sociologist Charles F. Emmons, folklorists David Hufford and Thomas E. Bullard; psychologists Stanley Krippner and Edward F. Kelly, and religious historians Jeffrey Kripal, Ann Taves, Gregory Shushan and Loriliai Biernacki. We were also joined by Esalen's founder Michael Murphy, and other members of the Esalen board. The symposium took place over four days in the Murphy House, perched on a cliff above the Pacific Ocean. The first day saw presentations from David Hufford on 'Modernity's Defences' against the supernatural, and Tanya Luhrmann on her current research comparing the experiences of voice hearers in Africa and the United States. Paul Stoller told of his experiences as an apprentice to a Songhay sorcerer, and Fiona Bowie presented a comparative study of afterlife narratives. The final session of the first day was from Jeff Kripal who spoke about the paranormal in the context of the study of religions. The second day kicked off with Ann Taves and her current research into Joseph Smith and the revelation of the book of Mormon. This was followed by Eddie Bullard's talk on ufology and its place amongst the sciences. Susan Greenwood then gave a paper on her experiences as a practitioner of magic and her experiences with 'magical consciousness,' and then I presented a brief historical overview of anthropology's engagement with the paranormal as an object of study. On the evening of the second day we sat around an open fire in Murphy House and told ghost stories. The third day opened with Antonia Mill's paper on the rebirth experiences of the Gitxsan and Witsuwit'en and her work with reincarnation researcher Ian Stevenson. Stanley Krippner then gave a particularly entertaining talk on his experiences investigating the Brazilian medium Amyr Amiden. Edith Turner's presentation followed this and explored the possibility of a self-organising force nudging the process of creation, and then Gregory Shushan gave an overview of his research comparing contemporary and ancient near-death experience accounts. After this Jeff Kripal, Ann Taves, Paul Stoller, Antonia Mills, Eddie Bullard and myself [sic] gave a community presentation about our symposium in the Huxley room. On the final day of the gathering, Rafael Locke and Edward F. Kelly gave an overview of parapsychology's main findings and explored the benefits of first-person approaches to the study of psi phenomena. Charles Emmons then presented a paper on 'Methodologies of the Mysterious' highlighting the broad spectrum of approaches to the study of anomalous phenomena. This was followed by Geoffrey Samuel's paper on the concept of the subtle body in the context of Tibetan Buddhism and Loriliai Biernacki's paper on Indian perspectives on the paranormal. On the evening of the last night we had a wonderful meal in Murphy House, watched the sun set over the Pacific, and then went down to the hot springs to relax under the stars. It was a wonderful experience.

Christopher Laursen: One of the things that has come out of the gathering at Esalen is a two-part podcast on *The Religious Studies Project* website, as well as the full interviews you did with participants. In the first part of the podcast, several of the speakers discuss the challenges of carrying paranormal studies into mainstream academia. Jeffrey Kripal and Ann Taves both say that one must adapt their passions for the paranormal into existing academic disciplines, more specifically, in fields that are actually hiring right now. Once you have the job and [have] proven yourself through the academic accomplishments you've made, then you can push forth on their passions as central to your research. (Of course, the humanities, in general, has a pretty tight job market, and entering a doctoral program, it can be hard to predict where things will be three to six years down the road.) Charles Emmons further suggested that the skills one gains in graduate school along with one's interest in the paranormal can be adapted to a variety of fields, not only academic studies, but perhaps palliative care in preparing people for death, near death experience research, cultural studies, and so forth. There certainly are more and more graduate students in the humanities exploring paranormal experiences now thanks to the new wave of humanities scholars over the past decade or so who have brought these topics further into mainstream academia. For me doing my doctoral studies, it's been a very exciting process that just seems to get stronger with each year. Being a graduate student yourself, and one who is very much making your own path in the field through paranthropology, I'm wondering what you thought of the responses you got to the relationship between academia and paranormal studies, and also in the time you have been studying the topic, how has it changed, opened up, or been challenging?

Jack Hunter: I wasn't too surprised by the cautious approach advised by the majority of participants. The paranormal (and even parapsychology) is still very much a taboo subject in academia, particularly when taken seriously. But there are ways of tackling the topic head on while still maintaining academic respectability, and there is a growing community of scholars who are doing it. This is one of the reasons anthropology is so well suited to an open-minded exploration of the paranormal – as a discipline it has been very open to taking alternative ways of conceiving of the world seriously. Religious Studies also serves as a useful discipline for exploring the paranormal: as Jeff Kripal stated in my interview with him, there is hardly an aspect of religion that can't be linked with the paranormal in some way. It's also useful to try to understand the paranormal as a component of a wider perspective, rather than as an isolated subject – the paranormal is, after all, complex, deeply embedded and multi-faceted. I also agree with Charlie Emmons about possible adaptations to other fields, such as palliative care. This has been one of the main focuses of David Hufford's work over the years. As for the job market, I hope things are changing, and that those of us who chose to take the paranormal seriously won't be treated unfairly when applying. The field seems to be flourishing at the moment, which I hope can be taken as a good omen for the future.

Christopher Laursen: Did you find the different disciplinary backgrounds of the speakers in tension with one another given their different approaches? Were these speakers pretty much already familiar with each other, or were there interdisciplinary breakthroughs evident in the process of discussions?

Jack Hunter: We had all circulated our papers before arriving at Esalen, so we were all pretty much aware of everyone's position from the outset. There were definitely differences in terms of the ways that things were approached between disciplines, though. One of the tensions that I noticed was the tendency to be distracted by definitions, which often seemed to halt our discussions in their tracks. For example, in a discussion about near-death experiences (NDEs) it is very easy to fall into the trap of constantly attempting to define the term without ever achieving any sort of consensus, which in itself prevents the discussion from making progress. This happened a couple of times over the course of the symposium, and could have something to do with tensions between those who generally adopt a textual approach, and those who are more concerned with lived experience in the field. This happened with a couple of other terms, including 'paranormal' and 'religion' (terms that have been debated for years without any definitive conclusions), which prevented us from digging deeper into the experiences themselves. But these were only really minor issues and didn't distract from the overall sense of excitement amongst the participants to be in such a wonderful place discussing such interesting stuff.

Christopher Laursen: At this point, what have you personally taken away from the gathering at Esalen? Any clues on where this meeting of wonderful thinkers may lead?

Jack Hunter: I thoroughly enjoyed the whole experience. Esalen provided an incredible setting for the meeting, and it was so wonderful to be able to meet up with such an exciting group of scholars. It was great to be able to meet people whose books and papers I had found so inspiring, useful and interesting. I felt like I was learning so much just listening to the discussions that took place during the daily sessions. I hope that the meeting will lead to the publication of a proceedings of some description, as the papers were all so interesting, and that we can all stay in touch and continue to work together on these subjects.

MISCELLANEOUS

My View: Ghosts
Paranormal Magazine, **April 2010.**

A brief perusal of the anthropological literature reveals a startling number of ghost stories from every corner of the globe. It is interesting to note, however, that different societies also have very different ways of conceiving of ghosts and their function. They also have different ways of dealing with them. In popular Chinese belief, for instance, ghosts require sustenance through offerings of food and paper money. For the Navajo of North America, ghosts visit the dying and guide them safely to the spirit world. Unlike in our own culture, the anthropologist Bronislaw Malinowski reported that the people of Kiriwina, Papua New Guinea, have no fear of the ghosts of the dead. It is clear, therefore, that the way we experience and understand ghosts is largely influenced by our cultural background.

Thanks to the Memorates
Paranormal Magazine, **September 2010.**

A peculiarity of the history of human thought is our apparent preoccupation with conceptions of unseen forces and invisible entities that would today be classed as supernatural, paranormal or even religious. Right across the world, from antiquity to the present day, human cultures have been built around metaphysical notions of an invisible world inhabited by spiritual beings, fairies, demons, ghosts and so on.

Life has been structured around paying homage to these entities, whether through offering sacrifices to gods and ancestral spirits, worshipping deities in ritualised ceremonies or through refusing to enter haunted houses. These activities serve to solidify ideas that are otherwise entirely abstract and invisible. The supernatural influences our behaviour, and our behaviour re-enforces the supernatural.

Now, one of the things I find so interesting about our species' widespread fascination with the supernatural is that despite its utter invisibility (for the most part) we nevertheless continue to be drawn to it. Even in our so-called 'modern secular society' the paranormal continues to play a significant role in our everyday lives. Our popular culture is, after all, riddled with references to the supernatural, in literature, films and other forms of art. Our everyday thoughts are often captivated by it.

Our enchantment can easily be seen when the supernatural arises in conversation: the discussion soon becomes a hotbed for the exchange of personal experience narratives, local ghost stories, and debate about the reality of the paranormal. We cannot help but be intrigued when we hear someone describe their encounter with divine beings; their abduction by extraterrestrial entities; or their having seen an apparition of a deceased loved one on the day they died, or soon after. We want to get involved in these stories, whether we believe them or not. We want to have our say.

For most of us, however, such experiences are infrequent, if they occur at all. So how does the notion of the existence of a supernatural order persist – on a broader socio-cultural scale than the personal – in the intervals between these relatively rare experiences?

In my opinion it is precisely through private conversation and the exchange of personal experience narratives that the supernatural continues to exert its influence on our thoughts. It is stories that keep the notion of the supernatural ticking over in the intervals between direct encounters. Traditions of folklore, urban legend and belief develop, which help to keep the experiences of others firmly embedded in our collective consciousness, even if we haven't had any such experiences ourselves.

Within the discipline of Folklore Studies, stories of events believed to be true are referred to as 'memorates.' Magazines such as this also help to perpetuate the idea of the supernatural on a broad scale, through allowing memorates to be shared and disseminated.

And here we find another interesting element of the supernatural's wider influence: those who have not had any encounters of their own, but who are nevertheless captivated by the *idea* of these experiences and their implications; those who, in the words of Fox Mulder of the *X-Files*, 'want to believe.' The experiences of others give us something to hold onto in a world that might otherwise seem devoid of mystery – a world that is geared towards financial gain and material possessions.

The idea that there is a supernatural order of reality may be taking the place in our minds that was once, in centuries past, occupied exclusively by religion. This fact has led many theorists to question the idea that the process known as 'secularisation' has really been occurring. If anything, paranormal beliefs appear to be more widespread than ever before, although the form these beliefs take has altered somewhat. Perhaps our society is not so secular after all?

EMFs and Spirit Mediumship: A Research Proposal
Seriously Strange Magazine, **Spring 2012.**

Since the nineteenth century, spirit mediumship has been associated with concepts of electricity and magnetism, and psychical research has a long tradition of trying to document and record anomalous electromagnetic radiations in the proximity of entranced mediums (Alvarado, 2006: 149-152). Indeed, anomalous electromagnetic effects have occasionally been recorded during attempts to document mediumship demonstrations with certain types of electromagnetic measuring equipment. Alvarado, for instance, describes the experiments of the French physician Hyppolyte Baraduc who, in 1893, used a delicately suspended needle to record movements effected when people put their hands near to the instrument. These movements, so Baraduc thought, were "tangible and recordable expressions of a superior force" (Alvarado, 2006: 149). Hereward Carrington describes experiments in which the physical medium Eusapia Palladino was able to discharge electroscopes at a distance, an observation that led Dr. Imoda to conclude that Palladino emitted "mediumistic rays" that could "become a conductor of electricity" (Carrington, 1919: 319). Albert von Schrenk Notzing (1920), in his investigations with the medium Eva C., noted "sensations of cold, heat and other radiations" and labelled them "thermoradiant" phenomena. He further suggested that such phenomena should be regarded "merely as preparatory and concomitant phenomena of one of the real manifestations." In a similar vein, Batcheldor (1984) noted that electrical and magnetic effects often accompanied the production of psychokinetic phenomena in sitter groups, but also suggested that these "may not necessarily be essential features of the PK process [...] but may themselves be created by PK" as epiphenomena. More recently, Wilson *et al.* (2010) used an 8-channel MESA measuring system in a séance-like situation to document fluctuations in environmental variables (infrared light, ultraviolet light, visible light, as well as changes in DC magnetic fields). The MESA system registered "notable changes in visible and infrared light, as well as changes in DC magnetic field strength," which coincided with observable PK phenomena during the session in which it was used (Wilson *et al.*, 2010: 630). In conclusion to their paper Wilson *et al.* suggest that the "specific interactions within the surrounding environment that may have led to the observed changes currently remain unclear, and any possible insight can only be guided by further research" (2010: 630). Bran (2011), using the PIP photography system, observed a distinct anomaly associated with her shamanic trance initiation procedure. During the initiation of her trance state, in which she called on her Upper World teacher to come closer to her, an unusual electromagnetic signature was seen to approach and merge with her own in the resulting PIP photographs. Could this be seen as evidence to suggest that unusual electromagnetic phenomena are associated with the induction of shamanic trance states? With the assistance of ASSAP, who have kindly provided us with two EMF meters, we intend to carry out some exploratory research into these possibilities with a Bristol based Spiritualist home-circle. Although the use of EMF measuring devices has been criticised on methodological and ethical grounds (Swale & Wood, 2009; Wood, 2009), it nevertheless remains true that such methods continue to be employed in both amateur paranormal and professional parapsychological investigations, and that the results of these preliminary studies demand further investigation. The experimental method will employ a "psi in process" approach and will be non-intrusive so as to maintain the ethnographic context, as though it were just a normal séance (cf. Giesler, 1984). This research would, therefore, be aimed at determining whether or not such effects can be independently documented with mediums in controlled, but normal, conditions, and at exploring whether there are correlations between apparently subjective trance experiences and physical/environmental fluctuations.

Beyond Culture Shock:
A Letter to the *Fortean Times*, 2012.

I was pleased to see Dr Edward Dutton's article 'Going Native' [FT289:44-49]. The paranormal experiences of anthropologists in the field are a particularly rich source of information on the nature of the anomalous, elucidating the social, cultural, physiological, psychological and emotional conditions that give rise to paranormal experiences.

Nevertheless, I feel the need to question Dr Dutton's use of the concept of 'culture shock' as a complete and satisfying explanation for the anomalous experiences recounted by Bronislaw Malinowski, E.E. Evans-Pritchard and Edith Turner. The problem lies in the fact that the experiences reported by these anthropologists matched very closely to the beliefs and experiences of the natives of the culture they were inhabiting. Evans-Pritchard, for example, described how his experience of an anomalous light in the Sudanese bush 'accorded well with Zande beliefs about witchcraft,' and that his informants immediately recognised the light as witchcraft substance when he described it to them. How, then, can the concept of 'culture shock' apply when these are precisely the kinds of experience reported by those who are native to that culture? Are they suffering from culture shock too?

I think Dr Dutton has missed the point in what these anthropologists were attempting to convey when they wrote about their anomalous field experiences. For Edith Turner, for example, to experience the extraction of a malignant spirit during a healing ceremony was to enter completely and deliberately into another culture, if only for a moment, to 'see what the Native sees,' without attempting to rationalise such experiences in terms of what our own culture deems acceptable. Turner asks us to take such experiences seriously, and to treat the belief systems of others with respect.

While I do not doubt that 'culture shock' might play a role in initiating the anomalous experiences of anthropologists (through psychophysiological arousal), I cannot accept it as a complete explanation because it ignores the embeddedness of such experiences within many of the world's cultures.

A Mind Altogether Stranger:
Microdose for *Metapsychosis Journal*, 2016.

Can we be certain that mind, or consciousness, is just an epiphenomenon of neurophysiological activity, that it is little more than a byproduct of brain function? How do we know that our current models are accurate explanations, even descriptions, of what consciousness *is*? The computer model of the mind and brain, with consciousness as software, is clearly outdated and oversimplified. The behaviorist assertion that consciousness does not exist is inaccurate. The history of science reveals a continuous succession of models and theories repeatedly replacing one another in light of new observations, discoveries, realizations and eventual paradigms of understanding.

My contribution to this debate, drawing from my own ethnographic observations, is to ask a simple question: *what if consciousness actually is something akin to the way it is experienced?* That is to say, perhaps taking heed of experience itself might tell us something about the nature of consciousness.

I am not simply referring to our everyday waking consciousness here, but am striving to be inclusive of the broadest range of conscious experiences – from the mundane to the sublime. Yes, for most of us, most of the time, consciousness is experienced as something that is fairly stable and continuous – a stream of mostly uninterrupted experience, usually characterized by intentional purpose as we steer through our lives. When we go to work, for example, we are usually clear and deliberate in our actions and experiences, we feel in control. But this narrow form of consciousness is not the only way we can experience our minds.

What about dreams, for example? In dreams consciousness is let loose. We can create whole worlds in our minds. Then there are mystical experiences, where consciousness is experienced as expansive and connected to all else in the universe (unity), and maybe even to God. What about astral travel and shamanic soul-journeys? Here consciousness is not confined to the physical body, but is something much more mobile, something capable of traveling through space and time to distant locales. Then there is spirit possession, and mediumship. Here consciousness is experienced not so much as a single bounded 'thing,' but rather as a conglomeration of minds, as made up of many different porous, interconnected, parts that coexist to form a whole. There are many more examples we could draw on to illustrate the fact that consciousness is often experienced in ways that are at odds with the dominant explanatory models of mind – time-slips, past-life experiences, precognition, psychedelic experiences, psychokinesis, near-death experiences, and so on.

Are we to assume, then, that such experiences tell us nothing at all about the nature of consciousness? *Must* we conclude that these experiences are purely illusory? I don't think that we do. Indeed, it seems, to my mind at least, that these experiences point towards an understanding of consciousness as something that is profoundly complex, deeply mysterious and altogether stranger than the dominant reductionist accounts seem to want to admit. We like things to be easily classifiable. We like simple explanations. But nature doesn't have to play by our rules – why would it?

BIBLIOGRAPHY

Alvarado, C.S. (2006). "Human Radiations: Concepts of Force in Mesmerism, Spiritualism and Psychical Research." *Journal of the Society for Psychical Research*, Vol. 70, No. 884, pp. 138-162.

Alvarado, C.S. (2011). 'Eusapia Palladino: An Autobiographical Essay.' *Journal of Scientific Exploration*, Vol. 25, No. 1, pp. 77-101.

Angoff, A. & Barth, D. (1974). *Parapsychology and Anthropology: Proceedings of an International Conference.* New York: Parapsychology Foundation.

Argyle, M. (1987). 'Innate and Cultural Aspects of Human Non-verbal Communication.' In. C. Blakemore & S. Greenfield (eds.) *Mindwaves: Thoughts on Intelligence, Identity and Consciousness.* Oxford: Basil Blackwell.

Ashby, R.J. (1972). *The Guidebook for the Study of Psychical Research.* London: Rider and Company.

Ashworth, P. (1996). 'Presuppose Nothing! The Suspension of Assumptions In Phenomenological Psychological Methodology.' *Journal of Phenomenological Psychology*, Vol. 27, No. 1, pp. 1-25.

Bargen, D. G. (1988). 'Spirit Possession in the Context of Dramatic Expression of Gender Conflict: the Aoi Episode of the Genji monogatari.' *Harvard Journal of Asiatic Studies*, Vol. 48, No. 1, pp. 95-130.

Barnard, A. (2000). *History and Theory in Anthropology.* Cambridge: Cambridge University Press.

Barrington, M.R. (2011). 'Archive No. 74: Researches With The Medium Eva C. (Marthe Beraud).' *The Paranormal Review*, Issue 54, pp. 3-6.

Bartlett, R. (2008). *The Natural and the Supernatural in the Middle Ages.* Cambridge: Cambridge University Press.

Batcheldor, K.J. (1984). 'Contributions to the Theory of PK Induction from Sitter-Group Work.' *Journal of the American Society for Psychical Research*, Vol. 78, pp. 105-122.

Bateson, G. & Bateson, M.C. (2005). *Angels Fear: Towards and Epistemology of the Sacred*. Cresskill: Hampton Press.

Beattie, J. (1977). 'Spirit Mediumship as Theatre.' *RAIN: Royal Anthropological Institute News*, No. 20, pp. 1-6.

Beischel, J., & Rock, A. J. (2009). 'Addressing the survival vs. psi debate through process-focused mediumship research.' *Journal of Parapsychology*, No. 73, pp. 71-90.

Beischel, J. (2014). 'Assisted After-Death Communication: A Self-Prescribed Treatment for Grief.' *Journal of Near-Death Studies*, Vol. 32, No. 3, pp. 161-165.

Bem, D. (2011). 'Feeling the Future: Experimental Evidence for Anomalous Retroactive Influences on Cognition and Affect.' *Journal of Personality and Social Psychology*, Vol. 100, pp. 407-425.

Bird-David, N. (1999). 'Animism Revisited: Personhood, Environment, and Rational Epistemology.' *Current Anthropology*, Vol. 40, Supplement, pp. 67-79.

Blackmore, S. (1992). *Beyond the Body: An Investigation into Out-of-the-Body Experiences*. Chicago: Academy of Chicago Publishers.

Blum, D. (2007). *Ghost Hunters: The Victorians and the Hunt for Proof of Life After Death*. London: Arrow Books.

Blackmore, S. (2005). *Consciousness: A Very Short Introduction*. Oxford: Oxford University Press.

Blum, D. (2007). *Ghost Hunters: The Victorians and the Hunt for Proof of Life after Death*. London: Arrow Books.

Boddy, J. (1988). 'Spirits and Selves in Northern Sudan: The Cultural Therapeutics of Possession and Trance.' *American Ethnologist*, Vol. 15, No. 1, pp. 4-27.

Bourguignon, E. Bellisari, A. & McCabe, S. (1983). 'Women, Possession Trance Cults, and the Extended Nutrient-Deficiency Hypothesis.' *American Anthropologist*, Vol. 85, No. 2, pp. 413-416.

Bourguignon, E. (2007). 'Spirit Possession.' In C. Casey & R.B. Edgerton (eds.) *A Companion to Psychological Anthropology*. Oxford: Blackwell Publishing.

Bowie, F. (2002). *The Anthropology of Religion*. Oxford: Blackwell Publishers.

Bowie, F. (2010). 'Methods for Studying the Paranormal (and Who Says What is Normal Anyway?)' *Paranthropology: Journal of Anthropological Approaches to the Paranormal*, Vol. 1, No. 1, pp. 4-6.

Bowie, F. (2013). 'Building Bridges, Dissolving Boundaries: Towards a Methodology for the Ethnographic Study of the Afterlife.' *Journal of the American Academy of Religion*, Vol. 81, No. 3, pp. 698-733.

Bowie, F. (2015). 'Miracles.' In M. Cardin (ed.) *Ghosts, Spirits and Psychics: The Paranormal from Alchemy to Zombies*. Santa Barbara: ABC-CLIO.

Bowker, J. (1973). *The Sense of God: Sociological, Anthropological and Psychological Approaches to the Origin of the Sense of God*. Oxford: Clarendon Press.

Bran, Z. (2011). 'Capturing Intention?: PIP Photography and Shamanic Intervention.' *Paranthropology: Journal of Anthropological Approaches to the Paranormal*, Vol. 2, No. 3, pp. 27-29.

Braude, A. (2001). *Radical Spirits: Spiritualism and Women's Rights in Nineteenth Century America*. Bloomington: University of Indiana Press.

Braude, S. (1997). *The Limits of Influence: Psychokinesis and the Philosophy of Science*. New York: University Press of America.

Braude, S.E. (2003). *Immortal Remains: The Evidence for Life After Death*. Oxford: Rowman & Littlefield.

Braude, S.E. (2007). *The Gold Leaf Lady and Other Parapsychological Investigations*. Chicago: University of Chicago Press.

Braude, S. (2010). 'Preliminary Investigation of a Spiritist Séance Group in Germany' [Lecture]. Available from: http://www.scientificexploration.org/talks/29th_annual/29th_annual_braude_investigation_spiritist_seance_germany.html [Accessed 18 November 2011]

Broughton, R. (1991). *Parapsychology: The Controversial Science*. London: Rider.

Brower, M. B. (2010). *Unruly Spirits: The Science of Psychic Phenomena in Modern France.* Urbana: University of Illinois Press.

Brown, D.E. (1991). *Human Universals.* Philadelphia: Temple University Press.

Bubandt, N. (2009). 'Interview with an Ancestor: Spirits as Informants and the Politics of Possession in North Maluku.' Ethnography, 10(3), 291-316.

Budden, A. (2003). 'Pathologizing Possession: An Essay on Mind, Self and Experience in Dissociation.' *Anthropology of Consciousness,* Vol. 14, No. 2, pp. 27-59.

Butler, T. & Butler, L. (2011). 'Stewart Alexander.' Available from: http://atransc.org/circle/stewart_alexander.htm [Accessed November 18th 2011]

Cameron, R. (2016). 'The Paranormal as an Unhelpful Concept in Psychotherapy and Counselling Research.' *European Journal of Psychotherapy and Counselling,* Vol. 18, No. 2, pp. 142-155.

Cardeña, E. (2014). 'Call for an Open, Informed Study of all Aspects of Consciousness.' *Frontiers in Human Neuroscience,* Vol. 8, No. 7.

Cardin, M. (2015). *Ghosts, Spirits and Psychics: The Paranormal from Alchemy to Zombies.* Santa Barbara: ABC-CLIO.

Carhart-Harris, R.L., Erritzoe, D., Williams, T., Stone, J.M., Reed, L.J., Colasanti, A., Tyacke, R.J., Leech, R., Malizia, A.L., Murphy, K., Hobden, P., Evans, J., Feilding, A., Wise, R.G. & Nutt, D. (2011). 'Neural Correlates of the Psychedelic State as Determined by fMRI Studies With Psilocybin.' *PNAS,* Vol. 109, No. 6, pp. 2138-2143.

Carrington, H. (1919). *Eusapia Palladino and Her Phenomena.* London: T. Werner Laurie.

Carter, C. (2012). 'Does Consciousness Depend on the Brain?' In D. Pinchbeck & K. Jordan (eds.) (2012). *Exploring the Edge Realms of Consciousness: Liminal Zones, Psychic Science, and the Hidden Dimensions of the Mind.* Berkeley: Evolver Editions. (pp. 331-343).

Castro, M., Burrows, R. & Wooffitt, R. (2014). 'The Paranormal is (Still) Normal: The Sociological Implications of a Survey of Paranormal Experiences in Great Britain.' *Sociological Research Online,* Vol. 19, No. 3, p. 16.

Caswell, J.M., Hunter, J. & Tessaro, L.W.E. (2014). 'Phenomenological Convergence Between Major Paradigms of Classic Parapsychology and

Cross-Cultural Practices: An Exploration of Paranthropology.' *Journal of Consciousness Exploration and Research*, Vol. 5, No. 5, pp. 467-482

Chalmers, D. (1995). 'Facing Up to the Problem of Consciousness.' *Journal of Consciousness Studies*, Vol. 2, No. 3, pp. 200-219.

Churchland, P.S. (1982). 'Mind-Brain Reduction: New Light From the Philosophy of Science.' *Neuroscience*, Vol. 7, No. 5, pp. 1041-1047.

Cohen, E. (2008). 'What is Spirit Possession? Defining, Comparing and Explaining Two Possession Forms.' *Ethos*, Vol. 73, No. 1.

Colborn, M. (2011). *Pluralism and the Mind: Consciousness, Worldviews, and the Limits of Science.* Exeter: Imprint Academic.

Colman, A.M. (2009). *Oxford Dictionary of Psychology.* Oxford: Oxford University Press.

Comte, A. (1976). 'The Positive Philosophy.' In K. Thompson & J. Tunstall (eds.) *Sociological Perspectives.* Harmondsworth: Penguin Books.

Crabtree, A. (1988). *Multiple Man: Explorations in Possession and Multiple Personality.* London: Grafton Books.

Csordas, T. (1990). 'Embodiment as a Paradigm for Anthropology.' *Ethos*, Vol. 18, No. 1, pp. 5-47.

Dawkins, R. (2006). *The God Delusion.* London: Transworld.

Dawson, A. (ed.) (2011). *Summoning the Spirits: Possession and Invocation in Contemporary Religion.* London: I.B. Tauris.

Delanoy, D.L. (2009). 'Parapsychology in a University Setting', in C.A. Roe, W. Kramer & L. Coly (eds.), *Utrecht II: Charting the future of parapsychology: Proceedings of an international conference held in Utrecht, The Netherlands, October 16-18, 2008.* pp. 289-304, Parapsychology Foundation, Inc., New York.

Delorme, A., Beischel. J., Michel, L., Boccuzzi, M., Radin, D., & Mills, P. J. (2013). 'Electrocortical activity associated with subjective communication with the deceased.' *Frontiers in Psychology*, Vol. 4, No. 834.

de Martino, E. (1975). *Magic: Primitive and Modern.* London: Tom Stacey.

Devereux, P. (1997). *The Long Trip: A Prehistory of Psychedelia.* London: Penguin Books.

Di Nucci, C. (2009). *Spirits in a Teacup: Questioning the Reality of Life and Death, Has Led One Housewife Along an Adventurous Path Towards Discovery*. Bristol: Bristol Spirit Lodge.

Di Nucci, C. & Hunter, J. (2009). *Charlie: Trance Communication & Spirit Teachings*. Bristol: Bristol Spirit Lodge.

Donovan, J. M. (2000). 'A Brazilian Challenge to Lewis's Explanation of Cult Mediumship.' *Journal of Contemporary Religion*, Vol. 15, No. 3, pp. 361-377.

Doyle, A.C. (2006). *The History of Spiritualism*. Teddington: The Echo Library.

Driesch, H. (1933). *Psychical Research*. London: G. Bell & Sons, Ltd.

Durkheim, E. (2008). *The Elementary Forms of the Religious Life*. Oxford: Oxford University Press.

Edwards, H. (1978). *The Mediumship of Jack Webber*. Guildford: The Harry Edwards Spiritual Healing Sanctuary.

Eliade, M. (1989). *Shamanism: Archaic Techniques of Ecstasy*. London: Arkana.

Emmons, C.F. (2000). 'On Becoming a Spirit Medium in a "Rational Society."' *Anthropology of Consciousness*, Vol. 12, No. 1-2, pp. 71-82.

Eriksen, T.H. (2001). *Small Places, Large Issues: An Introduction to Social and Cultural Anthropology*. London: Pluto Press.

Espirito Santo, D. (2014). 'Developing the Dead in Cuba: An Ethnographic Account of the Emergence of Spirits and Selves in Havana.' In J. Hunter & D. Luke (eds.) *Talking With the Spirits: Multidisciplinary Approaches to Spirit Mediumship*. Brisbane: Daily Grail Press.

Evans-Pritchard, E.E. (1965). *Theories of Primitive Religion*. Oxford: Clarendon Press.

Evans-Pritchard, E.E. (1976). *Witchcraft, Oracles and Magic Among the Azande*. Oxford: Oxford University Press.

Ferrari, F.M. (2014). *Ernesto de Martino on Religion: The Crisis and the Presence*. Abingdon: Routledge.

Firth, R. (1967). 'Ritual and Drama in Malay Spirit Mediumship.' *Comparative Studies in Society and History*, Vol. 9, No. 2, pp. 190-207.

Foley, K. (1985). 'The Dancer and the Danced: Trance Dance and Theatrical Performance in West Java.' *Asian Theatre Journal*, Vol. 2, No. 1, pp. 28-49.

Fort, C. (2008). *The Book of the Damned: The Complete Works of Charles Fort*. London: Tarcher.

Foy, R. (2007). *In Pursuit of Physical Mediumship*. London: Janus Publishing.

Frazer, J.G. (1993). *The Golden Bough*. London: Wordsworth Editions.

Freed, S. A. & Freed, R. S. (1964). 'Spirit Possession as Illness in a North Indian Village.' *Ethnology*, Vol. 3, No. 2, pp. 152-171.

Freud, S. & Breuer, J. (1974). *Studies on Hysteria*. Harmondsworth: Penguin Books Ltd.

Frijda, N.H. (1989). 'Aesthetic Emotions and Reality.' *American Psychologist*, pp. 1546-1547.

Gaskill, M. (2001). *Hellish Nell: Last of Britain's Witches*. London: Harper Collins.

Gauld, A. (1983). *Mediumship and Survival: A Century of Investigations*. London: Paladin.

Geley, G. (2006). *Clairvoyance and Materialisation: A Record of Experiments*. Whitefish: Kessinger Publishing.

Giesler, P.V. (1984). 'Parapsychological Anthropology: I. Multi-Method Approaches to the Study of Psi in the Field Setting.' *The Journal of the American Society for Psychical Research*, Vol. 78, No. 4, pp. 289-330.

Gilbert, H. (2010). 'A sociological perspective on 'becoming' a spirit medium in Britain.' *Rhine Online: Psi News Magazine*, No. 2, pp. 10-12.

Giles, L. L. (1987). 'Possession Cults on the Swahili Coast: A Re-Examination of Theories of Marginality.' *Africa: Journal of the International African Institute*, Vol. 57, No. 2, pp. 234-258.

Goffman, E. (1990). *The Presentation of Self in Everyday Life*. London: Penguin Books.

Gomm, R. (1975). 'Bargaining from Weakness: Spirit Possession on the South Kenya Coast.' *Man*, Vol. 10, No. 4, pp. 530-543.

Graham, F. (2011). 'Commentary on "Reflecting on Paranthropology."' *Paranthropology: Journal of Anthropological Approaches to the Paranormal*, Vol. 2, No. 3, pp. 20-21.

Graham, F. (2014). 'Vessels for the Gods: Tang-ki Spirit Mediumship in Taiwan and Singapore.' In J. Hunter & D. Luke (eds.) *Talking With the Spirits: Ethnographies from Between the Worlds*. Brisbane: Daily Grail.

Graham, R. (2017). *UFOs: Reframing the Debate*. Guildford: White Crow Books.

Greeley, A. (1975). *The Sociology of the Paranormal*. London: Sage.

Greenfield, S.M. (2008). *Spirits with Scalpels: The Culturalbiology of Religious Healing in Brazil*. Walnut Creek: Left Coast Press.

Greenwood, S. (2013). 'On Becoming and Owl: Magical Consciousness.' In G. Samuel & J. Johnston (eds.) *Religion and the Subtle Body in Asia and the West: Between Mind and Body*. Abingdon: Routledge.

Hageman, J.H., Peres, J.F.P., Moreira-Almeida, A., Caixeta, L., Wickramasekera II, I, & Krippner, S. (2010). 'The Neurobiology of Trance and Mediumship in Brazil.' In S. Krippner & H.L. Friedman (eds.) *Mysterious Minds: The Neurobiology of Psychics, Mediums and Other Extraordinary People*. Oxford: Praeger.

Hallowell, A.I. (2002) 'Ojibwa Ontology, Behaviour, and World View.' In G. Harvey (ed.) *Readings in Indigenous Religions*. London: Continuum.

Halloy, A. (2010) 'Comments on "The Mind Possessed: The Cognition of Spirit Possession in an Afro-Brazilian Religious Tradition" by Emma Cohen.' *Religion and Society: Advances in Research*, Vol. 1, pp. 164-176.

Hameroff, S. & Penrose, R. (1996). 'Orchestrated Re-duction of Quantum Coherence in Brain Micro-tubules: A Model for Consciousness.' *Mathematics and Computers in Simulation*, Vol. 40, pp. 453-480.

Hansen, G.P. (2001). *The Trickster and the Paranormal*. Bloomington: Xlibris.

Hansen, G.P. (2007, Nov 29). 'Marilyn Schlitz and Ian Stevenson: Embarrassed by Parapsychology', The Paranormal Trickster Blog, Viewed 19 November 2017, from http://paranormaltrickster.blogspot.com/2007/11/marilyn-schlitz-and-ian-stevenson.html.

Ianuzzo, G. (2009). 'Personal Reflections on Utrecht II: Discussion', in C.A. Roe, W. Kramer & L. Coly (eds.), *Utrecht II: Charting the future of parapsychology: Proceedings of an international conference held in Utrecht, The Netherlands, October 16-18, 2008.* p. 548, Parapsychology Foundation, Inc., New York.

Harner, M. (1990). *The Way of the Shaman.* San Francisco: Harper.

Harner, M. (2013). *Cave and Cosmos: Shamanic Encounters with Another Reality.* Berkeley: North Atlantic Books.

Hartley, R. (2007). *Helen Duncan: The Mystery Show Trial.* London: HPR Publishing Limited.

Harvey, G. (2005). *Animism: Respecting the Living World.* London: Hurst & Co.

Harvey, G. (2010). 'Animism Rather Than Shamanism: New Approaches to What Shaman's Do (For Other Animists).' In: Schmidt, Bettina & Huskinson, Lucy (eds.) *Spirit Possession and Trance: New Interdisciplinary Perspectives.* London: Continuum. pp. 14-34.

Haule, J.R. (2011). *Jung in the 21st Century, Vol. II: Synchronicity and Science.* London: Routledge.

Haynes, R. (1982). *The Society for Psychical Research: 1882-1982, A History.* London: MacDonald and Co.

Heath, P.R. (2000). 'The PK Zone: A Phenomenological Study.' *Journal of Parapsychology*, Vol. 64, pp. 53-72.

Holt, N.J., Simmonds-Moore, C., Luke, D. & French, C.C. (2012). *Anomalistic Psychology.* Basingstoke: Palgrave Macmillan.

Hufford, D.J. (1982). *The Terror That Comes in the Night: An Experience-Centred Study of Supernatural Assault Traditions.* Philadelphia: University of Pennsylvania Press.

Hughes, D.J. (1991). 'Blending with an Other: An analysis of Trance Channelling in the United States.' *Ethos*, Vol. 19, No. 2, pp. 161-184.

Hughes, D.J. & Melville, N.T. (1990). 'Changes in Brainwave Activity During Trance Channeling: A Pilot Study.' *Journal of Transpersonal Psychology*, Vol. 22, No. 2, pp. 175-189.

Hunter, J. (2009a). *Talking With the Spirits: An Experiential Exploration of Contemporary Trance and Physical Mediumship.* Unpublished undergraduate dissertation, University of Bristol.

Hunter, J. (2009b). 'The Issue of Fraud & Performance in Mediumship.' *PSI: Journal of Investigative Psychical Research*, Vol. 5, No. 2, pp. 17-25

Hunter, J. (2010a). 'Anthropology and the ontological status of the paranormal.' *Rhine Online: Psi News Magazine*, Vol. 2, No. 2, pp. 4-5.

Hunter, J. (2010b). 'Talking With the Spirits: Anthropology and the Interpretation of Spirit Communication.' *Anomaly: Journal of Research Into the Paranormal*, Vol. 44. pp. 34-49.

Hunter, J. (2010c). 'Contemporary Mediumship & Séance Groups in the UK: Speculations on the Bristol Spirit Lodge.' *Psychical Studies: Journal of the Unitarian Society for Psychical Studies*. No. 76, pp. 7-13.

Hunter, J. (2010d). 'Talking With the Spirits: More Than a Social Reality?' *Paranormal Review*. April 2010, Issue 54, pp. 9-13.

Hunter, J. (2011a). 'The Anthropology of the Weird: Ethnographic Fieldwork and Anomalous Experience.' In G. Taylor (ed.) *Darklore Vol. VI*. Brisbane: Daily Grail.

Hunter, J. (2011b). 'Talking With the Spirits: Anthropology and Interpreting Spirit Communication.' *Journal of the Society for Psychical Research*, Vol. 75.3, No. 904, pp. 129-141.

Hunter, J. (ed.) (2012a). *Paranthropology: Anthropological Approaches to the Paranormal*. Bristol: Paranthropology.

Hunter, J. (2012b). 'Contemporary Physical Mediumship: Is it Part of a Continuous Tradition?' *Paranthropology: Journal of Anthropological Approaches to the Paranormal*, Vol. 3, No. 1, pp. 35-43.

Hunter, J. (2013). 'Numinous Conversations: Performance and the Manifestation of Spirits in Spirit Possession Practices.' In A. Voss & W. Rowlandson (eds.) *Daimonic Imagination, Uncanny Intelligence*. Newcastle-Upon-Tyne: Cambridge Scholars.

Hunter, J. & Luke, D. (eds.) (2014). *Talking With the Spirits: Ethnographies From Between the Worlds*. Brisbane: Daily Grail Publishing.

Hunter, J. (2015a). *Strange Dimensions: A Paranthropology Anthology*. Llanrhaeadr-ym-Mochnant: Psychoid Books.

Hunter, J. (2015b). '"Between Realness and Unrealness": Anthropology, Parapsychology and the Ontology of Non-Ordinary Realities.' *Diskus: Journal of the British Association for the Study of Religions*, Vol. 17, No. 2, pp. 4-20.

Hunter, J. (2015c). 'Spirits are the Problem: Anthropology and Conceptualising Spiritual Beings.' *Journal for the Study of Religious Experience*, Vol. 1, No. 1, pp. 76-86.

Hunter, J. (2016). 'Introduction: Intermediatism and the Study of Religion.' In J. Hunter (ed.) *Damned Facts: Fortean Essays on Religion, Folklore and the Paranormal*. Paphos: Aporetic Press (pp. 1-14).

Hunter, J. (2017). *A Study of Spirit Mediumship in the UK: Towards a Non-Reductive Anthropology of the Paranormal*. Unpublished PhD Thesis, University of Bristol.

Huxley, F. (1967). 'Anthropology and ESP.' In J.R. Smythies (ed.) *Science and ESP*. London: Routledge & Keagan Paul.

Jahn, R.G. & Dunne, B.J. (1997). 'Science of the Subjective.' *Journal of Scientific Exploration*, Vol. 11, No. 2, pp. 201-224.

James, W. (2004). *The Varieties of Religious Experience*. New York: Barnes & Noble.

Jansen, R. (2010). 'The Soul Seeker: A Neuroscientist's Search for the Human Essence.' *Texas Observer*, May 28th 2010, pp. 17-20.

Jaynes, J. (1976). *The Origin of Consciousness in the Breakdown of the Bicameral Mind*. Boston: Houghton Mifflin Company.

Jokic, Z. (2008a). 'Yanomami Shamanic Initiation: The Meaning of Death and Postmortem Consciousness in Transformation.' *Anthropology of Consciousness*, Vol. 19, No. 1, pp. 33-59.

Jokic, Z. (2008b). 'The Wrath of the Forgotten Ongons: Shamanic Sickness, Spirit Embodiment, and Fragmentary Trancescape in Contemporary Buriat Shamanism.' *Sibirica*, Vol. 7, No. 1, pp. 23-50.

Jung, C. G. (2008). *Psychology and the Occult*. London: Routledge.

Kardec, A. (2006). *The Spirits' Book*. New York: Cosimo Inc.

Kastrup, B. (2011). *Meaning in Absurdity: What Bizarre Phenomena Can Tell Us About the Nature of Reality*. Alresford: Iff Books.

Kastrup, B. (2012). 'A Paradigm-Breaking Hypothesis for Solving the Mind-Body Problem.' *Paranthropology: Journal of Anthropological Approaches to the Paranormal*, Vol. 3, No. 3, pp. 4-12.

Keel, J.A. (2013). *The Eight Tower: On Ultraterrestrials and the Superspectrum.* San Antonio: Anomalist Books.

Keen, M. (2001). 'The Scole Investigation: A Study in Critical Analysis of Paranormal Physical Phenomena.' *Journal of Scientific Exploration*, Vol. 15, No. 2, pp. 167-182.

Kehoe, A. B. & Giletti, D.H. (1981). 'Women's Preponderance in Possession Cults: The Calcium-Deficiency Hypothesis Extended.' *American Anthropologist*, Vol. 83, No. 3, pp. 549-561.

Kelly, E.F. & Locke, R.G. (2009). *Altered States of Consciousness and Psi: An Historical Survey and Research Prospectus.* New York: Parapsychology Foundation.

Kelly, E.F., Kelly, E.E., Crabtree, A., Gauld, A., Grosso, M. & Greyson, B. (2009). *Irreducible Mind: Towards a Psychology for the 21st Century.* Lanham: Rowman & Littlefield.

Kiev, A. (1972). *Transcultural Psychiatry.* Harmondsworth: Penguin.

Kilson, M. (1971). 'Ambivalence and Power: Mediums in Ga Traditional Religion.' *Journal of Religion in Africa*, Vol. 4, pp. 171-177.

Kimbles, S. (2016). 'Phantom Narratives and the Uncanny in Cultural Life: Psychic Presences and their Shadows.' *European Journal of Psychotherapy and Counselling*, Vol. 18, No. 2, pp. 159-169.

Klass, M. (2003). *Mind Over Mind: The Anthropology and Psychology of Spirit Possession.* Oxford: Rowman & Littlefield.

Klimo, J. (1987). *Channeling: Investigations on Receiving Information from Paranormal Sources.* Los Angeles: Jeremy P. Tarcher Inc.

Kripal, J.J. (2010). *Authors of the Impossible: The Paranormal and the Sacred.* Chicago: University of Chicago Press.

Kripal, J.J. (2011). *Mutants and Mystics: Science Fiction, Superhero Comics and the Paranormal.* Chicago: University of Chicago Press.

Kripal, J.J. (2014). *Comparing Religions: Coming to Terms.* Chichester: John Wiley & Sons.

Krippner, S. & Friedman, H.L. (eds.) (2009). *Mysterious Minds: The Neurobiology of Psychics, Mediums and Other Extraordinary People.* Santa Barbara: Praeger.

Lambek, M. (1998). 'The Sakalava Poiesis of History: Realizing the Past through Spirit Possession in Madagascar.' *American Ethnologist*, Vol. 25, No. 2, pp. 106-127.

Lamont, P. (2005). *The First Psychic: The Peculiar Mystery of a Notorious Victorian Wizard*. London: Abacus.

Lang, A. (2010). *Cock Lane and Common Sense*. Bibliobazaar, LLC.

Lajoie, D.H. & Shapiro, S.I. (1992). 'Definitions of Transpersonal Psychology: The First Twenty-Three Years.' *Journal of Transpersonal Psychology*, Vol. 24, No. 1, pp. 79-98.

Laughlin, C. (1997). 'The Cycle of Meaning: Some Methodological Implications of Biogenetic Structural Theory.' In S. Glazier (ed.) *Anthropology of Religion: Handbook of Theory and Method*. Westport: Greenwood Press.

Laughlin, C.D. (2012). 'Transpersonal Anthropology: What is it, and What are the Problems We Face in Doing it?' In J. Hunter (ed.) *Paranthropology: Anthropological Approaches to the Paranormal*. Bristol: Paranthropology.

Laughlin, C.D. (2013). 'Dreaming and Reality: A Neuroanthropological Account.' *International Journal of Transpersonal Studies*, No. 32, pp. 64-78.

Leacock, S. & Leacock, R. (1975). *Spirits of the Deep: A Study of an Afro-Brazilian Cult*. New York: Anchor Books.

Lehmann, A. (2009). *Victorian Women and the Theatre of Trance*. Jefferson: McFarland.

Levy, R.I., Mageo, J.M., Howard, A. (1996). 'Gods, Spirits, and History.' In J.M. Mageo, & A. Howard (eds.) *Spirits in Culture, History, and Mind*. London: Routledge.

Lewis, I.M. (1971). *Ecstatic Religion: An Anthropological Study of Spirit Possession and Shamanism*. London: Penguin Books Ltd.

Littlewood, R. (1995). 'The Return of Multiple Consciousnesses.' In A.P. Cohen & N. Rapport (eds.) *Questions of Consciousness*. London: Routledge.

Littrell, J. (2008). 'The Mind-Body Connection: Not Just a Theory Anymore.' *Social Work in Health Care*, Vol. 46, No. 4, pp. 17-38.

Long, J.K. (1974). *Extrasensory Ecology: Anthropology and Parapsychology*. London: The Scarecrow Press.

Luke, D. (2010). 'Anthropology and Parapsychology: Still Hostile Sisters in Science?' *Time and Mind: The Journal of Archaeology, Consciousness and Culture*, Vol. 3, No. 3, pp. 245-266.

Luke, D. P., & Friedman, H. (2010). 'The Speculated Neurochemistry of Psi and Associated Processes.' In S. Krippner & H. Friedman (eds.), *Mysterious Minds: The Neurobiology of Psychics, Mediums and Other Extraordinary People*. Westport, CT: Praeger. (pp. 163-185).

Luke, D. P. (2012). 'Psychoactive Substances and Paranormal Phenomena: A Comprehensive Review.' *International Journal of Transpersonal Studies*, Vol. 31, pp. 97-156.

Mageo, J.M & Howard, A. (eds.) (1996). *Spirits in Culture, History, and Mind*. London: Routledge.

Marton, Y. (2010). 'A Rose by Any Name is Still a Rose: The Nomenclature of the Paranormal.' *Paranthropology: Journal of Anthropological Approaches to the Paranormal*, Vol. 1, No. 1, pp. 11-13.

Matthews, E. (2005). *Mind: Key Concepts in Philosophy*. London: Continuum.

McClenon, J. (1993). 'The experiential foundations of shamanic healing.' *Journal of Medicine and Philosophy*, Vol. 18, pp. 107-127.

McClenon, J. & Nooney, J. (2002). 'Anomalous Experiences Reported by Field Anthropologists: Evaluating Theories Regarding Religion.' *Anthropology of Consciousness*, Vol. 13, No. 2, pp. 46-60.

McLuhan, R. (2010). *Randi's Prize: What Sceptics Say About the Paranormal, Why They are Wrong and Why it Matters*. Leicester: Matador.

McCreery, C. (1973). *Psychical Phenomena and the Physical World*. London: Hamish Hamilton.

Melechi, A. (2008). *Servants of the Supernatural: The Night Side of the Victorian Mind*. London: William Heinemann.

Meintel, D. (2007). 'When the Extraordinary Hits Home: Experiencing Spiritualism.' In J-G. Goulet & B.G. Miller (eds.) *Extraordinary Anthropology: Transformations in the Field*. Lincoln: University of Nebraska Press. pp. 124-157.

Mesulam, M.M. (1981). 'Dissociative states with abnormal temporal lobe EEG: Multiple personality and the illusion of possession.' *Archives of Neurology*, No. 38, pp. 176 – 181.

Metcalfe, D. (2012). 'On Anthropological Approaches to Anomalous Phenomena: Explorations in the Science of Magic and the Narrative Structure of Paranormal Experiences.' In D. Pinchbeck & K. Jordan (eds.) *Exploring the Edge Realms of Consciousness*. Berkeley: Evolver Editions.

Monroe, R.A. (1972). *Journeys Out of the Body*. London: Souvenir Press.

Moreira-Almeida, A., Neto, F.L., & Cardena, E. (2008). 'Comparison of Brazilian Spiritist Mediumship and Dissociative Identity Disorder.' *Journal of Nervous and Mental Disease*, Vol. 196, No. 5, pp. 420-424.

Moreman, C.M. (2010). *Beyond the Threshold: Afterlife Beliefs and Experiences in World Religions*. London: Rowman & Littlefield.

Moss, D. and Andrasik, F., (2008). 'Foreword: Evidence-based practice in biofeedback and neurofeedback.' In C. Yucha & D. Montgomery (eds.) *Evidence-based practice in biofeedback and neurofeedback*. Wheat Ridge, CO: Association for Applied Psychophysiology and Biofeedback.

Muldoon, S. & Carrington, H. (1973). *The Phenomena of Astral Projection*. London: Rider & Company.

Myers, F.W.H. (1992). *Human Personality and its Survival of Bodily Death*. Norwich: Pelegrin Trust.

Nagel, T. (1974). 'What is it Like to be a Bat?' *The Philosophical Review*, Vol. 84, No. 4, pp. 435-450.

Nagel, T. (2012). *Mind and Cosmos: Why the Materialist Neo-Darwinian Conception of Nature is Almost Certainly Wrong*. Oxford: Oxford University Press.

Nahm, M. (2011). 'Phenomena seen/heard/felt at the séance Saturday, 10.04.2011 (my 8th sitting with Kai). Report written on the 11. and 12.04.2011 on the basis of notes taken in the hours after the sitting.' Available from: http://felixcircle.blogspot.com/2011/04/feg-spirit-team-holds-test-seance-for.html [Accessed 18 November 2011].

Nelson, G.K. (1969a). *Spiritualism and Society*. London: Routledge & Keagan Paul.

Nelson, G.K. (1969b). 'The Spiritualist Movement and the Need for a Redefinition of Cult.' *Journal for the Scientific Study of Religion*. Vol. 8, No. 1, pp. 152-160.

Nelson, G.K. (1972). 'The membership of a Cult: The Spiritualist National Union.' *Review of Religious Research*, Vol.13, No.3, pp. 170-177.

Newport, F. & Strausberg, M. (2001). 'Americans' Belief in Psychic and Paranormal Phenomena Up Over Last Decade.' Available online: http://www.gallup.org/poll/4483/americans-belief-psychic-paranormal-phenomena-over-last-decade.aspx [Accessed 14th October 2015].

Noll, R. (1985). 'Mental Imagery Cultivation as a Cultural Phenomenon: The Role of Visions in Shamanism.' *Current Anthropology*, Vol. 26, No. 4, pp. 443-461.

Ong, A. (1988). 'The Production of Possession: Spirits and the Multinational Corporation in Malaysia.' *American Ethnologist*, Vol. 15, No. 1, pp. 28-42.

Oohashi, T., Kawai, N., Honda, M., Nakamura, S., Morimoto, M., Nishina, E., Maekawa, T. (2002). 'Electroencephalographic Measurement of Possession Trance in the Field.' *Clinical Neurophysiology*, Vol. 11, No. 3, pp. 435-445.

Osborne, G. & Bacon, A.M. (2015). 'The Working Life of a Medium: A Qualitative Examination of Mediumship as a Support Service for the Bereaved.' *Mental Health, Religion and Culture*, Vol. 18, No. 4, pp. 286-298.

Otto, R. (1958). *The Idea of the Holy*. Oxford: Oxford University Press.

Parnia, S. & Fenwick, P. (2002). 'Near Death Experiences in Cardiac Arrest: Visions of a Dying Brain or Visions of a New Science of Consciousness.' *Resuscitation*, Vol. 52, pp. 5-11.

Pearsall, R. (2004). *The Table-Rappers: The Victorians and the Occult*. Stroud: Sutton Publishing.

Peres J.F, Moreira-Almeida A., Caixeta L., Leao F., Newberg A. (2012). 'Neuroimaging during Trance State: A Contribution to the Study of Dissociation.'*PLoS ONE*, Vol. 7, No. 11, pp. 1-9.

Peters, L. G. & Price-Williams, D. (1980). 'Towards an experiential analysis of shamanism.' *American Ethnologist*, Vol. 7, pp. 397-418.

Pilkington, R. (2004). 'The Mystery of Ectoplasm. In Panel: Perspectives in the Study of Mediumship.' *The Parapsychological Association Convention 2004, Proceedings of Presented Papers*, pp. 316-317.

Polidoro, M. (2001) *Final Séance: The Strange Friendship Between Houdini and Conan Doyle*. New York: Prometheus Books.

Prince, W.F. (1926). 'A Review of the Margery Mediumship.' *The American Journal of Psychology*, Vol. 37, No. 3, pp. 431-441.

Randall, J.L. (1975). *Parapsychology and the Nature of Life: A Scientific Appraisal.* London: Souvenir Press.

Rasmussen, S.K. (1994). 'The "Head Dance," Contested Self, and Art as Balancing Act in Tuareg Spirit Possession.' *Africa: Journal of the International African Institute*, Vol. 64, No. 1, pp. 74-98.

Rees, G., Kreiman, G., & Koch, C. (2002). 'Neural Correlates of Consciousness in Humans.' *Nature Reviews*, Vol. 3, pp. 261-271.

Rogo, D.S. (1988). *The Infinite Bounday: Spirit Possession, Madness, and Multiple Personality.* Wellingborough: The Aquarian Press.

Roxburgh, E. & Evenden, R.E. (2016). 'They Daren't Tell People: Therapists' Experiences of Working with Clients who Report Anomalous Experiences.' *European Journal of Psychotherapy and Counselling*, Vol. 18, No. 2, pp. 123-141.

Schechner, R. (1988). *Performance Theory.* London: Routledge.

Scott, J. & Marshall, G. (2009). *Oxford Dictionary of Sociology.* Oxford: Oxford University Press.

Schlitz, M., 2001, 'Boundless mind: Coming of age in parapsychology' [Parapsychological Association presidential address for year 2000]. *Journal of Parapsychology*, Vol. 65, No. 4, pp. 335-350.

Schrenk-Notzing, A. (1920). *Phenomena of Materialisation: A Contribution to the Investigation of Mediumistic Teleplastics.* London: Kegan Paul, Trench, Trubner & Co.

Schroll, M.A. (2005). 'Whither Psi and Anthropology? An Incomplete History of SAC's Origins, Its Relationship with Transpersonal Psychology and the Untold Stories of Castaneda's Controversy.' *Anthropology of Consciousness*, Vol. 16, No. 1, pp. 6-24.

Schwartz, S.A., (2000). 'Boulders in the Stream: The Lineage and Founding of the Society for the Anthropology of Consciousness,' Stephan A. Schwartz website, Viewed 19 November 2017 from http://www.stephanaschwartz.com/wp-content/uploads/2010/02/Boulders-in-the-stream-SA.pdf?x23564.

Searle, J.R. (1998). *The Mystery of Consciousness.* London: Granta Books.

Sessa, B. (2008). 'Is it Time to Revisit the Role of Psychedelic Drugs in Enhancing Human Creativity?' *Journal of Psychopharmacology*, Vol. 22, No. 8, pp. 821-827.

Shanafelt, R. (2004). 'Magic, Miracles and Marvels in Anthropology.' *Ethnos*, Vol 69, No. 3, pp. 317-340.

Sharf, R.H. (2000). 'The Rhetoric of Experience and the Study of Religion.' *Journal of Consciousness Studies*, Vol. 7, No. 11-12, pp. 267-287.

Sheldrake, R. (1987). 'Mind, Memory, and Archetype Morphic Resonance and the Collective Unconscious - Part I.' *Psychological Perspectives*, Vol. 18, No. 1, pp. 9-25.

Sheldrake, R. (2005). 'The Sense of Being Stared At: Is It Real or Illusory?' *Journal of Consciousness Studies*, Vol. 12, No. 6, pp. 10-31.

Sheldrake, R. (2012). *The Science Delusion: Freeing the Spirit of Inquiry*. London: Coronet.

Shorter, E. (1994). *From the Mind into the Body: The Cultural Origins of Psychosomatic Symptoms*. New York: The Free Press.

Sinclair, U. (2001). *Mental Radio*. Charlottesville: Hampton Roads Publishing Company.

Skultans, V. (1974). *Intimacy and Ritual: A Study of Spiritualism, Mediums and Groups*. London: Routledge & Keagan Paul.

Solomon, Grant & Jane (1999). *The Scole Experiment: Scientific Evidence for Life After Death*. London: Judy Piatkus.

Sommer, A. (2009). 'Tackling Taboos - From Psychopathia Sexualis to the Materialisation of Dreams: Albert von Schrenck-Notzing (1862-1929).' *Journal of Scientific Exploration*, Vol. 23, No. 3, pp. 229-322.

Sommer, A. (2016). 'Are You Afraid of the Dark?: Notes on the Psychology of Belief in Histories of Science and the Occult.' *European Journal of Psychotherapy and Counselling*, Vol. 18, No. 2, pp. 105-122.

Spencer, W. (2001). 'The Absent Friends: Classical Spiritualist Mediumship and New Age Channelling Compared and Contrasted.' *Journal of Contemporary Religion*, Vol.16, No.3, pp. 343-360.

St. Clair, D. (1971). *Drum and Candle: Accounts of Brazilian Voodoo and Spiritism*. New York: Bell Publishing Co.

Steinmeyer, J. (2008). *Charles Fort: The Man Who Invented the Supernatural*. London: Heinemann Books.

Stoller, P. (1994). 'Embodying Colonial Memories.' *American Anthropologist*, Vol. 96, No. 3, pp. 634-648.

Straight, B. (2007). *Miracles and Extraordinary Experience in Northern Kenya*. Philadelphia: University of Pennsylvania Press.

Strassman, R. (2001). *DMT: The Spirit Molecule*. Rochester: Park Street Press.

Sudduth, M. (2009). 'Super-Psi and the Survivalist Interpretation of Mediumship.' *Journal of Scientific Exploration*, Vol. 23, No. 2, pp. 167-193.

Sudduth, M. (2013). 'Is Postmortem Survival the Best Explanation of the Data of Mediumship?' In A.J. Rock (ed.) *The Survival Hypothesis: Essays on Mediumship*. Jefferson: McFarland & Company.

Swale, T. & Wood, D. (2009). 'Conclusions on Investigation Experimentation: EVP, ITC and Trigger Objects.' *PSI Journal of Investigative Psychical Research*, Vol. 5, No. 1, pp. 3-12.

Swanton, J.R. (1953). 'A Letter to Anthropologists.' *Journal of Parapsychology*, Vol. 17, pp. 144-152.

Tabori, P. (1968). *Companions of the Unseen*. New York: University Books.

Tallis, R. (2012). *Aping Mankind: Neuromania, Darwinitis and the Misrepresentation of Humanity*. Durham: Acumen Publishing Ltd.

Taves, A. (1999). *Fits, Trance and Visions: Experiencing Religion and Explaining Experience from Wesley to James*. Princeton: Princeton University Press.

Taylor, D. (1998). 'Spaces of transition: new light on the haunted house.' Retrieved from http://www.indigogroup.co.uk/foamycustard/fc019.htm on 17/11/09 at 19:17pm.

Thomas Jefferson University (2012, November 16). 'Brazilian Mediums Shed Light on Brain Activity During a Trance State.' ScienceDaily. Available from: http://www.sciencedaily.com/releases/2012/11/121117184543.htm [Accessed 11 January, 2013].

Turner, E. (1993). 'The Reality of Spirits: A Tabooed or Permitted Field of Study?' *Anthropology of Consciousness*, Vol. 4, No. 1, pp. 9-12.

Turner, E. (1998). *Experiencing Ritual*. Philadelphia: University of Pennsylvania Press.

Turner, E., (2006). 'Advances in the Study of Spirit Experience: Drawing Together Many Threads.' *Anthropology of Consciousness*, Vol. 17, No. 2, pp. 33-61.

Turner, E. (2010). 'Discussion: Ethnography as a Transformative Experience.' *Anthropology and Humanism*, Vol. 35, No. 2, pp. 218-226.

Turner, V. (1985). *On the Edge of the Bush: Anthropology as Experience*. Tuscon: University of Arizona Press.

Turner, V. (2002). 'Liminality and Communitas.' In M. Lambek (ed.) *A Reader in the Anthropology of Religion*. London: Blackwell Publishing Ltd.

Tylor, E.B. (1920). *Primitive Culture*. London: John Murray.

Tylor, E. B. (1930). *Anthropology: An Introduction to the Study of Man and Civilization*. London: C.A. Watts and Co. Ltd.

Tymn, M. (n.d). 'An Examination of Ectoplasm.' Association for Evaluation and Communication of Evidence for Survival. Available from: http://www.aeces.info/Library/Documents/Exam_Ectoplasm.pdf [Accessed 21 November 2011].

Vallee, J. (2016). *Passport to Magonia: From Folklore to Flying Saucers*. Brisbane: Daily Grail.

van de Port, M. (2011). *Ecstatic Encounters: Bahian Candomble and the Quest for the Really Real*. Amsterdam: Amsterdam University Press.

Velmans, M. (2007a). 'An Epistemology for the Study of Consciousness.' In M. Velmans & S. Schneider (eds.) *The Blackwell Companion to Consciousness*. New York: Blackwell. (pp. 711-725).

Velmans, M. (2007b). 'The Co-Evolution of Matter and Consciousness.' *Synthesis Philosophica*, Vol. 22, No. 44, pp. 273-282.

Walach, H., 2009, 'Spirituality: The legacy of parapsychology', in C.A. Roe, W. Kramer & L. Coly (eds.), *Utrecht II: Charting the future of parapsychology: Proceedings of an international conference held in Utrecht, The Netherlands, October 16-18, 2008*. pp. 363-386, Parapsychology Foundation, Inc., New York.

Wallis, J. (2001). 'Continuing Bonds: Relationships Between the Living and the Dead Within Contemporary Spiritualism.' *Morality*, Vol. 6, No. 2, pp. 127-145).

Watters, E. (2011). *Crazy Like Us: The Globalization of the Western Mind*. London: Constable & Robinson.

Webb, H.S. (2012). 'Clock System or Cloud System?: Applying Popper's Metaphor to the Study of Human Consciousness.' *Paranthropology: Journal of Anthropological Approaches to the Paranormal*, Vol. 3, No. 4, pp. 4-12.

Weiant, C.W. (1960). 'Parapsychology and Anthropology.' *Manas*, Vol. 13, No. 15, pp. 1-6

Wescott, R.W. (1977). 'Paranthropology: A Nativity Celebration and a Communion Commentary.' In J.K. Long (ed.) *Extrasensory Ecology: Parapsychology and Anthropology*. London: Scarecrow Books.

Whorf, B.L. (1956). *Language, Thought and Reality*. Massachusetts: MIT Press.

Williams, B. & Roll, W. (2007). 'Spirit Controls and the Brain.' *Proceedings of Presented Papers, The Parapsychological Association Convention 2007*, pp. 170-186.

Wilson, I. (1986). *The Bleeding Mind: An Investigation into the Mysterious Phenomenon of Stigmata*. London: Weidenfeld & Nicolson.

Wilson, M., Williams, B.J., Harte, T.M. & Roll, W.G. (2010). 'The Daniel Experiment: Sitter Group Contributions with Field RNG and MESA Environmental Recordings.' *Journal of Scientific Exploration*, Vol. 24, No. 4, pp. 611-636.

Wilson, P. J. (1967). 'Status Ambiguity and Spirit Possession.' *Man*, Vol. 2, No. 3, pp. 366-378.

Wilson, R.A. (1987). *The New Inquisition: Irrational Rationalism and the Citadel of Science*. Phoenix: Falcon Press.

Winkelman, M. (1982). 'Magic: A Theoretical Reassessment.' *Current Anthropology*, Vol. 23, No. 1, pp. 37-66.

Winkelman, M. (1986). 'Trance States: A Theoretical Model and Cross-Cultural Analysis.' *Ethos*, Vol. 14, No. 2, pp. 174-203.

Winkelman, M. (1990). 'Shamans and Other "Magico-Religious" Healers: A Cross-Cultural Study of Their Origins, Nature and Social Transformation.' *Ethos*, Vol. 18, No. 3, pp. 308-352.

Winkelman, M. (2000). *Shamanism: The Neural Ecology of Consciousness and Healing.* Westport: Bergin & Garvey.

Wood, D. (2009). 'Investigation Equipment: The Role of Chance.' *PSI: Journal of Investigative Psychical Research*, Vol. 5, No. 1, pp. 13-18.

Young, D.E. & Goulet, J-G. (1994). *Being Changed by Cross-Cultural Encounters: The Anthropology of Extraordinary Experience*. Ontario: Broadview Press.

Young, D.E. (2012). 'Dreams and Telepathic Communication.' In J. Hunter (ed.) *Paranthropology: Anthropological Approaches to the Paranormal*. Bristol: Paranthropology.

Zahavi, D. (2005). *Subjectivity and Selfhood: Investigating the First-Person Perspective*. Cambridge, Massachusetts: MIT Press.

ABOUT THE AUTHOR

Dr. Jack Hunter is an anthropologist exploring the borderlands of consciousness, religion and the paranormal, living in the hills of Mid-Wales. His doctoral research with the University of Bristol examined the experiences of spirit mediums and their influence on the development of self-concepts and models of consciousness, and is an effort towards a non-reductive anthropology of the paranormal. He is the founder and editor of *Paranthropology: Journal of Anthropological Approaches to the Paranormal*. He is the author of *Why People Believe in Spirits, Gods and Magic* (2012), editor of *Strange Dimensions: A Paranthropology Anthology* (2015), *Damned Facts: Fortean Essays on Religion, Folklore and the Paranormal* (2016), and co-editor with Dr. David Luke of *Talking With the Spirits: Ethnographies from Between the Worlds* (2014). He has served as a reviewer for the *Journal of Exceptional Experiences and Psychology* (JEEP), *Journal of the British Association for the Study of Religion* (JBASR), the *Journal for the Study of Religious Experience* (JSRE) and is a founding member of the Afterlife Research Centre (ARC). He is currently an Access to Higher Education tutor for Health and Social Care (Social Sciences) at North Shropshire College, where he teaches Psychology and Sociology. He completed a Permaculture Design Course at Chester Cathedral in 2017, and is currently working on a project to develop a mainstream permaculture curriculum for schools. He is also a musician and an ordained Dudeist Priest.

To find out more about his research and publications visit www.jack-hunter.webstarts.com

Paperbacks also available from White Crow Books

Elsa Barker—*Letters from a Living Dead Man*
ISBN 978-1-907355-83-7

Elsa Barker—*War Letters from the Living Dead Man*
ISBN 978-1-907355-85-1

Elsa Barker—*Last Letters from the Living Dead Man*
ISBN 978-1-907355-87-5

Richard Maurice Bucke—*Cosmic Consciousness*
ISBN 978-1-907355-10-3

Arthur Conan Doyle—*The Edge of the Unknown*
ISBN 978-1-907355-14-1

Arthur Conan Doyle—*The New Revelation*
ISBN 978-1-907355-12-7

Arthur Conan Doyle—*The Vital Message*
ISBN 978-1-907355-13-4

Arthur Conan Doyle with Simon Parke—*Conversations with Arthur Conan Doyle*
ISBN 978-1-907355-80-6

Meister Eckhart with Simon Parke—*Conversations with Meister Eckhart*
ISBN 978-1-907355-18-9

D. D. Home—*Incidents in my Life Part 1*
ISBN 978-1-907355-15-8

Mme. Dunglas Home; edited, with an Introduction, by Sir Arthur Conan Doyle—*D. D. Home: His Life and Mission*
ISBN 978-1-907355-16-5

Edward C. Randall—*Frontiers of the Afterlife*
ISBN 978-1-907355-30-1

Rebecca Ruter Springer—*Intra Muros: My Dream of Heaven*
ISBN 978-1-907355-11-0

Leo Tolstoy, edited by Simon Parke—*Forbidden Words*
ISBN 978-1-907355-00-4

Leo Tolstoy—*A Confession*
ISBN 978-1-907355-24-0

Leo Tolstoy—*The Gospel in Brief*
ISBN 978-1-907355-22-6

Leo Tolstoy—*The Kingdom of God is Within You*
ISBN 978-1-907355-27-1

Leo Tolstoy—*My Religion: What I Believe*
ISBN 978-1-907355-23-3

Leo Tolstoy—*On Life*
ISBN 978-1-907355-91-2

Leo Tolstoy—*Twenty-three Tales*
ISBN 978-1-907355-29-5

Leo Tolstoy—*What is Religion and other writings*
ISBN 978-1-907355-28-8

Leo Tolstoy—*Work While Ye Have the Light*
ISBN 978-1-907355-26-4

Leo Tolstoy—*The Death of Ivan Ilyich*
ISBN 978-1-907661-10-5

Leo Tolstoy—*Resurrection*
ISBN 978-1-907661-09-9

Leo Tolstoy with Simon Parke—*Conversations with Tolstoy*
ISBN 978-1-907355-25-7

Howard Williams with an Introduction by Leo Tolstoy—*The Ethics of Diet: An Anthology of Vegetarian Thought*
ISBN 978-1-907355-21-9

Vincent Van Gogh with Simon Parke—*Conversations with Van Gogh*
ISBN 978-1-907355-95-0

Wolfgang Amadeus Mozart with Simon Parke—*Conversations with Mozart*
ISBN 978-1-907661-38-9

Jesus of Nazareth with Simon Parke—
Conversations with Jesus of Nazareth
ISBN 978-1-907661-41-9

Thomas à Kempis with Simon
Parke—*The Imitation of Christ*
ISBN 978-1-907661-58-7

Julian of Norwich with Simon
Parke—*Revelations of Divine Love*
ISBN 978-1-907661-88-4

Allan Kardec—*The Spirits Book*
ISBN 978-1-907355-98-1

Allan Kardec—*The Book on Mediums*
ISBN 978-1-907661-75-4

Emanuel Swedenborg—*Heaven and Hell*
ISBN 978-1-907661-55-6

P.D. Ouspensky—*Tertium Organum:
The Third Canon of Thought*
ISBN 978-1-907661-47-1

Dwight Goddard—*A Buddhist Bible*
ISBN 978-1-907661-44-0

Michael Tymn—*The Afterlife Revealed*
ISBN 978-1-970661-90-7

Michael Tymn—*Transcending the
Titanic: Beyond Death's Door*
ISBN 978-1-908733-02-3

Guy L. Playfair—*If This Be Magic*
ISBN 978-1-907661-84-6

Guy L. Playfair—*The Flying Cow*
ISBN 978-1-907661-94-5

Guy L. Playfair —*This House is Haunted*
ISBN 978-1-907661-78-5

Carl Wickland, M.D.—
Thirty Years Among the Dead
ISBN 978-1-907661-72-3

John E. Mack—*Passport to the Cosmos*
ISBN 978-1-907661-81-5

Peter & Elizabeth Fenwick—
The Truth in the Light
ISBN 978-1-908733-08-5

Erlendur Haraldsson—
Modern Miracles
ISBN 978-1-908733-25-2

Erlendur Haraldsson—
At the Hour of Death
ISBN 978-1-908733-27-6

Erlendur Haraldsson—
The Departed Among the Living
ISBN 978-1-908733-29-0

Brian Inglis—*Science and Parascience*
ISBN 978-1-908733-18-4

Brian Inglis—*Natural and Supernatural:
A History of the Paranormal*
ISBN 978-1-908733-20-7

Ernest Holmes—*The Science of Mind*
ISBN 978-1-908733-10-8

Victor & Wendy Zammit —*A Lawyer
Presents the Evidence For the Afterlife*
ISBN 978-1-908733-22-1

Casper S. Yost—*Patience
Worth: A Psychic Mystery*
ISBN 978-1-908733-06-1

William Usborne Moore—
Glimpses of the Next State
ISBN 978-1-907661-01-3

William Usborne Moore—
The Voices
ISBN 978-1-908733-04-7

John W. White—
The Highest State of Consciousness
ISBN 978-1-908733-31-3

Stafford Betty—
The Imprisoned Splendor
ISBN 978-1-907661-98-3

Paul Pearsall, Ph.D. —
Super Joy
ISBN 978-1-908733-16-0

All titles available as eBooks, and selected titles available in Hardback and Audiobook formats from www.whitecrowbooks.com

Lightning Source UK Ltd.
Milton Keynes UK
UKHW01f1519070618
323896UK00001B/78/P